SELF+CULTURE+WRITING

SELF+CULTURE+WRITING

Autoethnography for/as Writing Studies

EDITED BY
REBECCA L. JACKSON AND
JACKIE GRUTSCH MCKINNEY

UTAH STATE UNIVERSITY PRESS
Logan

© 2021 by University Press of Colorado

Published by Utah State University Press
An imprint of University Press of Colorado
245 Century Circle, Suite 202
Louisville, Colorado 80027

All rights reserved

 The University Press of Colorado is a proud member of the Association of University Presses.

The University Press of Colorado is a cooperative publishing enterprise supported, in part, by Adams State University, Colorado State University, Fort Lewis College, Metropolitan State University of Denver, Regis University, University of Alaska Fairbanks, University of Colorado, University of Denver, University of Northern Colorado, University of Wyoming, Utah State University, and Western Colorado University.

ISBN: 978-1-64642-120-6 (paperback)
ISBN: 978-1-64642-121-3 (ebook)
https://doi.org/10.7330/9781646421213

Library of Congress Cataloging-in-Publication Data

Names: Jackson, Becky (Rebecca Lynn), editor. | Grutsch McKinney, Jackie, editor.
Title: Self+culture+writing : autoethnography for/as writing studies / edited by Rebecca L. Jackson and Jackie Grutsch McKinney.
Other titles: Self plus culture plus writing
Description: Logan : Utah State University Press, [2020] | Includes bibliographical references and index.
Identifiers: LCCN 2021015258 (print) | LCCN 2021015259 (ebook) | ISBN 9781646421206 (paperback) | ISBN 9781646421213 (ebook)
Subjects: LCSH: English language—Rhetoric—Study and teaching (Higher) | Academic writing—Study and teaching. | Ethnology—Biographical methods. | Ethnology—Authorship. | Narrative inquiry (Research method)
Classification: LCC PE1404 .S375 2020 (print) | LCC PE1404 (ebook) | DDC 808.06/692—dc23
LC record available at https://lccn.loc.gov/2021015258
LC ebook record available at https://lccn.loc.gov/2021015259

The University Press of Colorado gratefully acknowledges the support of Ball State University toward the funding of this book.

Cover illustration © DODOMO/Shutterstock.

To all of our students past and present who pushed our thinking on autoethnography as a research practice and genre and who trusted and often humbled us with their personal experiences and stories.

CONTENTS

Critical Introduction
Rebecca L. Jackson and Jackie Grutsch McKinney   3

PART ONE: WRITING STUDIES AUTOETHNOGRAPHIES

1. Her Own Voice: Coming Out in Academia with Bipolar Disorder
   Tiffany Rainey   29

2. Literate Vixens and Shameless Hijabis: An Automythnography
   Shereen Inayatulla   45

3. When Things Fall Apart
   Rebecca Hallman Martini   57

4. Critical Pedagogy and the Composition Classroom: Searching for a Middle Ground between Epistemological Despair and "Radical Hope"
   Leslie Akst   71

5. A Window into the Complex World of Factory-Floor Writing
   Elena G. Garcia and Guadalupe Garcia   85

6. Constructing a Transnational-Multilingual Teacher Subjectivity in a First-Year Writing Class: An Autoethnography
   Soyeon Lee   95

PART TWO: TEACHING WRITING STUDIES AUTOETHNOGRAPHY

7. Empowering Autoethnography in Two-Year College Reform
   Kirsten Higgins, Anthony Warnke, and Marcie Sims   115

8. "Say What You Want to Say!": Teaching Literacy Autoethnography to Resist Linguistic Prejudice
   Amanda Sladek   126

9. What the Students Taught the Teacher in a Graduate Autoethnography Class
   Sue Doe, Kira Marshall-McKelvey, Ross Atkinson, Caleb Gonzalez, Lilly Halboth, and Jennifer Owen   136

10. Agentic Discord in Writing Studies: Toward Autoethnographic Accounts of Disciplinary Lore
    William Duffy   149

11. Collaging the Classroom, the Personal, and the Critical: Autoethnographic Writing in the National Writing Project
    Trixie G. Smith   159

PART THREE: EXTENDING WRITING STUDIES AUTOETHNOGRAPHY

12. You Can't Do That Here: Black/Feminist Autoethnography and Histories of Intellectual Exclusion
    Louis M. Maraj   175

13. Writing *With* Not *About*: Constellating Stories in Autoethnography
    John T. Gagnon   186

14. Chaotic Constructions: Disabling the Autoethnography
    Autumn Laws   199

15. The Untapped Possibilities of Participatory Video as an Autoethnographic Method to Study Literacy
    Alison Cardinal, Melissa Atienza, and Aliyah Jones   210

Index   223
About the Authors   227

SELF+CULTURE+WRITING

CRITICAL INTRODUCTION

Rebecca L. Jackson and Jackie Grutsch McKinney

Toni Morrison once said in an interview, "If there's a book you really want to read, but it hasn't been written yet, then you must write it" (Brown, *Cincinnati Inquirer*, September 27, 1981). For us, this collection is one of those books. We'd both looked unsuccessfully for years for books on autoethnography we could use in our undergraduate and graduate writing studies courses. Books and articles on autoethnography existed, of course, but they were written primarily by qualitative researchers in the social sciences. There were some isolated exceptions—Linda Brodkey's "Writing on the Bias" (1994) and A. Suresh Canagarajah's "Autoethnography in the Study of Multilingual Writers" (2012a) come to mind—but there was no robust or sustained discussion of autoethnography in the field of writing studies. And while we could (and did) use texts representing our field's long engagement with personal narratives and critical personal narratives, we both viewed these genres as more autoethnographic than autoethnography.

Eventually, we realized we needed to craft the book we'd been searching for. Because it would be the first of its kind in writing studies, we knew the book needed to cover significant ground. It needed to define and explain autoethnography (translated literally as self + culture + writing) as both a method of inquiry and a genre of writing. It needed to include writing *about* autoethnography—unique approaches to and forms of autoethnography particularly suited to writing studies—and ideas about teaching autoethnography in different courses and contexts. Finally, the book needed to showcase actual autoethnographies written by practitioners and scholars in the field. These goals led us to shape the text as an edited collection. We have not regretted that decision; as you'll see, the authors included here offer compelling and competing ways for those of us in writing studies to think and rethink autoethnography as both a research process and product.

We imagine many readers will come to this book with some understanding of and affection for autoethnography. Perhaps readers are curious about how the personal narrative in writing studies is similar to and/or different from autoethnography. Perhaps these same readers have encountered autoethnography in other disciplines (communication studies, sociology, and medicine, for example) and wonder how those of us in writing studies conceptualize and practice it. For them, we hope this collection will inspire new thinking and new questions about teaching, doing, and reading autoethnographies in writing studies. Other readers may be coming to autoethnography for the first time. For them, the collection will offer solid grounding in autoethnography as a process and product and introduce them to emerging conversations about autoethnography in our field.

In the remaining sections of this introduction, we trace the origins of autoethnography, offer definitions of autoethnography as a qualitative research method and genre of writing, and briefly note common critiques of autoethnography. We then turn to autoethnography in writing studies, staking out a definition for writing studies autoethnography, reviewing existing literature, and drawing a fine but important distinction between what is autoethnographic and what is autoethnography.

WHAT IS AUTOETHNOGRAPHY?

By some accounts, autoethnography began as a research method and genre in the social sciences as a response to the "crisis of representation" in the second half of the twentieth century (Bochner 2012). The idea that researchers could write objectively, as they were traditionally trained to do, began to be seen as impossible and even unethical as it hid from readers the researcher's biases and effects of the researcher on the culture. Those doing qualitative research had to come to terms with the shift in thinking that an ethnographic account was not a simple recording of a culture. The crisis of representation meant the researcher could no longer be an omniscient narrator; the researcher was, in fact, very much present, even though positivist research conventions had required a researcher to be absent from (written out of) the report. The new perspective that emerged after this crisis was a subjective, emotional, and embodied view from the ground—one recognizing, in Arthur Bochner's (2017) words:

> Autoethnographers insist that the ideal of disinterested research and impartial analysis is an illusion. The "field" of our fieldwork necessarily includes the observer; it is a context of interactions and intersubjectivities. When the lived experiences, beliefs, and other subjectivities of the observer are excluded (or bracketed) to reach a more accurate, dispassionate

depiction of "reality," the product may have the aura but it will not have the authority of science. Adopting the cold, mathematical, and distant jargon of science does not make an account scientific. (69)

Simultaneously and relatedly, the traditional, colonial ways (mostly white) researchers entered into another culture to study its (nonwhite) people and report back to other (mostly white) researchers came under increased criticism.

As a result, some ethnographers worked to evolve the practice of ethnography to address its shortcomings. For example, some began to do "critical ethnography," which, according to Stephen May (1997), "adopts a perspective of social and cultural relations which highlights the role of ideology in sustaining and perpetuating inequality within particular settings" and "is not simply to describe these settings as they appear to be—as in conventional ethnography—but to change them for the better" (197). That is, critical ethnography pays attention to social forces and conventions that affect studying and writing about a culture, and critical ethnographers make a point to recognize those social forces in their relationships with participants and final research accounts. Feminist ethnography arose as another instantiation of critical ethnography, with careful attention paid to issues of gender, sex, sexuality, and power.

Other ethnographers moved further away from ethnography to something they called *autoethnography*. Writing in 2000, Bud Goodall suggested a "new ethnography" in which the researcher pays attention to personal experiences during and after time in the field as important to the study. His focus on writing, in *Writing the New Ethnography*, is a departure from early ethnographies in which the report of time in the field (the ethnography) was seen as a simple transmission of information—objective and therefore authorless. Thus, when Goodall writes that "the new ethnographers are not researchers who learn to 'write it up' but *writers* who learn how to use their research and 'get it down,'" he signals a major shift in ethnography (10; emphasis in original). Goodall says his approach might be called "autoethnographic," as it aims to tell the story of a culture through the eyes of the researcher. It may be impossible to report objectively and omnisciently on a culture, but it may be, Goodall suggests, possible, even desirable, to report on one's own experiences within a culture.

Despite the traction this version of the history of autoethnography has gained, an equally compelling, perhaps more "true" and just account of autoethnography's origins in the United States, can be traced, in part, to Black women writers and speakers in the nineteenth and early twentieth centuries (Maraj 2018). We take as one example Zora Neale Hurston, an African American anthropologist and writer who conducted (auto)ethnographic studies of her own community in the 1930s. While Hurston's (white) anthropology colleagues sought out "foreign" cultures to study, Hurston turned toward her hometown, because, as Layla D. Brown-Vincent (2019) writes,

> Hurston's familiarity with the subject matter and the producers of said subject matter, made the prospect of recording the tales of her youth not only seem possible but worthy of documentation as well as critical inquiry because she did not hold the racial biases many of her classmates and teachers held about southern Blacks. (111)

Hurston thus used her training in ethnography alongside her own experience and history in this culture to craft what is now understood as autoethnography. Equally important, Hurston actively and purposefully used her new version of ethnography (again, what we now call *autoethnography*) as a genre and method to disrupt dominant narratives and dominant interpretations, a tradition that remains strong today. For example, communications scholar Rachel Alicia (2012) calls for a Black feminist autoethnography that works as "an act of resistance" (also see Maraj [2018] and chapter 12 in this collection).

Carolyn Ellis, Tony Adams, and Arthur Bochner's (2011) definition of autoethnography reflects this latter tradition in which autoethnography is a "socially-just and socially-conscious act." They write,

> Autoethnography is an approach to research and writing that seeks to describe and systematically analyze personal experience in order to understand cultural experience. This approach challenges canonical ways of doing research and representing others and treats research as a political, socially-just and socially-conscious act. A researcher uses tenets of autobiography and ethnography to do and write autoethnography. Thus, as a method, autoethnography is both process and product. (273)

Marcelo Diversi and Claudio Moreira (2017) put an even finer point on autoethnography's social justice imperative, claiming that autoethnography is about decolonizing the way knowledge is made (and privileged) in the academy.

> We see autoethnography as a way of being and writing ourselves into the history of resistance against oppression, injustice, and exclusion happening every day around each of us, around the globe. We imagine autoethnography as a way to start from our common humanity in experiences between identities, as a way to defy the academic preference for sophisticated Foucauldian analysis of power over pedestrian narratives of blood and profanity. (41–42).

Autoethnography has emerged then as a "process and product," a method and a genre, in which, as Robin M. Boylorn and Mark P. Orbe (2014) note, "one could shift the ethnographic gaze from others and unto self" (14). This shift allows the autoethnographer to "write as an Other, and for an Other," which "invite(s) readers into the lived experience of a presumed 'Other' and to experience it viscerally" (15).

Much has been written about the contours, elements, and parameters of autoethnography: all try to articulate what it is and what it is not. In "Living Autoethnography," Faith Wambura Ngunjiri, Kathy-Ann C. Hernandez, and Heewon Chang (2010) assert three central components to autoethnography:

1. **Autoethnography is a qualitative research method.** Autoethnography demands "a systematic approach to data collection, analysis, and interpretation about self and social phenomena involving self" (2). This systematic approach to the "sociocultural understanding of self" is what distinguishes autoethnography from memoir and autobiography.

2. **Autoethnography is self-focused.** The researcher is at the "center" of the research inquiry as both "a 'subject' (the researcher who performs the investigation) and an 'object' (a/the participant who is investigated)" (2).

3. **Autoethnography is context conscious.** "Rooted in ethnography (the study of culture)," the researcher collects data about self while simultaneously exploring "how the context surrounding self has influenced and shaped the make-up of self and how the self has responded to, reacted to, or resisted forces innate to the context." Simply put, "ethnographic attention to the socio-cultural context is the foundation of this research method" (3).

In general, qualitative researchers endeavor to study complex phenomena in context to render a narrative of the person, phenomena, culture, or place under study. Autoethnography, as a qualitative research method, shares many of the same methods for collecting and analyzing data as ethnography; for example, an autoethnographer might collect interviews, artifacts, fieldnotes, photographs, or videos and might analyze these through reflection or coding and triangulation to discover and assert patterns and themes in order to make an interpretation. Less typical in ethnography, autoethnographers may also use memories, diaries, self-interviews, and systematic introspection on any or all of these as data points (Adams, Jones, and Ellis 2015; Crawley 2012). Perhaps the most well-known methods book on autoethnography, cited by several of the authors in this collection, is Heewon Chang's (2016) *Autoethnography as Method*. Chang walks readers through collecting and analyzing data for an autoethnography, as well as how to shape the writing of the final text.

A scholar might come to autoethnography as method when they realize they are a particularly good "case" for a specific area of inquiry. The scholar can "volunteer" as the subject of the study, which gives them (1) unlimited access: an ethnographer might have hours of interviews and months of fieldnotes, but an autoethnographer, potentially, has access to a lifetime of time "in the field," memories, artifacts, and potential interviewees, (2) the ability to ask the hard questions: autoethnographers can press themselves to think, feel, and remember things they might not press others to remember or process, (3) a dual role: the autoethnographer as both subject and researcher means they both produce and analyze the data, thus closing the gap in interpretation between a subject's and researcher's perspective.

The write-up of autoethnographic research can take different forms. Early on, two types emerged: analytic and evocative autoethnographies. Analytic (also called *interpretive autoethnography*) is typically characterized by the genre conventions we associate with social science writing; it likely includes specific and expected sections (literature review, methodology/methods, findings, and discussion) and directly engages other scholarship through citation, paraphrasing, or footnotes.

Evocative autoethnography, also called "heartful" autoethnography (Ellis 1999), typically takes the form of "stories that fuse ethnography with literary art" (Bochner 2017, 74). As Bochner explains further, evocative autoethnography is a

> blended, bended genre that blurs boundaries between nonfiction and fiction, research and reflection, memory and desire, poetry/literature/performance art and science and thereby shifts, expands, and transgresses traditional conventions and categories of expressing or "representing events that really occurred." (74)

Evocative autoethnographies require autoethnographers to engage in various forms of systematic reflection on experiences and memories to craft richly reflexive personal accounts that map onto or interrogate cultural attitudes, ideologies, practices, or times. Ellis, writing about her own approach to autoethnography, says she "starts with [her] personal life," paying careful attention to her "physical feelings, thoughts, and emotions." In a reflexive move, she then uses "systematic sociological introspection and emotional recall to try to understand an experience [she's] lived through" (Ellis and Bochner 2000, 737). Ronald J. Pelias (2019) explains that he "nudges" his memory about past events: asking others to help him remember details, interviewing people, and using such things as journals, letters, and photographs to spark memories and insights (23). Bochner (2017), speaking directly to the reader/ autoethnographer, explains that

> you must listen closely to yourself talking; you talk back to yourself, commenting directly on what you hear yourself saying; you don't stop there but rather insist on keeping the conversation going, interpreting and reinterpreting, to discover something strange about the self you started with as you try to transform yourself into a new being. (71)

For all of these reasons, evocative autoethnographies often read more like creative nonfiction because they draw upon literary conventions—concrete detail, characters, dialogue, and emotion—and because explicit discussions of research methodology and method are (typically) noticeably absent in this type. Thus, while evocative autoethnography arises from systematic research, the autoethnographer doesn't necessarily elaborate this process in the autoethnography itself, although autoethnographers may provide headnotes or footnotes that explain the methods used to gather and analyze data. Likewise, evocative autoethnographies may or may not explicitly reference secondary sources, although the cultural and disciplinary conversations the autoethnography engages are made clear through document features like headings, for example, and/or keen awareness of audience and the issues with which the audience would be familiar. (We'll have more to say on this later.)

Much of the writing about autoethnography in the social sciences thus far seems to be on evocative autoethnography, perhaps because it is such a departure from conventional social science research. Conventions that once dictated social science research writing—avoiding first person, for example—are flipped in evocative autoethnography, which demands rich, brave, vulnerable, creative first-person accounts (and even permits multi-genre work with poetry or plays). Scholars trained in the IMRAD tradition likely would need methods and models for evocative autoethnography because it differs so wildly from established social science conventions. However, we don't think it is easy or necessary to slice autoethnographies into an evocative versus analytic binary. Beyond evocative and analytic autoethnographies, in fact, dozens of other types of autoethnographies have emerged that are alike and different from each other in ideological orientations, methods, and genre conventions. These types include

- betweener (Diversi and Moreira 2018);
- Black feminist (Brown-Vincent 2019; Griffin 2012); feminist (Ettorre 2016);
- collaborative (Canagarajah and Lee 2013; Chang, Ngunjiri, and Hernandez 2016; Lapadat 2017);

- community (Toyosaki et al. 2009);
- critical (Boylorn and Orbe 2014); critical coconstructed (Cann and DeMeulenaere 2012);
- duoethnography (Breault 2017; Norris, Sawyer, and Lund 2012);
- exoautoethnography (Denejkina 2017);
- institutional (Taber 2010);
- Indigenous (Whitinui 2014);
- moderate (Stahlke Wall 2016);
- multispecies (Sheriff 2017);
- organizational (Herrmann 2017);
- performative (Spry 2016);
- postcolonial (Chawla and Atay 2018; Toyosaki 2018);
- rhetorical (Broad 2017; Lunceford 2015).

As Chang (2016) observes, the range of what is called or counts as autoethnography simply reflects the "diverging evolution of the genre" (48).

The practice of autoethnography of any type is not without critics and cautionary tales. For one, autoethnography can be less contained than other types of qualitative research. It may be difficult or impossible to plan in advance the data that will be collected, the timeframe for data collection, and even the sites of research—all of which raises questions about the methodological rigor of autoethnography and ethics (see Le Roux 2017). For instance, if an autoethnographer uses memories as a data point, those remembered experiences likely were not part of a sanctioned study; IRB was not consulted, and consent forms were not signed (Delamont 2009 offers a scathing critique of this practice). Moreover, autoethnography is by definition "backyard research," as the researcher is looking at a site or culture to which they belong (Creswell 2014). Thus, autoethnography is open to the same critiques that have plagued teacher research: as the researcher and the subject of the research simultaneously, can the researcher pay attention well enough? Will the researcher control the scene and unfairly shape the story that emerges? None of these limitations can be solved, only acknowledged and mitigated. Cheryl Le Roux (2017), for example, advocates doing member checks or interviews with persons who show up in memories or diaries, when possible, as a way to obtain their consent.

AUTOETHNOGRAPHY IN WRITING STUDIES

Given the multiplicity of types and approaches to autoethnography, what is writing studies autoethnography? Of what use is it and what forms ought it take? Adapting Ngunjiri, Hernandez, and Chang (2010), we define writing studies autoethnography as studies/texts in which

1. **the author writes from personal experiences within writing/writing studies.** What makes an autoethnography a *writing studies* autoethnography is that the writer has personal experiences with(in) the discipline or practices related to language and representation, literacy, writing, teaching writing, studying writing/writers, being a writer, and/or other related experiences at the heart of the study.

2. **the author uses an inductive, qualitative approach for project design, data collection, and analysis.** Autoethnography is an inductive approach to research that should start with inquiry and employ qualitative research methods in construction of the study; collection, analysis, and interpretation of data; and the resulting text. Autoethnographers are not using personal experiences to make an argument a priori; rather, autoethnographers pose a question, collect relevant data, and listen to the data to see what findings emerge. As Bochner (2017) puts it, "The shape of autoethnography is not the exclamation point but the question mark" (77).

3. **the author writes in conversation with other texts** (such as interviews, artifacts, or existing scholarship). Like Tony Adams, Stacy Holman Jones, and Carolyn Ellis (2015), we do not believe autoethnographers must cite specific secondary sources within the text in order to demonstrate engagement with important disciplinary conversations. In an evocative autoethnography, for example, we might find clear gestures to and analysis of disciplinary conversations those in the field are meant to recognize. Linda Brodkey's (1994) "Writing on the Bias" is an excellent example.

4. **the author writes back or intervenes in a cultural narrative or conversation.** Drawing on the tradition sparked by Zora Neale Hurston and others, autoethnographers in writing studies should attempt an interruption of dominant cultural narratives and interpretations through documentation and sharing of their "little narratives," as Jean-Francois Lyotard (1984) calls them.

We forward that all autoethnography is first-person scholarship, but not all first-person scholarship is autoethnography. We've seen in our discipline (and more outside our discipline) some haziness around this distinction: some scholarship calling itself "autoethnography" based solely on the disclosure of personal experiences within the scholarship. However, we worry if writing studies scholars were to use *autoethnography* to mean any first-person scholarship, nearly all our scholarship could be called *autoethnography*, making the term redundant and useless. The problem of defining an autoethnography for writing studies strikes us as not dissimilar to the problem scholars have faced in writing studies in defining multimodal texts over the last decade or two. Sure, it can be conceded that all texts are already multimodal (typeface, medium, size, binding, and so forth all help make the meaning of a text), but for the term to be useful we must be generous readers and consider intentionality. In that spirit, we don't think autoethnography should mean just anything and then, as a result, mean absolutely nothing. So, we have endeavored to bracket off what texts we see as being of a similar purpose and kind *and* texts that aren't something else already. If it's a literacy narrative, it's a literacy narrative. Autoethnography should not be used to rebrand an existing genre.

In addition, we want to underscore how autoethnography as a genre (product) complicates notions of what qualitative research ought to look like. Autoethnographies in the evocative tradition often do not have a methods discussion in which the researcher neatly lays out the research question, data-collection and analysis procedures, and the like within the text. This can make it difficult for readers to know whether a text is an autoethnography or not by looking at it. We think it's helpful for autoethnographers to find paratextual ways to communicate their methods for transparency and, potentially, replicability. For example, Tony Adams (2017) recommends using headnotes, footnotes, endnotes, or other forms to define autoethnography, articulate perspectives and methodology, and explain how personal experience is used. Doing so, autoethnographers preserve the coherence and impact of the autoethnographic narrative and discourage readers from "evaluating [the] work in unfortunate and untenable ways" (63). Following Adams's lead, we've asked contributors in this collection to use headnotes if they haven't discussed their methods within the texts of their autoethnographies.

Further, we concede there is a long history of personal critical scholarship within writing studies, of using first person, of respecting the lived experience of scholars as a way to theorize; we call some texts that result from that vein *autoethnographic* when the personal is used as a vantage point to understand/rewrite cultural narratives. What we're suggesting, however, is that autoethnography not only engages *self* and *culture* but is situated firmly within the qualitative tradition (and thus demands a systematic approach to gathering and interpreting data); an autoethnography is a research study. Though we think this distinction is relevant, this collection contains both autoethnographic pieces and autoethnographies (and discussions of autoethnographic writing/teaching and autoethnographies), as both do important work. (See also appendix 0.A: "Evaluating Autoethnography.")

We think it's important to stake out the territory of autoethnography for writing studies, as this collection endeavors to do, because when we look to existing writing studies scholarship to see how autoethnography is defined by others in writing studies, we don't find consensus. In fact, we don't find much at all about autoethnography. A genre/method that combines a focus on self + culture + writing seems as if it would find wide appeal in writing studies, a discipline in which so-called personal writing, cultural studies, and qualitative research have all taken root. However, at this point in time, it wouldn't be accurate to say autoethnography has been widely adapted. As of late 2020, when we last searched CompPile, the database for scholarship in writing studies (comppile.org), we found just over twenty sources with the keyword *autoethnography*, yet only a few of these engage autoethnography deeply within a writing studies journal or edited collection (Leack 2019; Maraj 2018; Passwater 2019; Rumsey 2009). One dissertation writer claims he found nearly one hundred instances of the term "autoethnography," "autoethnographer," or "autoethnographic" in peer-reviewed writing studies journals (doing a full-text word search not a keyword search), though he admits many of those instances were not in articles but in ads, announcements, and letters from the editors (Hopkins 2017). A search of recent CCCC programs (2014–18) reveals only eighteen presentations with *autoethnography* or *autoethnographic* in the title or one-sentence abstract. Fewer than a dozen writing studies dissertations using *autoethnography* have been completed.

It's possible that autoethnography isn't compelling to those in our discipline because we have existing scholarly conventions in which using personal perspective is the norm; writing studies scholarship is often written in first person and includes examples from personal experience to critique dominant cultural narratives. Said another way, writing studies scholars didn't need the turn toward autoethnography to encourage or justify writing the personal/critical into scholarship because we were already doing it in our work and teaching students to do the same.

Too, autoethnography might only now be rising in popularity because it raises questions about status and privilege—about who is "allowed" to write autoethnography and who is not. Though it is true autoethnography has long been employed by those on the margins to write back to those in the center, in the academic-publishing grind, autoethnography demands a vulnerability that may only be (safely) enacted by scholars who are tenured and established. Certainly, the chapters in this collection suggest one must lay bare quite a bit of the self in order to write a good autoethnography. As Deborah Holdstein (2002) notes, "I still believe, more often than not, that being 'too' personal is a luxury, the privilege of those who have somehow arrived" (9). It's commonly accepted that academics must commodify their scholarship to earn jobs, tenure, and promotion, but it's something else to ask academics to commodify their experiences and lives for the consumption of hiring and tenuring committees.

Nonetheless, some scholars in writing studies call their work *autoethnography* and use it as a method of inquiry. These scholars are often influenced by Mary Louise Pratt's (1991) "Arts of the Contact Zone." In this much-cited article, Pratt defines autoethnography as any text "in which people undertake to describe themselves in ways that engage with representations others have made of them" (7). One scholar influenced by Pratt is A. Suresh Canagarajah (1997, 2012a, 2012b, 2016), who has emerged as the foremost voice on autoethnography within writing studies/second language acquisition. For Canagarajah, the point of autoethnography is to inspire social change, and he sees autoethnography as a viable contact-zone methodology for studying and teaching multilingual writers in particular (2012a).

Though there are not currently many published works that call themselves *autoethnographies* in writing studies, we suggest there's a longer history of similar work in the field that was written under different names; a keyword search would obviously not suss out sources that used (near) synonymous terms. For example, Keith Gilyard calls his sociolinguistic work in *Voices of the Self* "autobiographical narrative" (1991, 11). Victor Villanueva (in Brandt et al. 2001) calls the approach he uses in *Bootstraps* and elsewhere "critical autobiography," and his description is similar to the moves a writer makes in autoethnography:

> There must be room for elements of autobiography, not as confession and errant self-indulgence, not as the measure on which to assess theory, not as a replacement for rigor, but as a way of knowing our predispositions to see things certain ways, of understanding what it is that guides our intuition in certain ways. That is the autobiographical as critique. (Brandt et al. 2001, 51)

Likewise, Daniel Mahala and Jody Swilky (1996) use the term "academic storytelling" to describe a hybrid genre that, much like autoethnography, "neither mimics the sentimental persona of the personal essay nor the impersonal personal of authoritative knowledge" (373). Instead, academic storytelling merges the personal and the social and asks that we "write the self reflexively as an historical subject who tells stories from lived experience yet also draws on ways of reasoning, arguing, and writing that empower [the academic storyteller] as a professional" (73).

Krista Ratcliffe (2004) theorizes "cultural autobiographics" as that which "interweaves the personal with the textual and the cultural, and exposes the material dimensions of language and written texts" (212), while Vershawn Young (2007) uses the term "narrative performance" to describe his purposeful mix of "creative" with "academic" in his arguments about the intersections of language and race (10). Finally, although there is certainly additional scholarship we could mention, Malea Powell (2012) promotes a self-reflexive move characteristic of autoethnography when she encourages writers to examine critically the stories they tell, to do the courageous yet difficult work of "stepping back" from their own narratives.

> In the writing classes that I teach, I often ask my students: "What is this story about?" and "What is this story doing?" I ask these questions to get my students to step back from the rush of events in their narratives, to reflect upon the action, to think through the effect their stories might have on their readers. As a writer and a scholar, I often have to do the same. This stepping back is hard; it takes a great deal of courage to stand outside our own narratives for a moment and ask, "What is this story about? What is it doing to those who may read it?" Stories have an effect. They are real. They matter. (390)

While some, including Louis Maraj (2018), have argued that the kinds of scholarship we cite here are indeed examples of autoethnography, we think it's tricky work to label others' scholarship after the fact with a name they didn't choose and a name that, perhaps until now, was overly malleable. Nonetheless, it's clear all autoethnographers in writing studies ought to be familiar with all these scholars, who have contributed to a tradition of scholarship that is, at minimum, very closely related to autoethnographic inquiry.

All that said, we see some evidence (and the projects proposed to this collection confirm this hunch to some degree) that autoethnography is taught more in writing classrooms than it is used by scholars in their research. So while writing studies folks talk about, define, and to some degree enact and theorize autoethnography, they mostly discuss its value in/as a genre for writing assignments. Perhaps this is because most in writing studies come to autoethnography by way Brodkey's (1994) "Writing on the Bias," which discusses the power of autoethnography for (student) writers. Deborah Mutnick (1998), for example, argues that for "students on the social margins," autoethnography creates a "bridge between their communities and the academy" (84). Mahala and Swilky (1996), Hannah Ashley (2001), Susan Hanson (2004), Jane Danielewicz (2008), Patrick Camangian (2010), Justin Hopkins (2017), and Ryan

David Leack (2019) each propose autoethnography for the writing classroom as a way, in Hanson's words, to merge the "autobiographical *Here*" with the "ethnographic *There*" (2004, 184). Elizabeth Wardle and Doug Downs's (2017) popular textbook *Writing about Writing* offers an autoethnography as a writing assignment, and Melissa Tombro's *Teaching Autoethnography* (2016) is a book-length guide to teaching autoethnography in writing studies.

OVERVIEW OF *SELF+CULTURE+WRITING*

We've divided the chapters in this collection into three sections. We begin with writing studies autoethnographies in part 1. These chapters are written by faculty, graduate students, and, in one case, a writing studies researcher in collaboration with her father who used writing extensively in his workplace. The topics range from teaching writing, which we might expect, to entering and navigating the profession and to exposing and resisting disciplinary, professional, and institutional narratives and practices that disenfranchise some, but not all. As autoethnographers do, the authors in this section reveal the multiple identities and related tensions that come to bear in their professional lives. For this reason, we find Pelias's (2019) taxonomy of available autoethnographic "selves" useful when reading chapters in this section. These "selves" include

- the disrupted or traumatized self,
- the diminished or marginalized/voiceless self,
- the confessional self who speaks what is culturally forbidden,
- the joyful self,
- the critical or activist self,
- the complicit self,
- the testifying or truth-telling self.

Last, the autoethnographies here are a bit different from each other in method and form; for this reason, we asked each author to include in or as a preface to their chapter a brief section discussing how they conducted their autoethnography and what they see as defining characteristics of autoethnography in writing studies. We organized the chapters in this section on a continuum from primarily evocative to primarily analytical, although we recognize each autoethnography in this section contains both evocative and analytical elements.

In chapter 1, "Her Own Voice," Tiffany Rainey writes an evocative autoethnography about her experience as a budding academic recently diagnosed with bipolar disorder. Drawing upon journal entries, medical forms, conversations, and reflective notes, Rainey examines what it might take to attain "rhetoricability" in the discipline and the culture at large. Related in spirit and form to Rainey's autoethnography, chapters 2 and 3 center the body as a site of knowledge production (Inayatulla) and means of interrogating constraints to identity and exploitative labor practices (Hallman Martini). In chapter 2, "Literate Vixens and Shameless Hijabis," Shereen Inayatulla employs what she calls "vulnerable automythnography" to address the power of gender, patriarchy, religion, sexuality, and family on literacy. In chapter 3, "When Things Fall Apart," Rebecca Hallman Martini deploys evocative autoethnography as disciplinary critique, narrating her experiences as a PhD student, exploited laborer in the academy, and burgeoning labor activist as catalysts of her emotional and physical breakdown. Chapters 4, 5, and 6 move incrementally toward the analytical autoethnography end of the spectrum. In chapter 4, "The Space Between: Searching for a Middle Ground between Epistemological Despair and Radical Hope," Leslie Akst offers an autoethnography of teaching and teaching autoethnography to examine the ways shame can occlude what is (supposed to be) hopeful about autoethnographic research and writing. Chapter 5, Elena C. Garcia and Guadalupe Garcia's collaborative autoethnography, titled "A Window into the Complex World of Factory-Floor Writing," shares with Akst's chapter features of analytic autoethnography while turning our attention away from the academy to the factory floor. Merging Elena G. Garcia's expertise in ethnography with Guadalupe Garcia's experiences as a factory machine operator, this autoethnography narrates factory-floor workers' refusal to write instruction manuals for their jobs on the floor as resistance to sharing workers' knowledge with others who could then easily take away their jobs. The last chapter in this section—Soyeon Lee's "Constructing a Transnational-Multilingual Teacher Subjectivity in a First-Year Writing Class"—takes us back to the academy and the classroom. In this piece, a clear example of analytic autoethnography, Lee positions her autoethnographic account of teaching first-year writing as a transnational, nonnative English speaker and graduate student in opposition to the numerous quantitative studies of NNES teachers' self-perceptions. Drawing upon "thick narratives" of her teaching read through transnational social field and translingual perspectives, Lee demonstrates her translingual teaching practices are "contingent on the material conditions that constitute the context of [her] migration experiences."

The chapters in part 2 offer arguments for and around teaching autoethnography within writing studies; contributors explore autoethnography as the locus of instruction in contexts ranging from the first-year writing classroom to the graduate-level seminar in writing studies to working with teachers in the National Writing Project. Each is concerned with autoethnography's effect on the writing student, asking, What do writers gain from this type of inquiry? To that end, and to greater and lesser degrees, each chapter shares what the authors' approaches look like on paper or screen—required course texts, required writing, project sequences, for example. Still, none of the chapters is a simple how-to on teaching autoethnography; rather, the writers merge course specifics with analysis of how autoethnography works and is taken up by student writers in vastly different contexts.

The first two chapters in this section address using autoethnography in first-year writing. In chapter 7, "Empowering Autoethnography in Two-Year College Reform," Kirsten Higgins, Anthony Warnke, and Marcie Sims discuss the use of autoethnography with community college writing students as a way to reform the reform movement allowing students to bridge their personal and academic lives, and in chapter 8, "'Say What You Want to Say!': Teaching Literacy Autoethnography to Resist Linguistic Prejudice," Amanda Sladek discusses the literacy autoethnographies of four multilingual writing students enrolled in a first-year writing course. Both these chapters argue that autoethnography, as a genre that intersects personal and academic writing, allows students a soft entry into college-level writing. In a similar way, chapters 9 and 10, "What the Students Taught the Teacher in a Graduate Autoethnography Course" by Sue Doe, Kira Marshall-McKelvey, Ross Atkinson, Caleb Gonzalez, Lilly Halboth, and Jennifer Owen, and "Agentic Discord in Writing Studies" by William Duffy, make the case for teaching autoethnography to graduate students as a way to help them understand and interrogate their complex, often contradictory, positions as newcomers to the discipline. Finally, in the last chapter in this section, chapter 11, "Collaging the Classroom, the Personal, and the Critical," Trixie Smith uses a multigenre collage essay to argue the connectedness of the method of autoethnography and the National Writing Project. Taken as a whole, the chapters in this section make the case that entry points into disciplines are ripe moments for autoethnographic study by establishing what students and teachers learn from assigning autoethnographic projects.

Finally, part 3 contains chapters whose authors extend, and at times challenge, conventional histories of and methodological approaches to autoethnography and propose ways of thinking about and doing autoethnography that are more inclusive, nuanced, and media rich. Collectively, these chapters push us to interrogate what we think we know about autoethnography—to ask important questions about who is allowed to author and police histories of autoethnography; how particular theoretical frames and attendant metaphors invite us to see autoethnography from new vantage points; how autoethnography contributes to and bolsters dominant cultural narratives rather than, as our disciplinary narrative suggests, how autoethnography resists and subverts them; and how particular autoethnographic tools engender insights other tools may not.

In chapter 12, "You Can't Do That Here: Black/Feminist Autoethnography and Histories of Intellectual Exclusion," Louis Maraj traces the roots of Black feminist autoethnography to nineteenth-century Black women writers and speakers whose work "squares the personal with the political" but has been (and continues to be) devalued or ignored altogether. Such "intellectual exclusion," Maraj argues, is grounded in "white respectability politics and hegemonic ideologies" that determine who gets to produce knowledge in the field (and who doesn't). Chapters 13 and 14 echo the call to revision Maraj advances in chapter 12. In chapter 13, John Gagnon proposes "constellational autoethnography" (adapted from Indigenous research traditions and methods) as a methodological approach "centered in making an effort to understand the shared reality that participants and researchers inhabit by being brought together to create knowledge and make meaning." Merging "the cultural rhetorics idea of constellational practice with that of critical autoethnography," constellational autoethnography replaces traditional (often reified) notions of autoethnography as "interpersonal" with an invigorated understanding of "shared realities." Autumn Laws, in chapter 14, "Chaotic Construction: Disabling the Autoethnography," argues that autoethnography proper, as a primarily academic practice and genre, is inaccessible to the disabled because "the academy has always been a space that reifies ableism." Laws proposes disability life writing, the "chaos narrative" in particular, as a useful substitute for disability autoethnography, arguing chaos narratives "resist the nondisabled expectations that other autoethnographic methods might presume." In chapter 15, Alison Cardinal, Melissa Atienza, and Aliyah Jones turn to our attention to participatory video as a media-rich qualitative tool for gathering autoethnographic data on literacy. They suggest participatory video offers researchers and participants "the opportunity to discover different aspects of literacy that composing a written autoethnographic text alone does not," including the "embodied, visual and affective nature of literacy." Yet they also warn against uncritical acceptance of participatory video as a tool, noting that successful participatory video experiences require student investment, motivation, and trust.

Certainly, readers will notice several chapters could fit in more than one of the parts and see ideas and themes that carry throughout the collection. As we arranged the chapters, we noticed issues of identity and (not) belonging, trauma, and labor running through the collection, particularly in part 1. We argue that other methods of study likely would not have rendered these issues as well as the autoethnographic approach does, and the discipline needs to acknowledge and own these issues. Many in our discipline, particularly adjunct faculty and graduate students, are laboring in unfair, unsustainable positions. Many (still) hold a precariously thin strand of connection to the discipline that still operates as if members are all white, American, English speaking, straight, cis, neurologically typical, and from the academic/professional class. The authors in this collection reveal how far the line of connection is stretched, almost to the point of breaking, as they try to fit into and try to resist a discipline and a vocation not built for them.

At the same time, we see in this collection the dogged, perhaps unreasonable, hopefulness of educators and their desire to enact Paolo Freire's call for education to be the practice of freedom. Teachers of writing want students to believe the future can be different from the present, and autoethnography becomes an almost therapeutic tool for students to take control of their stories and to correct dominant narratives that misrepresent or omit them entirely.

We believe this collection will change readers and change writing studies. We believe this collection shows the possibility of autoethnography to open up space for writers and how autoethnography can be utterly persuasive to readers. We began soliciting chapters for this collection with curiosity and end this process with a much clearer sense of purpose and commitment. Autoethnography as a way of making meaning, as a method of inquiry, as a teachable genre, has much to offer writing studies. Bochner (2012) has written, "If our research is to mean something to our readers—to be acts of meaning—our writing needs to attract, awaken, and arouse them, inviting readers into conversation with the incidents, feelings, contingencies, contradictions, memories, and desires that our research stories depict" (158). We hope by the end of this collection that writing studies readers will recognize the power of autoethnography to be an act of meaning.

APPENDIX 0.A

EVALUATING AUTOETHNOGRAPHY

Subjectivity
- The self is primarily visible in the research. That is, the researcher reenacts or retells a noteworthy or critical personal relational or institutional experience—generally in search of self-understanding (Le Roux 2017).
- The researcher is self-consciously involved in the construction of the narrative that constitutes the research (Le Roux 2017).
- The text embodies a fleshed-out, embodied sense of lived experience (Richardson 2000).
- The text reveals the self (Schroeder 2017).
- The text enables the reader to enter the subjective world of the teller—to see the world from their point of view (Adams, Jones, and Ellis 2015).

Credibility
- The experiences the narrator describes are believable; they could have happened (Adams, Jones, and Ellis 2015).
- The text seems "true"—a credible account of cultural, social, individual, or communal sense of the "real" (Richardson 2000).
- There is evidence of verisimilitude, plausibility, and trustworthiness in the research (Le Roux 2017).
- The research process and reporting are permeated by honesty (Le Roux 2017).

Reflexivity
- There is evidence of the researcher's intense awareness of their role in and relationship to the research, which is situated within a historical and cultural context (Le Roux 2017).
- There is evidence of self-awareness, self-exposure, and self-conscious introspection (Le Roux 2017).
- The author is committed to ethical practices in research and representation (Richardson 2000).

Resonance or Impact
- The text affects the reader emotionally and/or intellectually (Richardson 2000).

- The text generates new questions (Richardson 2000).
- The text moves the reader to write, try new research practices, act (Richardson 2000).
- Readers are able to enter into and engage with the writer's experience or connect with the writer's story on an intellectual and emotional level (Le Roux 2017).
- There is a sense of commonality between the researcher and the audience—an intertwining of lives (Le Roux 2017).
- Readers are encouraged to think about how and why lives are similar and different (Adams, Jones, and Ellis 2015).

Contribution
- The piece contributes to our understanding of social life (Richardson 2000).
- The writer demonstrates a deeply grounded human-world understanding and perspective (Richardson 2000).
- The piece extends knowledge, generates ongoing research, liberates, empowers, improves practices, and/or makes a contribution to social change (Le Roux 2017).
- The piece is useful (Adams, Jones, and Ellis 2015).

Aesthetic Merit
- The piece (or relevant sections of the piece) succeeds aesthetically (Richardson 2000).
- The use of creative analytical practices opens up the text and invites interpretive responses (Richardson 2000).
- The text is artistically shaped, satisfying, complex, and not boring (Richardson 2000).
- The text reflects storycraft (Schroeder 2017).

REFERENCES

Adams, Tony. 2017. "Autoethnographic Responsibilities." *International Review of Qualitative Research* 10 (1): 62–66.

Adams, Tony E., Stacy Holman Jones, and Carolyn Ellis. 2015. *Autoethnography: Understanding Qualitative Research*. New York: Oxford University Press.

Ashley, Hannah. 2001. "Playing the Game: Proficient Working-Class Student Writers' Second Voices." *Research in the Teaching of English* 35 (4): 493–524.

Bochner, Arthur P. 2012. "On First-Person Narrative Scholarship: Autoethnography as Acts of Meaning." *Narrative Inquiry* 22 (1): 155–64.

Bochner, Arthur P. 2017. "Heart of the Matter: A Mini-Manifesto for Autoethnography." *International Review of Qualitative Research* 10 (1): 67–80.

Boylorn, Robin M., and Mark P. Orbe. 2014. "Critical Autoethnography: Implications and Future Directions." *Critical Autoethnography: Intersecting Cultural Identities in Everyday Life*. New York: Routledge.

Breault, Rick. 2017. "Dialogic Life History in Preservice Teacher Education." In *Theorizing Curriculum Studies, Teacher Education, and Research through Duoethnographic Pedagogy*, edited by Joe Norris and Richard D. Sawyer, 63–84. New York: Palgrave Macmillan.

Brandt, Deborah, Ellen Cushman, Anne Ruggles Gere, Anne Herrington, Richard E. Miller, Victor Villanueva, Min-Zhan Lu, and Gesa Kirsch. 2001. "The Politics of the Personal: Storying Our Lives against the Grain. Symposium Collective." *College English* 64 (1): 41–62.

Broad, Bob. 2017. "So Many Data, So Much Time: Living with Grounded Theory in A Rhetorical Autoethnography." In *Reflections on Qualitative Research in Language and Literacy Education*, edited by Seyyed-Abdolhamid Mirehosseini, 91–104. New York: Springer.

Brodkey, Linda. 1994. "Writing on the Bias." *College English* 56 (5): 527–47.

Brown-Vincent, Layla. D. 2019. "Seeing It for Wearing It: Autoethnography as Black Feminist Methodology." *Taboo: The Journal of Culture and Education* 18 (1): 109–25.

Camangian, Patrick. 2010. "Starting with Self: Teaching Autoethnography to Foster Critically Caring Literacies." *Research in the Teaching of English* 45 (2): 179–204.

Canagarajah, A. Suresh. 1997. "Safe Houses in the Contact Zone: Coping Strategies of African-American Students in the Academy." *College Composition and Communication* 48 (2): 173–96.

Canagarajah, A. Suresh. 2012a. "Autoethnography in the Study of Multilingual Writers." In *Writing Studies Research in Practice: Methods and Methodologies*, edited by Lee Nickoson, Mary P. Sheridan, and Gesa Kirsch, 113–24. Carbondale: Southern Illinois University Press.

Canagarajah, A. Suresh. 2012b. "Teacher Development in a Global Profession: An Autoethnography." *TESOL Quarterly* 46 (2): 258–79.

Canagarajah, Suresh. 2016. "Translingual Writing and Teacher Development in Composition." *College English* 78 (3): 265–73.

Canagarajah, Suresh, and Ena Lee. 2013. "Negotiating Alternative Discourses in Academic Writing and Publishing: Risks with Hybridity." In *Risk in Academic Writing: Postgraduate Students, Their Teachers and the Making of Knowledge*, edited by Linda Cooper and Lucia Thesen, 59–99. Bristol: Multilingual Matters.

Cann, Colette N., and Eric J. DeMeulenaere. 2012. "Critical Co-constructed Autoethnography." *Cultural Studies, Critical Methodologies* 12 (2): 146–58.

Chang, Heewon. 2016. *Autoethnography as Method*. New York: Routledge.

Chang, Heewon, Faith Ngunjiri, and Kathy-Ann C. Hernandez. 2016. *Collaborative Autoethnography*. New York: Routledge.

Chawla, Devika, and Ahmet Atay. 2018. "Introduction: Decolonizing Autoethnography." *Cultural Studies, Critical Methodologies* 18 (1): 3–8.

Covington, Dennis. 2009. *Salvation on Sand Mountain: Snake Handling and Redemption in Southern Appalachia*. 15th ann. ed. Cambridge, MA: Da Capo.

Crawley, Sara L. 2012. "Autoethnography as Feminist Self-Interview." In *The SAGE Handbook of Interview Research: The Complexity of The Craft*, edited by Jaber F. Gubrium and James A. Holstein, 143–61. 2nd ed. Thousand Oaks, CA: SAGE.

Creswell, John. 2014. *Research Design*. 4th ed. Thousand Oaks, CA: SAGE.

Danielewicz, Jane. 2008. "Personal Genres, Public Voices." *College Composition and Communication* 59 (3): 420–50.

Delamont, Sara. 2009. "The Only Honest Thing: Autoethnography, Reflexivity and Small Crises in Fieldwork." *Ethnography and Education* 4 (1): 51–63.

Denejkina, Anna. 2017. "Exo-Autoethnography: An Introduction." In *Forum Qualitative Sozialforschung/Forum: Qualitative Social Research* 18 (3).

Diversi, Marcelo, and Claudio Moreira. 2017. "Autoethnography Manifesto." *International Review of Qualitative Research* 10 (1): 39–43.

Diversi, Marcelo, and Claudio Moreira. 2018. *Betweener Autoethnographies: A Path Towards Social Justice*. New York: Routledge.

Ellis, Carolyn. 1999. "Heartful Autoethnography." *Qualitative Health Research* 9 (5): 669–83.
Ellis, Carolyn, Tony E. Adams, and Arthur P. Bochner. 2011. "Autoethnography: An Overview." *Historical Social Research / Historische Sozialforschung* 36 (4): 273–90.
Ellis, Carolyn, and Arthur P. Bochner. 2000. "Autoethnography, Personal Narrative, Reflexivity: Researcher as Subject." In *The SAGE Handbook of Qualitative Research*, edited by Norman K. Denzin and Yvonna S. Lincoln, 733–68. 2nd ed. Thousand Oaks, CA: SAGE. https://scholarcommons.usf.edu/spe_facpub/91.
Ettorre, Elizabeth. 2016. *Autoethnography as Feminist Method: Sensitising the Feminist "I."* New York: Routledge.
Gilyard, Keith. 1991. *Voices of the Self: A Study of Language Competence*. Detroit: Wayne State University Press.
Goodall, H. L. (Bud) Jr. 2000. *Writing the New Ethnography*. Vol. 7 of Ethnographic Alternatives Book Series. New York: AltaMira.
Griffin, Rachel Alicia. 2012. "I AM an Angry Black Woman: Black Feminist Autoethnography, Voice, and Resistance." *Women's Studies in Communication* 35 (2): 138–57.
Hanson, Susan. 2004. "Critical Auto/Ethnography: A Constructive Approach to Research in the Composition Classroom." In *Ethnography Unbound: From Theory Shock to Critical Praxis*, edited by Stephen Gilbert Brown and Sidney I. Dobrin, 183–200. Albany: SUNY Press.
Herrmann, Andrew F. 2017. *Organizational Autoethnographies*. New York: Routledge.
Holdstein, Deborah. 2002. Introduction to *Personal Effects: The Social Character of Scholarly Writing*, edited by Deborah Holdstein and David Bleich. Logan: Utah State University Press.
Hopkins, Justin. 2017. "The Story of Them: Outcomes of Practicing Autoethnography in Undergraduate Writing Courses." PhD diss., Indiana University of Pennsylvania.
Jackson, Michael. 1989. *Paths toward a Clearing: Radical Empiricism and Ethnographic Inquiry*. Bloomington: Indiana University Press.
Lapadat, Judith C. 2017. "Ethics in Autoethnography and Collaborative Autoethnography." *Qualitative Inquiry* 23 (8): 589–603.
Leack, Ryan David. 2019. "From Chaos to Cosmos, and Back: Place-Based Autoethnography in First-Year Composition." *Composition Forum* 41. http://compositionforum.com/issue/41/chaos-cosmos.php.
Le Roux, Cheryl S. 2017. "Exploring Rigour in Autoethnographic Research." *International Journal of Social Research Methodology* 20 (2): 195–207.
Lunceford, Brett. 2015. "Rhetorical Autoethnography." *Journal of Contemporary Rhetoric* 5 (1–2): 1–20.
Lyotard, Jean-Francois. 1984. *The Postmodern Condition*. Minneapolis: University of Minnesota Press.
Mahala, Daniel, and Jody Swilky. 1996. "Speaking Personally: Reconsidering the Place of Lived Experience in Composition." *JAC* 16 (3): 363–88.
Maraj, Louis M. (2018). "'Are You Black, Though?': Black Autoethnography and Racing the Graduate Student/Instructor." In *Precarious Rhetorics*, edited by Wendy S. Hesford, Adela C. Licona, and Christa Teston, 212–33. Columbus: The Ohio State University Press.
May, Stephan A. 1997. "Critical Ethnography." In *Encyclopedia of Language and Education*, edited by Nancy H. Hornberger and P. Corson. New York: Springer.
Mutnick, Deborah. 1998. "Rethinking the Personal Narrative: Life-Writing and Composition Pedagogy." In *Under Construction: Working at the Intersections of Composition Theory, Research, and Practice*, edited by Christine Farris and Chris M. Anson, 79–92. Logan, UT: Utah State University Press.
Ngunjiri, Faith Wambura, Kathy-Ann C. Hernandez, and Heewon Chang. 2010. "Living Autoethnography: Connecting Life and Research." *Journal of Research Practice* 6 (1): Article E1.

Norris, Joe, Richard D. Sawyer, and Darren Lund, eds. 2012. *Duoethnography: Dialogic Methods for Social, Health, and Educational Research.* New York: Routledge.

Passwater, T. 2019. "Precarious Spaces, Institutional Places." *Composition Forum* 41. http://compositionforum.com/issue/41/precarious-spaces.php.

Pelias, Ronald J. 2019. *The Creative Qualitative Researcher: Writing That Makes Readers Want to Read.* New York: Routledge.

Pratt, Mary Louise. 1991. "Arts of the Contact Zone." *Profession*: 33–40.

Powell, Malea. 2012. "Stories Take Place: A Performance in One Act." *College Composition and Communication* 64 (2): 383–406.

Ratcliffe, Krista. 2004. "Cultural Autobiographics: Complicating the 'Personal Turns' in Rhetoric and Composition Studies." In *The Private, the Public, and the Published*, edited by Barbara Couture and Thomas Kent, 198–215. Logan: Utah State University Press.

Richardson, Laurel. 2000. "Evaluating Ethnography." *Qualitative Inquiry* 6 (2): 253–55.

Rumsey, Suzanne Kesler. 2009. "Heritage Literacy: Adoption, Adaptation, and Alienation of Multimodal Literacy Tools." *College Composition and Communication* 60 (3): 573–86.

Schroeder, Robert. 2017. "Evaluative Criteria for Autoethnographic Research: Who's to Judge?" In *The Self as Subject: Autoethnographic Research into Identity, Culture, and Academic Librarianship*, edited by Anne-Marie Deitering, Robert Schroeder, and Richard Stoddar, 315–46. Chicago: Association of College and Research Libraries.

Sheriff, Robin E. 2017. "A Cat for All Senses: A Multispecies Autoethnography." *Anthropology and Humanism* 42 (1): 8–10.

Spry, Tami. 2016. *Body, Paper, Stage: Writing and Performing Autoethnography.* New York: Routledge.

Stahlke Wall, Sarah. 2016. "Toward a Moderate Autoethnography." *International Journal of Qualitative Methods* 15 (1): 1–9.

Taber, Nancy. 2010. "Institutional Ethnography, Autoethnography, and Narrative: An Argument for Incorporating Multiple Methodologies." *Qualitative Research* 10 (1): 5–25.

Tombro, Melissa. 2016. *Teaching Autoethnography: Personal Writing in the Classroom.* Albany: Open SUNY Textbooks.

Toyosaki, Satoshi. 2018. "Toward De/Postcolonial Autoethnography: Critical Relationality with the Academic Second Persona." *Cultural Studies, Critical Methodologies* 18 (1): 32–42.

Toyosaki, Satoshi, Sandra L. Pensoneau-Conway, Nathan A. Wendt, and Kyle Leathers. 2009. "Community Autoethnography: Compiling the Personal and Resituating Whiteness." *Cultural Studies, Critical Methodologies* 9 (1): 56–83.

Wardle, Elizabeth, and Doug Downs. 2017. *Writing about Writing.* 3rd ed. Boston: Bedford/St. Martin's.

Whitinui, Paul. 2014. "Indigenous Autoethnography: Exploring, Engaging, and Experiencing 'Self' as a Native Method of Inquiry." *Journal of Contemporary Ethnography* 43 (4): 456–87.

Young, Vershawn Ashanti. 2007. *Your Average Nigga: Performing Race, Literacy, and Masculinity.* Detroit: Wayne State University Press.

PART ONE

Writing Studies Autoethnographies

1
HER OWN VOICE
Coming Out in Academia with Bipolar Disorder

Tiffany Rainey

This project began in a graduate course on autoethnography as a research method for/as writing studies. Because I had recently experienced a psychotic break and was dealing with the social and professional fallout, I chose to explore my experiences with mental illness; specifically, I wanted to gain a critical understanding of my experience as a graduate student and faculty member with bipolar disorder.

The process was broken into recursive steps in which I searched my memories; wrote them narratively; coded, analyzed, and interpreted primary data; and consulted existing literature. Because themes of fear of accepting a diagnosis and problems with disclosing mental illness emerged at nearly every step, my research quickly became an interrogation of the dominant narrative that has led to stigmatization of persons with mental illness.

Stigmas surrounding mental illness run deep in our culture, so deep that sufferers often internalize them: "Stigma says I am not to be trusted. I am not to be trusted." Or "Stigma says I am incompetent. I am incompetent." We don't say these things aloud. We don't necessarily think them. But deep down, many of us believe them. Before I began my research, it had not occurred to me that the dominant narrative could be wrong. This autoethnography changed me. Now, I want to change the dominant narrative.

Carolyn Ellis, Tony Adams, and Arthur Bochner (2011) write, "Autoethnographies are socially-just acts that change us and the world we live in for the better" (284). Certainly, the world would be better without stigma. If the most effective way to fight stigma is through empathy, and we develop empathy through perspective taking, then we should be telling stories of mental illness in ways that help others—and ourselves—understand our lived experiences. Thus, it is through "deep disclosure" (Uthappa 2017, 166)—a detailed, evocative, and sometimes disturbing account of how I experience my illness—that I attempt to show readers what having bipolar disorder means for me.

The story goes that a person with mental illness is "quite thoroughly bad, or dangerous, or weak" (Prendergast 2001, 3). Further, she is wildly irrational, unpredictable, and incompetent. She is lost, often unaware or in denial of her illness.

If one were to ask a person with mental illness her thoughts on this story, she would say that while some of these things are true some of the time, her symptoms are not permanent, and her illness does not make her bad or dangerous or weak. She is more than just her illness; in fact, she is a dynamic and complex human, much like anyone else (Myers 2004, 258). Perhaps no one would listen, though, because the story has damaged her ethos.

How can a person with bipolar disorder secure an audience so she can tell the true story of her illness? Much of the literature on the subject says she cannot because mental illness "supplants one's position as a rhetor"; her personal expression has "no bearing outside of itself, no transactional worth" (Prendergast 2001, 57). It rarely matters if a stigmatized person has a wholesome or valuable message—they are silenced by their "kakoethos," or mark of "bad character." Jenell Johnson (2010) writes,

> If one's attributes make a claim, it is a claim of character—a stigmatized attribute breaks that claim by offering a more persuasive argument for a particular audience, and much like the ancient Greek mark [of stigma], it drowns out other forms of "speech" about character. One might be unfailingly kind, breathtakingly beautiful, and a whiz at calculus, but if one walks with a cane, wears the hijab, or is known to have bipolar disorder, these attributes tend to shout down the others in rhetorical environments where cane use, the hijab, or bipolar disorder are stigmatized. (465)

It is no wonder people with bipolar disorder are so hesitant to accept a diagnosis. While we might have felt relief initially at finally having a name for our monster and at the realization we are not inherently bad, perhaps relief turns to denial, or panic, or terror when it starts to sink in, when we begin to question what it means to "be" mentally ill (Young 2009, 58). Not least on the list of what it means is that stigmas associated with mental illness can rob us of voice. *Everyone knows psychos can't speak for themselves.* Because, you know, we're crazy.

I want to believe there is transactional worth in an alternative story of mental illness. I want to talk back to the cultural narrative that frames mental illness "as personal weakness, as something shameful, utterly destructive, and permanent" (Young 2009, 58). I want to say I am not weak, that I "do not necessarily, nor passively, accept the negative consequences of this group membership" (Michalak et al. 2010, 22). I want to say all the things I don't yet believe because if I say them loudly enough, confidently enough, powerfully enough, just *enough*, maybe I will persuade someone they are true. And when they believe, maybe I can believe too.

* * *

I didn't know I was sick. I knew, though, *I always knew*, I was off.

People who suffer from mental illness often don't know they have it. I was fully a woman—a wife and mother of three—when I was diagnosed with bipolar disorder in the spring of 2009.

James was out of town on business. It was rare that he left home for several days at a time, but it wouldn't be a problem, we said. With family nearby, I and our children had plenty of support. We were doing well, only missing him, when I abruptly found myself in our garage, hysterical, suicidal. Like most of my memories of this sort, I can't remember the important pieces that might help me understand why I ended up in this state. It's almost always a blur.

While my young children watched cartoons just steps away, I lay screaming and sobbing violently on the cold concrete floor of my garage. I don't know how long I was there. It was dark when I called James—I imagine a strained conversation because I can't recall our actual one—and he came home quickly. In the weeks following, there were fits of screaming, broken things, tears. My torment became James's torment; he carried our children on eggshells for me. We kept my instability from our family and friends, but there were times hiding out would have given away our secret. I went to family dinners. Smiled for pictures. Said all the things a normal, not-crazy person would say. It wasn't working. I was sure they knew.

* * *

I went alone to the psychiatrist's office, arrived early, and sat in my car for a very long time, deliberating on whether I should go inside. I didn't want to. I wanted to hide—from the psychiatrist, from James, from the crazy that welled up in me randomly, angrily. A burly, sour-faced woman greeted me from the other side of a thick, plexiglass window as I entered the office. It was dark and smelled of leather. There seemed to be a fog coming from somewhere, or there was a fog in my head. "The doctor is with a patient. Wait there." I heard men's voices through the wall. I tried not to listen. *Will someone overhear me talking with the doctor, too?* I was embarrassed.

He motioned for me to sit. *The couch? The chair?* I opted for the couch and regretted it. A precariously tall stack of papers shifted as I sat, and it's all I thought about as I answered stock questions for what felt to me like hours. "History of violence?" *No.* "Criminal record?" *Not really.* "Neurological disorders?" *Not that I'm aware of.* "Thoughts of harming yourself?" *Yes.* "Others?" *No.* When the questions stopped, there was a long pause as he scratched at his notepad. I asked for a copy of what he had written. I don't think he answered, or I didn't ask aloud. Bipolar disorder, he said finally, as he handed me a prescription. I was exhausted. As I walked to my car, I considered what I might say to James. *Which one of the characters in Girl, Interrupted has bipolar disorder?* My diagnosis didn't register; I didn't see myself in the images I had of mental illness.

* * *

There is an official story of bipolar disorder, one that clinicians tell. In this story, it is a randomly occurring cycling of mood states "between the extremes of mania and depression" (Guest 2018, 79). Assessed behaviorally, people with bipolar disorder have "distinct period[s] of elevated or irritable mood that can take the form of euphoria" (80). These cycles are linked to an "apparent increase in energy, a decreased need for sleep, racing thoughts, poor attention span, increased risk taking, increased self-importance and a heightened sex drive" (80). A case study might present the bipolar patient in a manic state as crazed and promiscuous, noting these patients often believe they are brilliant or invincible. When in depression, also called "mixed mood state" or dysphoria, they are unpredictable, potentially a danger to themselves and others. In this confused state, they "frequently experience[s] additional symptoms such as agitation, anxiety, guilt, impulsiveness, ideas of suicide and paranoia" (80). The clinical language of bipolar disorder extends beyond behavioral assessments and, in fact, becomes even more detached from the individual's experience of their illness. According to Paul Guest, definitive evidence of bipolar disorder lies in "altered glucose metabolism and insulin signaling, growth factor pathways and immunological alterations" (79) and can be observed in "abnormal function in the prefrontal cortex, hippocampus and amygdala emotion-processing circuits" (80).

While there is value in describing bipolar disorder in clinical terms, particularly to clinicians, it does little to fight stigma. "If stigma is a matter of values rather than facts, whether mental illness has its origins in genes, chemistry, biography, environment, bad character, God's will, or the cycles of the moon is of little importance" (Johnson 2010, 475). But clinical stories of bipolar disorder "are not the only stories there are to tell or the only languages in which to tell them" (Kafer 2016, 6).

* * *

Lithium and Cymbalta, and I felt nothing. "You're a zombie," James said. "Come back to us." It was unsettling for him, restful nothingness for me. For months, we tried to get used to the new me. Finally, though, we agreed it was the wrong way and I stopped taking the medication. To our relief, nothing happened. *I'm fine. I'm better.* I stopped seeing the psychiatrist too. *Talking to him is difficult, anyway.* White coat, notepad, too little or too much eye contact.

* * *

By the following summer, I was no longer fine. It began with lists. Lists for everything. Chores, sorted spatially and resorted by estimated time to completion. Shopping, sorted by where I would put things, again by price, and again by where I would find them in the store. I began writing my lists in pencil. I was compelled to buy an abundance of certain items: notebooks, hand sanitizer, batteries. *Batteries, because it's hurricane season, and we need to be prepared.* When there was no money to buy things, I shoplifted. *Batteries and groceries, groceries and clothing.* By the time James knew there was a problem, I was in crisis.

I needed to talk to someone who could help me understand what was happening to me. I knew I shouldn't—we don't talk about these things—but I had to. While talking with a family member I knew had been diagnosed with bipolar disorder, I said that I was cycling rapidly between depression and mania, that I had been shoplifting and I couldn't stop. Instantly, I regretted it. His expression when I told him was enough to shut me up. *Disgusting.* James was angry with me. "Why would you tell him, of all people?" I was ashamed all over again. We were still pretending it was only postpartum depression.

* * *

I returned to the psychiatrist's office to find Dr. Achilles was gone and a new sign on the door. The receptionist couldn't tell me anything. Along with my medical records, my doctor had just vanished. James wanted me to find someone else, this time someone who wouldn't be so quick to prescribe drugs. Our health insurance did not cover mental-health services, but through James's employee-assistance program, I was entitled to three therapy sessions. I was surprised at the relative ease of getting in with no wait to see a therapist at a small, nonprofit clinic. The receptionist had a kind voice. No judgment from her.

On the day of my appointment, I pulled into one of the four parking spaces in front of the small brick building that housed Samaritan Counseling Center. *This is it. Fix it or you'll lose everything.* My counselor's office was long and narrow with windows that opened to the low branches of an old oak tree, the leaves reflecting off the walls and giving the air a green hue. There was a single bookshelf, tidy and full. Throughout our sessions, she talked with me about self-care, motherhood, and spirituality. To my relief, she respected my reluctance to take medication and my aversion to the diagnosis. She suggested self-help books I never looked for but mostly only listened as I worked through feelings of guilt and worthlessness, fear I would do nothing, be nothing, fail at everything. After my last session, I felt buoyant, as if I was floating on hope, but I couldn't point to any specific thing my counselor said that made my world seem brighter. When anyone asks, I half-joke that she used magic. Within a month of my last visit, I was enrolled in college. I was fine again. I packed the diagnosis away and focused my energy on my studies.

* * *

Toward the end of the final semester of my undergraduate career, I took a playwriting course in the Honors College. For our final project, Professor Hood split us into groups of three. Because it was a mixed-enrollment course, each group included a graduate student. Our assignment was to adapt a stage play for the screen, and we chose *Trifles*. For some reason, or for no reason at all, I felt uneasy about the group dynamic, specifically about Carol, the graduate student. *She doesn't like that I have talent. She feels threatened.* Early in the project, I came to firmly believe she intended to sabotage our project and take my ideas for her own.

I fought fiercely to protect the integrity of my work, my creative property, just as anyone else would do in those circumstances, I thought. I called my professor. I had taken two other classes with him. He was my thesis director. He knew me. I was certain he would intervene on my behalf. I was stunned by his response. In my mind, I can still hear him.

"Tiffany, do you have anger problems?"

That conversation marked the very beginning of a suspicion that it was me, not her. It made no sense at all that another student—a graduate student—would disrupt her own progress in the course for forty-two mediocre pages of *Trifles*, the screenplay. *But she would, wouldn't she?* I couldn't make out the truth. *If this isn't reality, what is it?*

At that time, I was historian for the Honors Student Association. My fellow officers were my friends. We got along well, and I cherished their deference to my insight as a first-generation, nontraditional, seasoned student. *I'm needed, valued.* I was motherly with them, and they encouraged me to be. But because I was graduating, we needed a new historian. Mari was older than the others, a nontraditional student like me, and more assertive than any of us. I don't know that I had any specific reason to believe she disliked me, but I felt she wanted me to know she did not need my help settling into her new position. I was offended, and I was hurt my friends didn't notice her animosity toward me. For a while, I heeded the small voice in my mind. *Let it go.*

It got worse. When the time came to recruit members for the following year, the officers came together to make decisions on such particulars as recruitment strategies, meeting times, and membership dues. We agreed on the design of the flyers. We agreed on a meeting place and time. We did not agree on one thing: I felt that recruits should have the option to pay a lower amount if they were willing to forgo the t-shirt, that we would recruit more members by setting dues lower. When several of the officers disagreed, I convinced myself that they were elitists, that they were using dues to limit membership to only those who could afford t-shirts. I obsessed. I couldn't let it go.

The change in our relationship was sudden. Some of the officers began to look at me pityingly, others were aloof. Alex, who had deferred to me the most, spoke to me curtly, as if annoyed. It was infuriating. I blamed Mari. *She's whispering in their ears.* Mari blamed me. "You're doing this to yourself, Tiffany. It's you." With hard feelings, I resigned. But when the smoke began to clear, a confusion washed over me. *How could this have happened? Why?*

When I couldn't make sense of it, I tearfully confided in my husband—who had been my champion through it all, who had encouraged me to stand up for myself, who had been as puzzled at their behavior as I, and who was offended on my behalf—that I wasn't sure anymore if Mari and Carol had been the problem. *Maybe it's me.* I was losing my mind.

When it became clear that what I was experiencing would delay the completion of my undergraduate thesis, I confided in my committee that I believed I was having a mental-health crisis.

Then, crickets.

They don't care about me.

Ironically, the Common Experience theme that year was mental health, professed to "explore how perceptions of mental health and illness affect our thinking, laws, actions, and quality of life."

* * *

Destructive. Impulsive. Obsessive. Distrustful. Angry. Wretched. Vile. Shameful. Worthless. Me.

I didn't hate myself always, and I don't hate myself all the time. The self-loathing came over me in my adolescence as I began making terrible mistakes, ones with consequences far more serious and lasting than an ass whooping from Mimi, ones we didn't talk about openly. I was often aware I was making a mistake even as I made it, unable to stop, and when held to account, I made no apologies. They were my mistakes. *I am a shitty person. This is what shitty people do.* For years, I begged God to fix me. *Cleanse my heart and mind, oh Lord.* As a teenager and into adulthood, I sometimes fantasized about my death. *Close your eyes, yank the wheel, let go, die.*

Standing in the ruins of my undergraduate career, the thing I spent more than a decade building, I began to hate myself again. For everything. Since the beginning of time. For the relationships I destroyed. The people I hurt. *I'm so sorry, love.* The things I took that weren't mine to take. The pieces of me I threw to the dogs. I was disgusted with myself. Furious. I raged. I lay in bed at night, hating, sobbing, cursing myself. Quietly so I wouldn't wake James, quietly so I wouldn't have to lie about why I sobbed. *How can I tell him the reasons he shouldn't love me?* I couldn't. I was alone.

And in my hatred, I made more ruins to hate myself for.

Poor babies. They deserve a mother, but they got you. You're shit. That's why Brooke wouldn't stay. That's why Kiersten doesn't try to hug you anymore. That's why Logan won't make eye contact with you. What have you done to James? He didn't sign up for this. You're shit. Fuck you. Load the gun, pull the trigger, die.

For months after graduation, I didn't sleep. I went days, weeks without leaving home. There were bugs crawling on me—I saw them, I felt them, and no one could convince me they weren't there.

Something has to give.

I made an appointment with Dr. Heller, the psychiatrist at the Student Health Center. The receptionist said they could treat me for three months, until my grace period ended. The doctor wouldn't speculate on the name of my affliction without a psychological evaluation, but she agreed to treat my symptoms. *Ambien, 5 mg by mouth at bedtime. Store the bottle in a cabinet away from the bed. Lamotrigine, 50 mg by mouth at bedtime.* It wasn't working. *Lamotrigine, 100 mg. 150 mg. 300 mg.* The bugs were gone. The anger turned to a deep sadness and regret. *Better.* Still, over and over, I saw myself die.

Then, my grace period ended. I couldn't see Dr. Heller anymore. James was working under contract, so we did not have health insurance through his job. We purchased insurance on the Health Insurance Marketplace, but I searched and searched and couldn't find a single provider who would accept it. Dr. Heller said to make an appointment with the Department of Assistive and Rehabilitative Services. DARS, a place where people with *disabilities* go for help getting jobs.

* * *

It was a run-down building, smelling of insecticide and mildew. The people there didn't look like me. I was sure they noticed. I, with fully functioning arms and legs, able to see, hear, and speak, was not there for help finding a job. *Just say that's why you're there.* I felt guilty, ashamed. I told her the truth. *I can't afford a psychiatrist. I can't work. I can hardly function.* She was reassuring. Treatment now, job later. She said I would need an evaluation. We scheduled an appointment at Austin Center for Therapy and Assessment. I looked forward to the evaluation. I was finally ready to call my monster out by its name.

I arrived an hour early. The waiting room was confining. I waited in my car, smoking cigarettes one after another. It was a yellow day—red is worst, green is best—and I was especially anxious. I called my husband. *Maybe today isn't a good day for this. Maybe my anxiety will skew the results.* "Perfect," he said. "They need to see you in a bad place, they need a baseline." I heard a hint of desperation in his voice. He needed me to stay.

The evaluation took four hours. I wasn't warned I would be coaxed into talking about my mistakes, the traumas of my childhood, my absentee father, *my mistakes, my mistakes,* everything I hate about myself. Then there was an IQ test. I wasn't prepared for it.

My entire life, I believed I was especially intelligent. I had internalized how my family saw me, what they said about me. *Jaime is the pretty, mature one. Robbie is the charming one. I am the smart one.* It was part of my identity. But the report read, "Ms. Rainey's current level of overall intellectual functioning lies in the average range, scoring higher than 66% of same age adults." James laughed. "It's a silly, irrelevant test." I didn't laugh. *If I'm not the smart one, who am I?* I obsessed. *I wasn't ready. This is wrong.* I wanted a do-over. In the following weeks, I left half a dozen messages for my counselor. Finally, she returned my call. "Ms. Rainey, when can you come in for a therapy session?"

On my second visit, the therapist handed me two vibrating, egg-shaped, silver balls. "Concentrate. Find the little girl whose needs went unmet. Tell her she's going to be okay." I couldn't concentrate. I was holding what looked to me like a sex toy. *They can't help me.* I didn't return.

* * *

The world kept spinning. Ready or not, I applied for a directorship at a local education nonprofit. I wanted and needed it more than anything. A phone interview turned into a second, then a third. "Can you come in for a working interview?" I hesitated. "Of course, I'd love to," I lied. The task was to prepare and conduct a thirty-minute lesson on a topic of my choice with a small group of nontraditional college students. I chose resilience. The interview came on a red day, and I bombed it spectacularly. I cringe now at the memory of it. Me: wild-eyed and flushed, disheveled, stammering, sweating, paralyzed by anxiety. I wonder, If I had told them I have bipolar disorder and asked for a second chance, how would they have responded? Would they have been gentler in their rejection?

* * *

One Sunday in May, James said, through tears, that he'd been laid off from work the week before. He couldn't tell me sooner because he worried I would sink further into my madness. As he said it, something in his eyes startled me. *He's afraid.* Like a snap of the fingers, I was suddenly able to see outside myself. *He's hurting.* It was surreal. I realized at that moment that, for the first time since we married, my husband felt he couldn't tell me something important. *I did that.* "It isn't your fault," he said. "There's nothing to be ashamed of." It didn't feel that way to me, but it mattered that he said it.

It was then that the crazy began to subside. For the first time, I accepted my diagnosis completely, but as something outside me. *It isn't who I am,* I told myself. *I'm not a shitty person.* Things began to look up. James got a new job, and eventually, I did too. We had health insurance. It didn't matter that psychiatry wasn't covered—my primary-care doctor agreed to manage my medication. The medication affected my memory and focus, made my lips and fingers numb. It zapped my creativity. I felt sluggish and dim. When I caught myself wondering if it was worth the trouble, I reminded myself that the real me, the me who loves herself, wouldn't miss a dose because she knows it's the only thing holding it all together. I replaced negative self-talk with new mantras. *They're not out to get me. I am loved. Darkness isn't permanent. Light will shine on me too.* I worried it would happen again, and I was afraid, but I also thought if I really tried, I would recognize my symptoms in time to stop the spiral.

* * *

In the fall of 2017, two weeks before I began my first semester in graduate school, it was happening again. This time, though, the stakes were much higher. It started with a hum as I busied myself preparing for what was to come. I made lists. I would need books, notebooks, pens, pencils, highlighters, paper clips, a lamp. A new desk. A moderately professional wardrobe. *What do instructional assistants wear?* I cleaned and reorganized my house. *Who knows if I'll have the time later?* The hum became more frenzied as I cleaned and reorganized again. High on adrenaline, I became irritable, impatient. My husband recognized the mania. So did I. *Wooosahhhh.* Then, the old familiar self-doubt began to creep in. It had been four years since I was in school. I would be surrounded by smart people, most of whom had either just finished undergraduate studies or were continuing their careers. In the time since I was an undergraduate, I'd done nothing significant.

My apprehension mounted at the orientation for new instructional assistants. As I listened to the previous years' instructional assistants talk about the ups and downs of teaching, their strenuous schedules, and balancing coursework with job expectations, I was hateful to myself. *You don't belong here. They'll know it soon.* Then, during introductions on my first day at the writing center where I had been assigned, I rambled. On realizing I was rambling, I rambled more. I was losing control. I scribbled mean things to myself on a handout. *You're an idiot. Shut up. Shut up. Shut up.* I was sure they were rolling their eyes at me. *Who could blame them?* At home, James said, "Stop it. You're doing that thing again."

Each day was worse than the last. I watched as the other instructional assistants grew more confident. They seemed be transitioning into their positions and taking on projects with ease. When a lead tutor turned the session over to me, I rambled. My peers were taking over their sessions, and I was still watching. I was forgetting important meetings. I couldn't tell them why, so I offered partial truths: "I had class. I was finding parking." Supervisors noticed. By the middle of the term, it was obvious I wasn't adapting. My midterm performance review was a testament to my failure. The director of the center wrote,

> A lead staff member provided "mixed feedback." Tiffany "seems eager to do well, but that doesn't necessarily translate into productivity or effective tutoring sessions." The most common bit of constructive feedback from lead tutors is that she sometimes goes on tangents. It is more than halfway through the semester and she is not, yet, tutoring on her own.

I was devastated, but it was the truth. I was derailing cotutoring sessions, and the lead tutors were fed up. The review very concisely summed up the problem. "The problem escalates, then, because tutors become irritated and, thus, send nonverbal signals that they are frustrated. . . . [W]hen she reads their behavior, it undermines her confidence, thus interfering with her ability to focus." It was exactly that. The review crushed me—even more so because I knew it would be sent on to the director of the writing program, someone I desperately needed to impress—but it was all true. Then, more hate. *Go away. No one wants you here.* I was sinking. I wandered around campus in a heavy fog, inspecting roof tops and estimating which buildings were tallest. *Climb to the top, jump, die.*

* * *

While bipolar disorder is tangible in the body, it is also observable in speech. During periods of mania or mixed-mood states, and sometimes even when there are no other obvious symptoms, a person with bipolar disorder contends with thought disorder, a linguistic phenomenon that affects their ability to think and speak coherently. Simply put, persons with bipolar disorder are both physiologically and rhetorically challenged. The challenges are even greater when the spaces we inhabit make us especially vulnerable. In kairotic spaces such as writing centers, "the moments are fleeting, the timing is precise and quick, the cues for appropriate behavior both rigid and subtle" (Price 2014, 73).

* * *

What I did next, although the realization of it was furthest from my mind at the moment of doing, could have promptly ended my career prospects. On an impulse, I confessed to my supervisor that I have bipolar disorder, that I was not in control. *Something is happening to me and I can't stop it.* I asked for her mercy.

Instead, she gave me grace and said, "Tell that cruel inner bitch to fuck off."

An impulsive decision made in the throes of a bipolar cycle fully changed my trajectory. It wasn't bravery. I was thrust into coming out by the same invisible source that has compelled me to make lists and steal batteries. All the same, I was out to someone, and instead of distancing herself, this someone picked me up and drew me closer. It did not matter that I was so anxious and tearful I could barely speak. She heard me. She reminded me my erratic and disruptive behavior was temporary. My symptoms would subside. I would be myself again. All this because she had a prior understanding of my illness.

Then, the fog began to dissipate.

* * *

As much as it hurts to remember what others have said in their reports and evaluations—I imagine cruel things being whispered about me—I still look at them sometimes. Buried under the evidence of my inadequacies are a handful of words that give me hope. When my supervisor at the writing center says, "I see her potential," I hear, *don't give up.* And when the psychologist writes, "Ms. Rainey has the cognitive and academic abilities to obtain gainful employment in her chosen field and will likely do well in positions that allow her to work independently and emphasize her strong academic skills," I hear, *you are good enough, you belong.*

My cruel inner bitch rarely speaks to me these days. I'm teaching and learning, and I have allies who recognize the value of my voice, not despite my mental illness but because of it and all the other things that make me, me. My cycles aren't all of me; the memories I share here aren't everything. In between, there are long stretches of green days, yellow days. On yellow days, when I feel the madness creeping in, I chastise myself. *Snap out of it, Tiffany. Don't go back there.* I sometimes feel helpless to stop it, but I try anyway, and sometimes it works. These memories are reminders that, for me and other people with mental illness, stability is fleeting. But it gets better. Awareness makes it better. Having allies makes it better. Being able to talk openly about it makes it better.

* * *

There are obvious problems with coming out with our illnesses. We risk "infantilizing responses, dramatic changes in attitude, and negative repercussions" (Kerschbaum 2014, 57). Many of us have been or will be passed over, cast aside, invalidated because disability is understood as incompetence (69). There is always the possibility we won't get the job or the promotion after disclosing our illnesses to those "who do not know us personally and therefore cannot see the ways in which we competently navigate professional and social responsibilities" (Myers 2004, 258). This is especially true in the academy, where the opposite of collegiality is neuroticism, a trait "inimical to academic achievement" (Price 2014, 65).

There are also problems with *masking* our illnesses. For me, masking bipolar disorder requires unsustainable emotional labor. On top of having to contend with symptoms of irrational paranoia and anxiety, there is the valid concern that something will slip, I'll be found out. Because "there is no rhyme or reason, no pattern, to how the fatal flaw works itself in and through my life" (Sparkes 1996, 483), eventually, a public coming out will happen with or without my permission, as it nearly did in the fall of 2017. I was lucky then. I won't always be lucky. Further, keeping secret this part of my identity has caused feelings of isolation, loneliness, and shame. I will continue to feel this way until I give someone—the right someone—the chance to help me make sense of those feelings and to tell me that I am not alone, that I shouldn't feel ashamed.

But my decisions on whether, when, or how to come out with bipolar disorder do not hinge only on risks and harms; there are *benefits* to consider as well. Disclosing on her own terms, in her own time, and in "*her own voice*, a personal voice telling what illness has imposed on her and seeking to define for herself a new place in the world" (Frank 1995, 7) gives her agency in self-representation. Kimberly Myers (2004) writes, "Coming out with illness can be liberating—a move from a 'resistance identity' of defensiveness stemming from a devalued sense of self, to a 'project identity' where one proactively constructs a new identity that redefines her position in society" (268). Similarly, other scholars have found strategic disclosure can foster our "sense of power over the experience of mental illness and stigma" (Corrigan, Kosyluk, and Rüsche 2013, 3). And when we no longer have the stress of hiding our illnesses, we gain the ability to be "more open, encouraging engagement with people who are supportive or who share similar experiences" (Michalak et al. 2010, 220).

* * *

I began working on my "project identity" not long after my psychotic break in the fall of 2017. I made short, tentative strides here and there by talking occasionally with family members and close friends about symptoms I was experiencing or adjustments to my medications. I began sharing mental-health resources on social media. I gently intervened in discussions when I thought stigmas were being reinforced. The project took on a more formal structure when I enrolled in a graduate course on autoethnography the following year.

Before I began my research, I had only allowed myself brief glimpses of my bipolar self; when I had looked too long or too closely at my illness, I had been overwhelmed with shame. Autoethnography allowed me to investigate rather than look. With a new sense of purpose, I asked, What am I ashamed of? Why? Throughout the process, I was in a perpetual state of reflexivity. In turns, I was able to see the patterns of my illness both introspectively and with critical distance. It was uncomfortable and sometimes even painful, but it was enlightening and encouraging as well. Through my research, I learned more about myself and my illness in six months than I had in the decade since my first diagnosis. And not only that, I discovered allies in the literature. I was not alone.

The decision to share my autoethnography outside my immediate circles was a difficult one. Mental illness, one's own mental illness anyway, is not at all a safe subject for study. Patrick Corrigan, Kristen Kosyluk, and Nicholas Rüsch (2013) warn that while "broadcast experiences," or "seek[ing] out people with whom to share past history and current experiences with mental illness," can fight stigma by adding momentum to the mad studies movement, the disclosed information can also be misused or misinterpreted by others (794). At worst, I'll be unemployable after coming out. (Scenes of volatile "crazies" are ever present in many people's images of mental illness.) At best, I'll have to navigate awkward conversations about my research.

I have other concerns about sharing my research. Many scholars take issue with autoethnography on the grounds that it is subjective and resists generalization. Given that the sciences tend to prize *logos* and *ethos* while rejecting *pathos*, I am braced for a swift dismissal by some. Even more, *evocative* autoethnography draws criticism from scholars who believe it tends toward "navel-gazing" (Freeman 2011, 215). However, narrative is more than a rhetorical device or an act of self-indulgence. Autoethnographers use storycraft to "make personal experience meaningful and cultural experience engaging" (Ellis, Adams, and Bochner 2011, 277). When audiences find our stories meaningful and engaging, they are more willing and better able to empathize with us. Further, because evocative texts are more accessible to nonacademics, they may "reach wider and more diverse mass audiences that traditional research usually disregards, a move that can make personal and social change possible for more people" (277).

* * *

Scholars and researchers have found over and again that narrative self-disclosure of mental illness works against stigma by offering occasions for perspective taking, thus fostering empathic bonds. Elizabeth Young (2009) notes that when readers immerse themselves in mental-illness narratives, they practice "an act of inclusion and empowerment that challenges the dominant story of mental illness as something shameful and isolated" (67). The importance of perspective taking, Chung and Slater (2013) write, "is that it can motivate audience members to perceive stigmatized characters as individuals reminiscent of ourselves . . . thus encouraging greater in-group perception" (906). In other words, when readers are able to see themselves in us or us in themselves, we bond. Then, "these bonds expand as the stories are retold. Those who listened then tell others, and the circle of shared experience widens" (Frank 1995, xii). As we press on, more and more people "reformulate their understanding of stigmatized others" (Chung and Slater 2013, 898) and we begin to see microshifts in the social construction of mental illness (Young 2009, 67).

* * *

Ultimately, I decided to let go and let God because, at this moment, other more persuasive conversations are being whispered by those who have nothing nice to say. I can't shake the idea that if I don't do my part, however small, to challenge the dominant narrative, those conversations won't change, and stigma will continue to thrive. Through this autoethnography, I offer my voice to others "not to speak for them, but to speak *with* them as a fellow sufferer who . . . has a chance to speak while others do not" (Frank 1995, 132).

WORKS CITED

Chung, Adrienne H., and Michael D. Slater. 2013. "Reducing Stigma and Out-Group Distinctions Through Perspective-Taking in Narratives." *Journal of Communication* 63 (5): 894–911.

Corrigan, Patrick W., Kristen A. Kosyluk, and Nicholas Rüsch. 2013. "Reducing Self-Stigma by Coming Out Proud." *American Journal of Public Health* 103 (5): 794–800. EBSCOhost, libproxy.txstate.edu/login?url=http://search. ebscohost.com.libproxy.txstate.edu/log in.aspx?direct=true&db=edsfra&AN=edsfra.27541057&site=eds-live&scope=site.

Ellis, Carolyn, Tony E. Adams, and Arthur P. Bochner. 2011. "Autoethnography: An Overview." *Historical Social Research/Historische Sozialforschung* 36 (4): 273–90. doi: 10.1002/9781118901731.iecrm0011.

Frank, Arthur W. 1995. *The Wounded Storyteller: Body, Illness, and Ethics*. Chicago: University of Chicago Press.

Freeman, John. 2011. "Solipsism, Self-Indulgence and Circular Arguments: Why Autoethnography Promises Much More Than It Delivers." *Journal of Arts and Communities* 3 (3): 213–27. doi:10.1386/jaac.3.3.213_1.

Guest, Paul C. 2018. *Biomarkers and Mental Illness: It's Not All in the Mind*. Springer.

Johnson, Jenell. 2010. "The Skeleton on the Couch: The Eagleton Affair, Rhetorical Disability, and the Stigma of Mental Illness." *Rhetoric Society Quarterly* 40 (5): 459–78. EBSCOhost, doi:10.1080/02773945.2010.517234.

Kafer, Alison. 2016. "Un/Safe Disclosures: Scenes of Disability and Trauma." *Journal of Literary and Cultural Disability Studies* 10 (1): 1–20. doi:10.3828/jlcds.2016.1.

Kerschbaum, Stephanie L. 2-14. "On Rhetorical Agency and Disclosing Disability in Academic Writing." *Rhetoric Review* 3 (1): 55–71.

Myers, Kimberly R. 2004. "Coming Out: Considering the Closet of Illness." *Journal of Medical Humanities* 25 (4): 255–70. EBSCOhost, libproxy.txstate.edu/login?url=http:// search.ebscohost.com. libproxy.txstate.edu/login.aspx?direct=true&db=edsovi&AN= edsovi.00002036.200425040.00003&site=eds-live&scope=site.

Michalak, Erin., James D. Livingston, Rachelle Hole, and Melinda Suto. 2010. "'It's Something That I Manage but It Is Not Who I Am': Reflections on Self-Management Strategies and Stigma in Bipolar Disorder." *Journal of Affective Disorders* 7 (3): 209–24. EBSCOhost, doi:10.1016/j.jad.2010.02.041.

Prendergast, Catherine.2001. "On the Rhetorics of Mental Disability." *Embodied Rhetorics: Disability in Language and Culture*, edited by James C. Wilson and Cynthia Lewiecki-Wilson. Carbondale: Southern Illinois University Press.

Price, Margaret. 2014. *Mad at School: Rhetorics of Mental Disability and Academic Life*. Ann Arbor; University of Michigan Press.

Sparkes, Andrew C. 1996. "The Fatal Flaw: A Narrative of the Fragile Body-Self." *Qualitative Inquiry* 2 (4): 463–94. doi:10.1177/107780049600200405.

Uthappa, N. Renuka. 2017. "Moving Closer: Speakers with Mental Disabilities, Deep Disclosure, and Agency through Vulnerability." *Rhetoric Review* 36 (2): 164–75. doi:10.108 0/07350198.2017.1282225.

Young, Elizabeth. 2009. "Memoirs: Rewriting the Social Construction of Illness." *Narrative Inquiry* 19 (1): 52–68.

2
LITERATE VIXENS AND SHAMELESS HIJABIS
An Automythnography

Shereen Inayatulla

I define autoethnography as a written account of the mirrored and cyclical ways intersectional identities shape our cultural subject positions. Autoethnography can reverberate, blend, bolster, and intervene in genres of first-person writing (beyond the scope of autobiography or memoir) but does so in order to make sense of the coconstitutive relationship among culture/bodies/experience/knowledge. I have come to practice what I call vulnerable automythnography (Inayatulla 2016), a term inspired by the work of Ruth Behar, Suresh Canagarajah, Audre Lorde, and Dorothy Allison. Vulnerable automythnography employs autobiography, literacy narrative, myth, and embroidered memories; it centers the body as a site of knowledge production.

This chapter explores the critical awakening of a brown queer Muslim raised by South Asian settler-immigrants on the prairies of Treaty One territory: Anishinaabeg, Cree, Oji-Cree, Dakota, and Dene peoples, and the homeland of Métis Nation. This piece describes the complexities of cloistering, rebellion, passing, and consensual assimilation. Armed with overlapping and sometimes competing literacies learned at home and school, the narrator formulates queer scripts for navigating a sexist and heteronormative reality—one that frequently Others immigrants and Muslims as dangerous, subhuman subjects. Employing literacy narrative, myth, and embroidered memories, this piece challenges fact/fiction and anecdote/theory binaries that historically shape autobiographical writing conventions in the field of composition. This narrative contributes a version of personal reflection that posits storytelling as intellectual currency and historical archive.

SCIENCE AND CREATION

They have a house and HE has a universe. Theirs stands on a small plot of weed-free grass, mowed so short it needles bare feet. HIS floats in a pool of black with silvery dots visible between the streetlights. They furnish the house with blue sofas and ruby carpet, wall-to-wall. HE paints HIS universe with sapphire skies and yellow fields yawning into the horizon.

According to Her, we fell to the earth from an insect-free garden because of bad apples and bad choices, and we deserve to be punished, for insolence and nudity are shameful. According to Him, our fallen ancestors resembled apes and had dinosaur companions, for one can have one's evolutionary cake and eat it, too. There are Einstein, Newton, the Imam, and Allah. She insists we take sides. He believes we ought to reconcile. *Einstein split the Adam.*

They build their house with wood and bricks. A rusty nail gets loose and pierces His bare foot. At the hospital, they chide Him for wearing chapals, then prick Him with a needle to stop the poison. We are thereafter forbidden from playing on the construction site because His tools might make us bleed. The garden they plant grows weeds that snake into the neighbors' yard, eliciting over-the-fence insults and instructions on how things are done *around here*. To remedy the situation, They use chemical sprays that poison bare skin. I am commanded to stay off the grass and play inside the safety of Their house. I spend summer afternoons with my pallid paper doll and her wardrobe. She has four dresses, two hats, and no family. I find stiff, multicoloured cardstock under a tower of telephone bills and attempt to create a paper-doll companion. But the scissors are dull and the experiment fails. I collapse on the cool linoleum, imagining what I would create if only sharp tools weren't forbidden. *Einstein used an X-Acto knife to split the atom.*

Poised with my bedtime snack, prewashed and peeled, I wait to hear Her stories. They feed my imagination and teach me good and desirable ways of being. My head pressed against Her fleshy arms, fingers wedged between Her folds of belly, I linger in wide-eyed anticipation. I absorb Her twisted plots into my sun-toasted skin. She tells and retells the one about Her near-fatal childbirth and the doctors who forbade her from future pregnancies. She recreates images so vividly I can see Her, lifeless, in the ICU, tubes inserted into every part of her body, not lucid enough to ask if my sister had survived. I imagine Her, limp and yellow, under a maze of wires, doctors with clipboards peering into her window—*I see you.* It was a uterine haemorrhage, but the exact origin couldn't be found. Haemorrhage . . . *hammers can make you bleed.* After six years of healing and sister's nightly prayers for a baby to play with, She risked her life on a second pregnancy. *You were born fair and beautiful with long black hair. Like a princess.* A risky hybrid created from hammer blood, prayers, and apes.

Her stories, tragic and nonlinear, still my curiosity in confusion and terror: *Baby princess. But then you grew up.* I absorb Her words into my sunburned skin. One story stars a beautiful cousin, admired for her blood-red lips and fair skin, *you wouldn't even know she was desi.* She died mysteriously in her thirties. Her husband, who matched her beauty in wealth, was devastated.[1] *What can you do? It's Allah's will.* Cousin-Could-Be-White appears before me every time I open the oversized pages of my red, hardcover fairy tales. Perhaps she had been poisoned—bad apples, bad choices. *It was stomach cancer but Backhome medicines are no good and doctors backwards.*

Beauty is a family recipe that transgresses borders, shuttling East to West and East again: chocolate hair, milky skin, apple-red lips. Blend well. Add marriage. Serve and Enjoy. I pour over the illustrations in my giant red storybook, dodging Her insistent demands that I *read* the words *like a good girl* instead of *making nonsense stories* from the pictures. My sister is good. She reads books like chain smokers light cigarettes. She escapes to worlds of redheaded orphans and empowered girl detectives.[2] *Be good and read like your sister instead of playing with imaginary friends in hot sun. Look at you! Getting too dark.* I have ruined my chances of looking like Cousin-Could-Be-White. Tanning is a backyard tragedy, which She grieves to no end: *You were so white and good. A princess. But then you grew up.* Blackenedeverafterthheend.

Moms create babies and dads rule them. But HE is the creator and ruler of moms&dads. HIS job is to boss and watch our every move, even when we take off the paper doll's dress to examine her sketched-on bra. *HE knows when you are sleeping, HE knows when you're awake.* I am explicitly instructed not to picture George Burns whenever I pray to HIM. So I replace that image with a footless, floating Santa Claus, but once They find out, this, too, is forbidden. God&Mom are mighty creators. They know the origins of everything familiar and foreign—how bacteria becomes yogurt, where to sew a button, why Lucy Lunenfeld was blessed with blonde hair and I wasn't. God&Dad are the rulers of the land, equipped with lessons on how not to hold a hammer, why deep water can drown you, and what happens to girls who don't come directly home from school. Kidnappers are urban wolves. GodMom is to be honored, GodDad obeyed, and GodSanta feared.

Her stories are about people, His are about wildlife and poverty. His terrifying parables hold me in hair-chewing agony but always deliver a happy ending. There's the one about a sad baby butterfly that wanted to soar through the sky: *It was scared at first but then one day flapped its wings putter, putter, putter.* The butterfly story circles through my mind whenever I'm afraid to confront insects and deep water. I yearn to escape the limitations of my body, to be better than I am, to be good. He curves His hairy-knuckled index finger[3] like a hook, describing the venomous scorpion that bit his ankle on his way home from grade school. I squeeze his finger, releasing a yelp as He describes the stinger piercing His flesh. Naniamma had to put *big white tablet on the bite to draw out poison* or else He *would have died.*

Backhome is dangerous. You might meet a snake in the outhouse, find a convention of cockroaches in the sugar bowl, or get chased by a monkey when you try to make away with the mangoes falling from the sky. Technically the mangoes belong to the monkeys and temptation makes you the thief. The monkeys do the heavy lifting, shaking the fruit off the trees. But Newton's law of gravity works in hungry children's favor. Most kids in His village only have two shirts, two shorts, and one flimsy pair of chapals that serve as an open invitation to street-walking rodents. There are no after-school cartoons or bedtime snacks, only a chalky slate on which to do math homework. People there fall into deadly comas, like His mom and sister, six months apart, sending the younger kids to various homes of relatives where *sometimes there was nothing to eat.* But He was a good student, got scholarships, and flew to *The New World.*[4] He puttered across the Atlantic, East to West, which is backwards according to our world map. On the plane, He filled out an immigration card, last name first and first name last, like they did Backhome, *backwards.* The card was stamped, and His name stayed permanently reversed. But He moved forward with his studies, *created a good life from nothing,* and so it is expected that I *be good and grateful for bedtime apples and an abundance of paper for homework and doll clothes.* I should feel protected in Their house and HIS universe—a little Once-Was-White-Princess under open, cloudless, prairie skies, contented butterflies, and grass that's scorpion free.

I fuss and whine, faking fevers to get out of school. She gets savvy and starts taking temperatures under my armpit so I can't drink a cup of hot water to cheat the thermometer. *Good girls go to school. If you don't go you'll end up starving to death and you won't even have two shirts and chapals.* Good stories aren't abundant at school. You have to read them by yourself in silence, your butt pressed into a hard plastic chair. *Stop wiggling!* Miss Rose simply doesn't allow it when I squirm and insist that stories are supposed to be animated.[5] They are meant to putter, putter, putter with hooked fingers and skin crushing skin, so close you don't even know whose warmth is whose.

The stories at school are sterile and solitary, so I resort to writing my own. I start with a fat, red pencil—shaky printed letters spanning four horizontal lines. At home, They approve of my efforts. She encourages me to read the story in front of The Aunties, who pinch my cheeks and press me to their multicolored, perfumed blouses. He staples the pages together and saves them in Their closet for safekeeping. Mary Jane, my protagonist, is a fair-skinned, blue-eyed, fairy-tale version of me. She wears dresses that twirl and has baby sisters because her mom never got any tubes tied. Writing is a good indoor activity: no hammers, no scissors, no conflicts and commands.

Good girls go to school to learn how to be good, stop fidgeting in their seats, and come home with stories. It is how they prepare for the marriage and magic promised to them, princes and fairies waiting with stallions along the horizon. It's a recipe for success: read, write, and marry. Serve and enjoy! At school, I learn about desire—to be like the other girls, own Barbie corvettes, decorate X-mas trees, and flaunt brand-name jeans. The desire to worship Jesus instead of HIM and host birthday parties that serve hot dogs. The desire to eat hot dogs with everyone so I no longer have to fester in HIS pork-forbidden, peanut-butter prison. For protection, She tells me to lie, to tell the birthday-party-goers and their moms I am allergic to wieners. She discourages the truth, *what vould people say? They will think our family is a terrorist. What more we need now?* I learn about the desire to talk back, demanding a good reason I shouldn't wear shorts in gym class like *normal* girls, arguing against the holy trinity of Santa-Mom-Dad and their scrolls of forbidden pleasures. *Have you no shame? You must keep your izzat intact.* Allah is our indoor word for God. Except when the normal girls come over to play and make disapproving faces at our illegible wall hangings. They're ancient scrolls. Stories about Jesus. I don't understand them because I only speak English. Like I am allergic to wieners, I am allergic to Arabic.

At school, I learn about the desire to kick Meron Salinger in the dink for getting his insults confused, calling me a string of racial slurs before remembering the "right" one: *Pack Up Paki.* The desire to know just what a dink is, and why Jennifer Avalon thought she had one until we watched those videos about girl and boy bodies. *Oh.* So binary. I learn why girls don't have dinks and why good girls aren't allowed to talk about them. Dinks create orgasms (although the video didn't tell us that) and girls who say *dink* or *orgasm* are ungodly. God is good minus the *o*. God, a swift, sharp prick of good, there's no double *o* for HIM.

I'm not supposed to talk about dinks and orgasms, but they are all over my library books. GodMomDad says I should be grateful for a library full of stories much smarter than my red, hardcover fairy-tale nonsense. They insist my brain needs *stimulation*. The library is where I learn about blonde teenage twins who kiss boys and wear string bikinis. I discover some girls desire their brothers and have unwanted pregnancies. I consume their dramas like a bloodthirsty serial killer, opening one book as I close another. These heroines give tiny titless teens with bad perms something to strive toward, incentive to mail order skin-lightening creams and arm-hair bleach made especially for darkies like me. It eases Her mind that I've discovered the library, *well at least now you're reading*, although She's oblivious to all the erotic teen sex that has me hooked. These stories incite private desires made even more shameful with God-Formerly-Known-As-Allah hovering overhead. *Oh no.* These stories stir desires for boyfriends, B-cups, and bosom buddies who can be trusted to remain loyal to their tiny teen friend forbidden from school dances and shared sips of beer. I consume these stories of dirty girls who French bad boys and wear short skirts. I absorb them and they feed my cloistered addiction.

I create my own versions of these coming-of-age stories, secret networks of heroines stashed under the mattress. These girls experience all the things God-Mom-Dad forbid.[6] They break rules and take risks in a universe of musky, pressed paper. I write breathlessly in my private laboratory, the starlit streets refracting, shadowy pages spread across my bed. And the more I read, the faster I write. Filling pages like the Day of Judgement is coming to split me into atomic bits. The Once-Was-White princess dying a little death, in wide-eyed, hair-chewing agony, riding off into the stallion-lined, storybook horizon, happily ever after swallowing me whole.

بسم الله الرحمن الرحيم

One part princess, one part ape. Split, exact, irreconcilable. Imagined Figure 1: A room with tattered curtains, sinking bed, snow-caked baseboards closing in. Crooked shadows line the walls, curling scrolls of poetry. Imagined Figure 2: Mustard acres and winding roads spill over the horizon. A field lined with crab apple trees trembles in the open wind. The ape princess hooks the branches and devours the fruits whole.

HONOUR KILLINGS AND SEMICOLONS

Academia is a cult and books can turn good girls into sluts and homos, sometimes both at once. I putter off to a disorienting campus that yawns into the horizon. Our faces like sunflowers, rows of students sit bright eyed and poised to absorb beams of wisdom. In Introduction to Women's Studies, I make a friend. She is kind and thoughtful and drives me home when class runs late. I fear her but not in the way I once feared footless Santa. Just like *Backhome*, Lesbian is dangerous. It is an outspoken-front-row emblem of resistance with heavy piercings and stiff, multicoloured hair. GodMomDad flare nostrils, their eyebrows curving into hairy hooks every time our nation's cleanly pressed anchorman repeats the word *homosexual* on the evening news. They sputter insults at the self-absorbed deviants destroying HIS glorious universe, pricking holes in the fabric of society one piercing at a time. Above all, there's *sex* in *homosexual*, which makes it off limits for conversation unless you wish to fall into HIS eternal pit of flames. *Those Women* are unworthy of stories, and for speaking up, their tongues *will be cut out in hell*. Wouldn't the searing flames be enough? Might HE make an exception for my new friend and split Those Women into categories of good lesbian and bad lesbian? So binary. I wonder if "good lesbian" means having a kind and generous soul or if it's just someone who's good *at* being lesbian. I pull out the passage I've been carrying around with me and reread to myself it in a whisper: "Those of us who stand outside the circle of this society's definition of acceptable women; those of us who have been forged in the crucibles of difference—those of us who are poor, who are lesbians, who are Black, who are older—know that survival is not an academic skill. . . . It is learning how to take our differences and make them strengths. For the master's tools will never dismantle the master's house" (Lorde 1984, 112). Which tools have been used on me? Which tools do I want to use? Which tools make the best weapons?

For Her, izzat is what makes girls good and keeps them that way. It's what girls lose when they are raped, which is why walking home with "the boys" is strictly forbidden. Boys are Godless, hormonal, predators. Professor LeBlanc insists that rape is about power. She presses her finger on the overhead projector to emphasize this point. Those Women ask me to join their study group and offer to drive me to our mandatory excursions. I watch their sunflower bonnets nod and sway as Professor LeBlanc paces the front of the room.

The Boys are a captivating secret. They walk me halfway home and call the house in code. Crushes are about power, and we crush the power out of each other, carving names into the old, wooden library carrels tagged already with jagged flowers and cartoon dinks.

I flip through the diagrams in my thick red hardcover textbooks, mapping stories about female anatomy. *Figure 1: Malignant Ovarian Cyst. Figure 2: White stretch marks from childbirth.* Feminism shows up in poetry classes, blurring the grammars and discourses I am absorbing into my brain. I am asked to describe this poem in one word—*stimulating*.

. . . acknowledging in myself
the rebel traitor thief the one who asked too many questions . . .
(Brandt 1987)

Chesty, perfumed aunties gather in Her kitchen, spooning heaps of yellow rice onto my plate. *What you are studying? We must get you married!* Serve and enjoy. Feminism and cayenne are giving me an ulcer. I excuse myself from the house to attend my study group. *Homosocial.* Together, Those Lesbians and I practice saying *neoliberal hegemony*, rolling it over our tongues and teeth until it feels right (because it's so wrong). We explore the outskirts of the city on our way back from the women's art excursion, speeding past Mennonite farms, searching for towns that aren't dry. If you drive fast enough, the flax fields look like ocean under storm clouds, their blue crimped flower tips rippling in the wind.

In class, bell hooks and e. e. cummings free us from the ideological strongholds of capital letters, although one is a revolutionary and the other is a prick. In the car, lifeless fields bloom into homogenous rows of colour; fallow is dark and depressing but wheat is blonde and heartening. I absorb Those Lesbians' front-seat debates about what it means to be a Marxist, postmodernist, third waver. *Stimulating.* Their conclusions are soothing, like milk on an ulcer. I begin to fuck with line breaks in prose and use the word *fuck* with confidence whether or not HE is hovering. Feminism fucks my insides out. I create columns of *hers* and *ours*:

> So why is it that a woman loses her Izzat when she's raped and the rapist's izzat goes undiscussed?

> If this Woman Study teaches you to talk like you know everything then YOU BETTER TAKE OTHER CLASSES.

> "Maybe I'm abnormal or something, I mean I have fantasies about handsome strangers coming in through the window too, like Mr. Clean, I wish one would, please god" (Atwood 1996, 2225).

> "this is how to hem a dress when you see the hem coming down and so to prevent yourself from looking like the slut I know you are so bent on becoming" (Kincaid 1996, 2335).

> "Well bred girls don't answer back" (Anzaldúa 1999, 76).

Professor LeBlanc encourages me to write from my experience as a *woman of colour*, to put texts in conversation with each other instead of creating disconnected lists of block quotations. I respond by writing about back-seat landscapes, *canola/ flax/ alfalfa/ extending so far you can see other people's weather/ rainclouds drenching fields on the horizon/ creeping steadily closer*. Professor LeBlanc discourages me from fucking with grammar conventions, *a sentence needs a verb; this is not the correct use of a semicolon and why is your essay centered on the page?* I respond by enrolling in Postmodern Prairie Lit. My Lesbians pull over on service roads and we sit on the hood of the car. *yellow/ blue/ green/ plump rain like summer thigh sweat/ pressed against the vinyl/ the perfumed back of HER neck.* The fields are flecked with crooked barns that someone built and abandoned. I peel off my layers, too loose, too long, too sleeved, and let my skin absorb the poisonous beams of light.

Imagined Figure 1: Carbon Atom Bonding
Imagined Figure 2: Adam's Apple Resizing

Neither religion nor science has a grammar for gender and attraction. Professor LeBlanc asks us to list the things that influence our ideas about womanhood. Being good and being a girl were once inseparable: *If you eat two apples every day you will have pink cheeks and red lips; if you pat baby powder on your neck it will make you look fair; anise seed freshens breath; alum cleans your teeth; never wash your underwear and socks in the same basin; almonds make you smarter; grapes will sharpen eyesight so you can thread the smallest needle; V-necks are revealing; if you want something done properly, do it yourself; learn to roll roti and honour your customs; be a good daughter and wife, it is rude and arrogant for you to ask why.* Grammar and gender are imperative. I read my textbooks in secret, placing stiff cardstock across the pages in case They look over my shoulder at the kitchen table. There is *sex* in *intersexual,* which makes it off limits for conversation unless you wish to fall into HIS eternal pit of flames with scissored tongues. Some things cannot be reconciled, not even with a semicolon. I grow convinced that white is right, dark is backwards, and there are lists for everything important.

The Black List:	LeBlanc List:
pantheism	socialism
abortion	emancipation
adultery	polyamory

The aunties and professors twist my insides into irreconcilable lists of antis and pros. Rebellion is a homemade recipe: to missed curfews add alcohol and cut class. Beat well. Light flames to burn off alcohol. Indulge and atone. Within one growing season, flood, drought, and twisters ravage the farmland. Desperate to escape disasters at home, my place of refuge becomes the library. Farmers burn stubble. Smoke fills the maze of stacks, and the pages absorb the poison. I find an article about a teenage girl whose father lit her on fire for betraying the family's customs. I pull an X-Acto knife out of my bag, cut out her smoky photograph, and fold it into the copy of *Grapefruit* I've been carrying around with me—my blueprint for rethinking binary space in the context of a "goldfish swimming across the sky":

> . . . Let it swim from the West to the East.
> . . . Let it swim from the East to the West.
> (Ono 2000, "Drinking Piece for Orchestra")

Professors cover every subject familiar and foreign: how mass dairy farming is exploiting the land, where garment workers have unionized, why skin bleaching is directly linked to internalized racism. Professors are the rulers of the classroom, equipped with lessons on how not to split the infinitive, why religion is oppressive, and what orgasms can do to improve your writing. Illicit temptations fuel curious minds. Mom is uncritical, Dad is illogical, and God is a dink or dead as a doornail.

Professor Docktor advises me to embrace my culture. *Such beautiful customs and costumes.* Professor Docktor has traveled The East and learned to eat rice with the tips of his fingers, *it makes so much more sense to eat with your hands.* After class, he asks me to step into his office. The walls are covered with Arabic scrolls. Professor Docktor insists I am too critical of "third world practices." *You write cultural vignettes, like ethnic stand-up comedy routines that only reinforce the problematic stereotypes most westerners hold.* In Docktor's class there are westerners and foreigners, cowboys and Indians, all of whom now occupy Indigenous land. *We are squatters and thieves. All of us complicit. Colonization is about power.* I agree to learn more about settler politics. Professor Docktor presses his thigh against the arm of my chair to emphasize his point. But I didn't agree to this.

He encourages me to rethink my grammatical choices. *Fuck is a verb, noun, and adjective. Use it, overuse it, then use it again. This is what makes a writer.* I fear the rough brush of his arm hair against mine when he leans in close to guide and advise: *You insist that spiritual belief systems are for the feeble, but aren't you alienating your own lineage? Where does ancestor worship enter your theory?* Arm hair on ape fur tangled so close we cannot feel whose is whose, repelling atoms, fused then split. His words leave me wondering if I should be grateful or ashamed and either way he's knocked me to my knees, a righteous saviour towering above me, ivory skin aglow, a storybook stallion naming my internalized racism and settler ignorance. I consider how we dig up the earth without asking for consent. I think of the hubris we embody as settlers and the ways the prairie poets I revere reflect our landscape back to us:

> Carrots are fucking the earth. a
> permanent erection, they push deeper . . .
> (Crozier 1985, "Carrots")

The cowgrrrlz and Indienne, tongues intact, return from the horizon where blond fields have swallowed the darkened, falling sun. Our prairie sky transforms jagged, fiery streaks into hushed petals of pink, layered like petticoats under ruched clouds. We drive the wild, dusty road, eastbound, backwards. It forks and we stop, unsure of which route is right. *Do you really have a curfew? You could say it's our fault for getting you lost.* The Wild West is dangerous. You might take a wrong turn and get lost on the prairies, with a gas tank running low and nothing in sight but other people's sunsets.

I part the tattered curtains and sponge mildew off the baseboards. I cut out poetic vignettes printed on onion paper, press them against stiff, black cardstock and hang them wall to wall. At night I hear the paper curling in the humid air and I lie coiled like zucchini vines tugged by gravity along the soil, my sweat-drenched thighs against the cotton bed skirt. I am thinking of forked roads and forked tongues—*fork* is a verb, noun, and adjective. "For people who live in a country in which English is the reigning tongue but who are not Anglo . . . what recourse is left to them but to create their own language? . . . We speak a patois, a forked tongue, a variation of two languages" (Anzaldúa 1999, 77). Sleepless in wide-eyed, hair-chewing ecstasy, I see the shadows of dead ancestors dance on the walls. Cousin-Could-Be-White hovers over me where GodSanta once loomed. SHE admonishes my disregard for heritage and rituals, my denunciation of the very institutions SHE so wished to have experienced long into old age.

Every day I cut my hair shorter and shorter with scissors so sharp they crunch and swish with every calculated snip. The dark hair falls and falls in gravitational euphoria, like Rapunzel's braid snaking down the tower.

The Boys creep secretly to my window, crushed palms against the glass. I have no hair for them to climb, there's no entry, no way to come up. Hair is about power.	My Lesbians drive quietly to my window, perfumed necks craned up. I devise creative escapes, there's always an exit, a way to break out. Power is about consent.

The ape princess wiggles out from under forbidden spells, bursts through the petri dish, and putters off into the horizon where airplanes fight gravity flying upward and forward and into the sun, fearless. Far from Backhome jungles and the Wild West plains, with a toolbox containing nails, knives, hammers, and needles, I build stories and plant ideas. And the more I produce, the easier it is to understand the narrative. I fill gaps with fiction like salve on a sunburn. The Once-Was-White princess testing the horizon, reaching into that crease where air meets earth, confirming the theory that the world isn't as flat as paper.

NOTES

1. *Beauty brings you wealth. That's why I ended up vith your father and we have no money.*
2. Once upon a time, in a place far away from the screaming and fighting in the kitchen, far from His angry glare, His fist on the kitchen table, Her raging shouts diminishing in fear, far from the imminent threat of raised hands and fat lips, and a little sister crying in her bedroom (she should've cooperated during the Arabic lesson so they wouldn't have fought in the first place), there lived a dashing sultan/lucrative career that would rescue the good girl from her wickedly backward family.
3. His dark, brown finger bent in sharp angles like a witch holding an apple. I am starting to look like His sisters, who are all dark and sharp, too. *And if you're not careful you'll end up looking like them,* She warns, *or worse, ugly like me.*
4. He landed in Gainesville, Florida, *vith just fifteen US dollars in pocket.*
5. Your daughter fidgets in class, doesn't complete assignments, and scored two years behind in math and reading comprehension.
6. Forbidden from watching soap operas and movies with the word "dirty" in the title (*Dirty Dancing, Dirty Rotten Scoundrels,* even *Dirty Harry*); no coed socializing: roller skating parties, or Nintendo at Genevieve Penner's when her brothers are home but her mother is not; no phone calls from boys, even to discuss math homework and newspaper club; no sleepovers at Genevieve's in case her brothers are sexually perverse (people here don't have morals like they do backhome); jeans are too tight, skirts are too short, shirts don't have enough sleeve.

REFERENCES

Anzaldúa, Gloria. 1999. *Borderlands/La frontera: The New Mestiza.* San Francisco: Aunt Lute Books.

Atwood, Margaret. 1996. "Rape Fantasies." *Norton Anthology of Literature by Women,* edited by Sandra M. Gilbert and Susan Gubar, 2222–28. New York: Norton.

Brandt, Di. 1987. Forward to *questions i asked my mother.* Winnipeg: Turnstone.

Crozier, Lorna. 1985. *The Garden Going On Without Us.* Toronto: McClelland and Stewart.

Inayatulla, Shereen. 2016. "Brown Queer Compositionistas and the Reflective Practice of Automythnography." *Journal of Lesbian Studies* 21 (4): 1–12.

Kincaid, Jamaica. 1996. "Girl." *Norton Anthology of Literature by Women,* edited by Sandra M. Gilbert and Susan Gubar, 2335–36. New York: Norton.

Lorde, Audre. 1984. "The Master's Tools Will Never Dismantle the Master's House." In *Sister Outsider,* 110–13. Berkeley, CA: The Crossing.

Ono, Yoko. 2000. "Drinking Piece for Orchestra." In *Grapefruit,* 31. New York: Simon and Schuster.

3
WHEN THINGS FALL APART

Rebecca Hallman Martini

This is an evocative autoethnography that uses personal experience to understand the intersections of labor conditions, mental health, and activism among graduate students in writing studies. Most conversations about contingent labor focus on part-time faculty, adjunct labor, and writing program administration (Kahn, Lalicker, and Lynch-Biniek 2017; McClure, Goldstein, and Pemberton 2017). Discussions of both mental health/disability and activism are largely dominated by faculty and professional perspectives (Babcock and Daniels 2017; Kahn and Lee 2010; Price et al. 2017; Rand 2014). This piece brings these threads together through the telling of a story that raises questions about what counts as the disciplinary work of writing studies. In particular, I use autoethnography in both method and form because it opens space for the consideration of disciplinary conversations about labor and writing instruction alongside both public stories (in articles, press releases, and social media) and private stories (across internal institutional email exchanges, collaborative core-committee documents, and personal notes). (To this end, images are included throughout the text to highlight relevant activity and to show the tfsunite community in action. They are meant to be considered alongside the text, but are not directly referenced in the narrative itself for rhetorical effect.) Rather than focusing on labor as a collective experience, this research focuses on how ethnographic study of the whole self—the academic and the personal—can shed light on cultural practices and shape how we understand the work of writing studies.

Sophie Tamas (2009) raises questions about how our representation of trauma within autoethnographic scholarship often requires a rational, recovered authorial voice that misrepresents the messy, broken, and not always knowable experiences. This, in turn, "may reinforce the expectation that our trauma ought to make sense, and if it doesn't, we must be somehow inadequate or failing." When we create neat, tidy narratives of trauma in our scholarship, we may be "doing [ourselves] harm" (1). The problem here is that "clean and reasonable scholarship about messy, unreasonable experiences is an exercise in alienation" when what is really needed is an "empathetic connection" (3). In autoethnographic writing, there is a "need to make my voice match my words no matter how much my audience and I just want to be reassured and comforted" (23). Tamas admits, "I do not know how to write this way, close to the bone. . . . But there are some stories I cannot tell any other way" (24).

* * *

I remember my excitement on the evening of Sunday, March 31, 2013, when I read an email about a meeting for English teaching fellows (TFs) and all supporting faculty the next afternoon to discuss our working conditions and pay. During the meeting, there would be a "vote on how to proceed." The group had been meeting for the past seven months, since the fall 2012 "accidental" charge of $121.05 to each graduate student for tuition. While the university refunded the money, an opportunity to fight for a pay increase began to develop. Had someone not been paying attention, perhaps the charge would have gone unnoticed, even though it directly violated our full tuition remission contracts. This was the tipping point, as TFs and several faculty members were already angry we had not received a raise in twenty years. We were being paid $9,600 as MFA students and $11,200 as PhD students for teaching two twenty-seven-student sections of first-year writing, with no health insurance and $1,685.70 to pay in annual fees. A petition had been signed and circulated, but not acknowledged. It was time to act.

I didn't attend the earlier meetings. As a first-year PhD student in writing studies, I was taking three graduate courses, working twenty hours a week in the writing center, teaching an online class for another university, and teaching a section of first-year writing at a community college where I also worked hourly in the writing center. Even though having additional jobs was technically against the rules, the department was complicit in helping us find extra work. They sent us job ads for adjuncts at nearby colleges. Everyone knew we couldn't survive on the TF stipend alone.

That Sunday night when I got the email, I immediately planned on attending the meeting. With the momentum of the end of the semester, I thought maybe something real was going to happen. As someone who was better friends with literature and creative writing graduate students and somewhat of an outcast among the those in the writing studies program, I also thought this provided an opportunity for the whole department to come together over a shared concern about the exploitation of graduate student labor. In the seven months I had been in the English Department, I had learned the politics were tough—we had the creative writing program (one of the top programs of its kind), literature (the home discipline of most faculty in the department), and writing studies (the newest concentration with the fewest number of faculty members and the heaviest administrative load). The departmental politics were complicated, and the faculty seemed divided. I sensed the inequality and saw the divisions trickle down.

Yet, the issue of graduate student labor seemed to represent a somewhat common experience (all of us had to teach the same number of classes, regardless of concentration). The potential of what lay ahead gave me a sense of relief.

I couldn't have been more wrong about how the next week's events would unfold.

* * *

On Monday, April 1, 2013, my professor ended class an hour early per the request of a few students who wanted some time to "organize ourselves" before heading into the afternoon's English TF meeting. I wasn't sure why.

These students, who were all in the writing studies concentration, seemed to already feel left out of the larger English TF group. I think some of them had made suggestions that weren't being taken. Others had no idea a group had been meeting about TF working conditions at all. They all seemed to agree that the larger English TF group was in the wrong and said things like, "They're asking for too much money. This isn't going to work"; "We need to be in conversation with the other graduate students across campus before we can actually take a stand"; "They're making all of these decisions without us and we should have been informed earlier"; "I'm taking my name off of that petition."

I didn't agree but said nothing.

These writing studies students/composition teachers seemed to share some attributes with what Susan Miller (1991) refers to as the "stigmatized individual," an identity common in English departments, "where ego identities from both literature [and might we add creative writing?] and composition complexly conflict as privileged and subordinate, or healthy and 'spoiled,' identities" (128). Important, Miller also notes that "no feature intrinsic to composition teaching urges stigma on its participants. The discrepancy between a felt identity and social treatments of those who allow themselves to be perceived as 'in' composition causes stigmatized relations" (130). These writing studies students liked to position themselves as "the good teachers," in contrast to the other graduate students, and to claim the bullied identity. I'm not sure why.

We walked into the English TF meeting, and I mostly listened. I learned the petition was now in its second form and had been updated with more hard data. I learned that the original one sent to the associate dean had received no reply and that the updated petition was sent to the president with no response. The updated petition had also gone to the *Houston Press*, and the *Houston Chronicle* had interviewed students and contacted administration for a forthcoming article. We had a Facebook page and Twitter handle. The movement was named TfsUnite.

A comment was made about urgency and needing to get things done this semester, as time was not on our side and the administration had been dragging on a response for months. One of my writing studies peers raised a question about why there was little focus on drawing other departments into the conversation. Someone mentioned the difference in the amount of work we were doing as instructors of record compared with teaching assistants in other departments who were only assisting or grading. Someone else said, "Publicity is our biggest weapon" and that other departments might join in when we start making noise. Efforts had been made to connect with other departments and progress was slow. We needed to move.

We talked about our options—sick out (everyone call in sick to teaching responsibilities until the university agrees to negotiate our pay), sit-in (go to the president's office and sit outside her door from the time the building opens until it closes each day until we receive a meeting with her to discuss a pay increase), an occupy-style action (perhaps appearing at a university event).

Someone moved to vote on the sit-in idea. I raised my hand. Every single one of the writing studies students voted no, except for one who abstained. It was decided the sit-in would begin on Wednesday morning. Someone asked what would happen if administration tried to force sitters to move out of the area. Someone said we would stay in place until we were arrested. It was decided the core committee would give more details about the plan the next day so we could be prepared.

The writing studies students who voted *no* asked for their names to be removed from the petition. The core committee, made up primarily of creative writers, asked if there were others from writing studies or literature who wanted to join. I raised my hand and signed up.

* * *

When I got home, I had an email from my professor who had ended class an hour early that day. The email said, "Although I did grant you all time by ending my class early to discuss issues surrounding the TA action, I am requesting that you find a way to remember your OTHER and perhaps MORE IMPORTANT identity this week—that of graduate students . . . I do not want to discuss the matter any further." They wanted to "keep fractious discussions and hurt feelings out of the classroom and our concentration."

My identity as a "graduate student" was exactly what led me to participate in TfsUnite. The graduate students had already fractured.

Tony Scott argues that graduate courses in writing studies tend to focus on what Donna Strickland has called the "'official' scholarly field": the academic conversations, theories, and research that help students "build their professional careers," while the "'unofficial' education happens in the broader material sites within which most graduate courses are situated" (quoted in Scott 2016, 18). Rarely, it seems, are there opportunities for the "unofficial" education to seep into the "official," course-based education. Here was such an opportunity. Why didn't we bring a discussion of our own lived practices of labor into the classroom?

* * *

On Wednesday, April 3, around 9 a.m., I met approximately twenty other TFs to sit in the president's office lobby. The day before, I worked with the core committee to develop "Sit-In Procedures" so we would all be consistent, respectful, and professional. As we sat, we worked quietly. An excel sign-up sheet circulated and at least three TFs signed up for each hour of the day. I spent two hours sitting in. Someone from a local newspaper came with his camera and took pictures.[1]

By Wednesday afternoon we had received an email from the provost and dean that said they "ha[d] taken very seriously the teaching fellows funding issues" and that they "plan[ned] to deal with this through the annual budget planning process." The core committee wrote back, thanking them for their response but also letting them know "the promise of an annual budget planning process is too vague to be reassuring." Instead, we requested a meeting we "required" by April 5 to discuss a wage increase. The provost and dean set up a meeting with the core committee for Thursday.

An email was sent to the group by a single mother who was concerned about care for her seven-year-old daughter should she be arrested during the sit-in. She also suggested a hunger strike in place of a sick-out should we get that far so as not to impact our students. Someone researched university policies about occupying space to make sure we followed rules that would prevent such an arrest from occurring. Others offered to take care of the seven-year-old, should her mother get arrested.

* * *

On Thursday, April 4, there was a meeting with the provost and dean. I don't remember much of what was said except that the dean referred to our TfsUnite Facebook and Twitter activity as an "annoyance" and requested that it stop. We said we wouldn't stop until we received an official wage offer. The social media involvement was gaining attention from across the state and well beyond. We were expanding participation in our movement through gathering people who could act as "enabler[s] of a politics without being-with" (North 2012) while still rooting our activism in physically situated practice, a move necessary for serious political engagement (Pettman 2016; Read 2014). More people were signing our petition as we exposed the reality of our (over)working lives by listing a typical day's work, posted images of the bathroom in the president's suite next to pictures of the ones in the crumbling English Department building, questioned the university's claim to tier-one status and posted flyers around campus.

* * *

On Friday, April 5, one faculty member in my concentration met privately with me to voice support. They even mentioned attending a planning meeting with the group.

The faculty member meant well but never showed up.

* * *

On Sunday, April 7, after a TfsUnite meeting to discuss the teach-out we were planning for the following week, another faculty member in my concentration I had never met before started to show up. They were on sabbatical but came to participate in the sit-in, as faculty were now joining us. They took me out for dinner and acknowledged how difficult a position I was in. I agreed and cried a little. That meal was the first I had eaten all day.

The faculty member meant well, but it was already too late.

According to a recent study with students at 234 institutions, "Graduate students are over six times as likely to experience depression and anxiety as compared to the general population" (Evans et al. 2018, 282). Over half of the students with anxiety or depression felt a lack of support or mentorship from their advisors.

* * *

And then everything started to fall apart.

Things moved fast; I had no control. I stopped doing—called in sick to work at my second and third jobs, didn't read for class. It felt great.

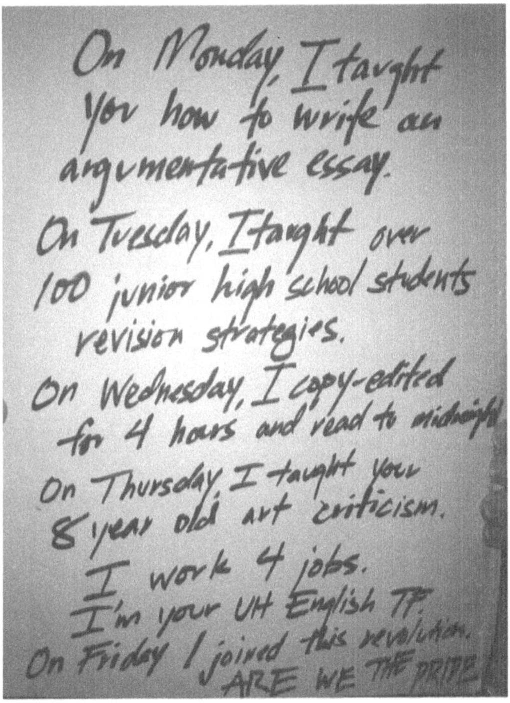

Figure 3.1. April 8: Another anonymous note from a UX English TF. "On Friday, I joined this revolution." #AreWeThePride #TierOne

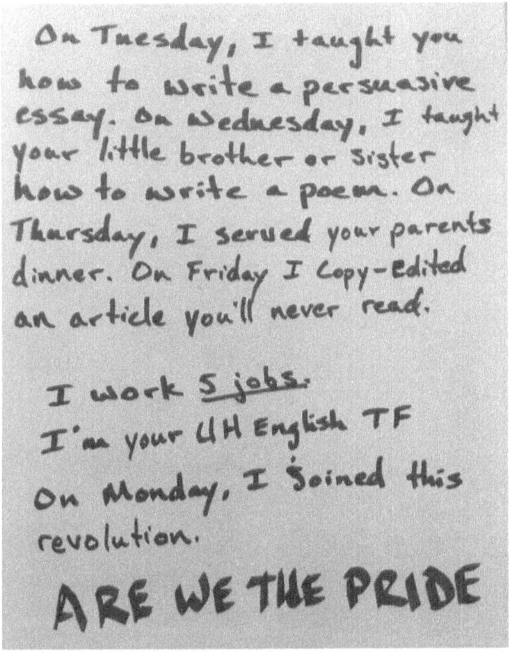

Figure 3.2. April 8: An anonymous note from a UX English TF. #AreWeThePride #TierOne

Figure 3.3. April 5: Breaking News from the President's Office Bathroom: The complementary mouthwash in a decorative, faux-crystal vial is deliciously refreshing, too. We know, because we tried. #AreWeThePride

A TIER ONE SCHOOL
WHERE YOUR ENGLISH TEACHER
CAN'T PAY RENT

$19,213
Living Wage in Houston

$11,490
Federal Poverty Line

$11,200
Your English Teacher's
Maximum Salary

UNIVERSITY of **HOUSTON**
#AreWeThePride

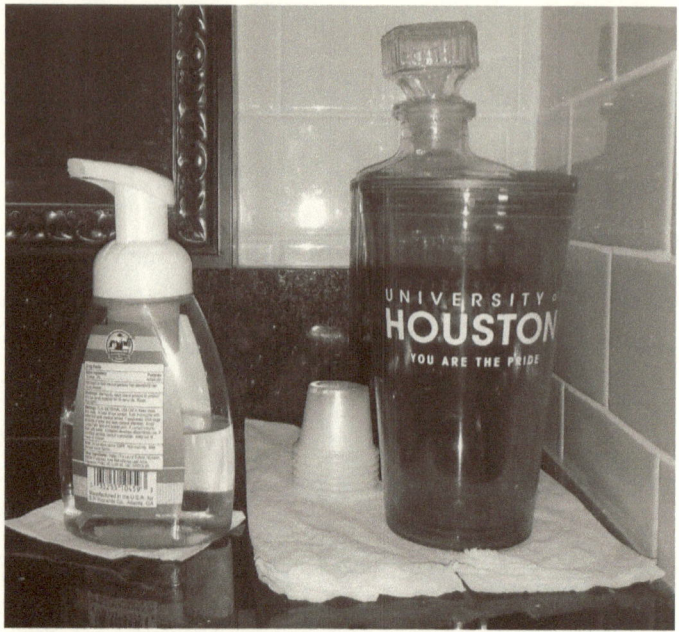

Figure 3.4. Image printed on t-shirts worn by TFs

Figure 3.5. April 5, 2013: Twenty years without a raise would make any coog a little cranky. #HungryTierOneTFsThings got personal. People noticed.

Reacting without thinking. Not writing things down. I could do it all! TfsUnite was working! I stopped eating, but I wasn't hungry. I stopped sleeping, but I wasn't tired.

I constantly felt sick—going to class, hearing my professors' disapproval (publicly and privately), trying to communicate TfsUnite action with a couple of interested writing studies students too wimpy to participate but curious.

This was mania, I later learned, after filling out a questionnaire in my psychiatrist's office.

But the mania didn't last.

It became paranoia. And that stayed.

It first came on Monday. One week after the first TfsUnite meeting.

I couldn't decide what to wear. Nothing fit me. I was too skinny. I had a meeting with a business professor whose class I would be coteaching in the summer. I took my bright yellow bracelet off. I didn't want to do TfsUnite anymore. Things had gone too far.

I went to the sit-in. Couldn't log into my university account, one of many accounts I had—a local university account, a couple of bank accounts, a computer password, two accounts at other universities. Each had different numbers and symbols and letters with maximums and minimums. I had to keep the passwords separate. My password isn't working. Someone must have hacked my account.

We met with the president. She promised one million dollars. I didn't go. I don't want to play anymore.

I was elated but uncomfortable. I went to class, unprepared. No one said anything about one million dollars.

I didn't say a word.

I had a conversation I wouldn't remember with the professor at the end of class. I left, crying and confused.

Later, I watched my college basketball team play in and win the NCAA championship game with a few friends at a local bar. How is this happening? So much good in one day. I can't handle it.

I had only one beer but had surely convinced everyone I was drunk. I asked a friend to walk me home. I didn't tell her, but I didn't know how to get there on my own.

One in two PhD students experiences psychological distress, and one in three is at risk for a psychiatric disorder, with work and organizational context identified as significant predictors of well-being (Levecque et al. 2017). The number of undergraduate students who experience psychological distress is also on the rise (American Psychological Association 2017).

* * *

Too many roles: student, girlfriend, daughter, sister, friend, teacher, tutor, core committee member, writing studies student, friend of creative writer, Louisvillian, Houston resident
Too many secrets
Too much pressure
Too many performances
Too many tests
One that day
hadn't studied. Could no longer perform.
I was crying
I was laughing
I was hiding
I was pacing
No one knew what to do with me.

My partner came home. I called my mom. I got her and him to talk. They knew something wasn't right. They knew they needed to turn somewhere for help. But who knew what to do?

I was taken to Healthcare Services on campus.

A woman named Beatrice questioned me. Lots and Lots of Questions Over and Over again. Are you going to hurt yourself? Are you going to hurt someone else? Do you want to go home? Are you going to hurt yourself? Do you miss your family? Are you going to hurt yourself? Are you tired? Are you going to hurt yourself? Do you want to take a nap? Are you going to hurt yourself?

Eventually, I said I was going to hurt myself. It was an accident. I tried to change my mind. I said "Yes . . . I mean no." I meant no. I wasn't allowed to change my mind.

I became crazy.

A phone call was made.

We waited.

We went outside. A police car came. My partner looked terrified. I didn't understand why. He told me everything would be okay. I believed him. I was put in handcuffs. I was put into the back of a police car. I didn't know where I was going.

And yet, I felt eerily calm.

The kind brown eyes of the police officer, darting back and forth between the road and me, through the rearview mirror, confused and sad and a little scared.

But really, as I would decide later, I had done something wrong and I was being punished.

* * *

Tuesday, April 9, 2013, was my first of fourteen days in the Bellaire Behavioral Hospital, where I would eventually learn I had a stress-induced psychotic break. The story above is just the beginning. It doesn't include being forced by a nurse into cold water through sobbing tears for my first shower in days. It doesn't include frantically pushing on hospital doors the moment I realized I was locked in. Being scratched by the tech. "Let this be your medicine," she said. It doesn't include telling my family this and hearing their voices not believe me. It doesn't include the terror of thinking people I knew were pacing the hallways looking for me, angry at me. Or that over the course of a few days, I felt I had caused my parents to get a divorce, the death of my friend's father, and the Boston Marathon bombing, or that the patients in the hospital were students who were signing in to go on a hunger strike to get me out of there, that I was on a hunger strike to get me out of there, that I had taken it all too far, that I had an eating disorder, an alcohol problem, and every disorder in the DSM-5. It doesn't include feeling that the patients in the hospital could understand and hear my thoughts and that they were using this to control me, or briefly taking up smoking for the first time in my life so I could go outside twice a day for five-minute breaks. It doesn't include losing language—losing the ability to talk, struggling to write one word, balling up and shaking my left hand as if loosening thoughts into phrases, tapping the pencil in my right hand until I could squeeze a letter out. It doesn't include starting to feel better and sitting in group therapy with people who had tried to commit suicide multiple times who looked at me like I was crazier than them when I said I was a graduate student and a writing teacher.

All of those rules I didn't know about how to survive that nobody told me, but I had to learn.

I wasn't allowed to fill my Styrofoam cup with water and put it on my nightstand when I went to sleep.

And I haven't even mentioned my relapse in May, the experience of actually recovering my memories from the past weeks, embodying them, coming to terms with the fact that I had been absolutely out of my mind. Remembering the narratives my mind had pieced together to explain who I was and where I was and what I was doing there. It doesn't include the second trip we made to the hospital to make sure I wasn't still so crazy I needed to be put away, or seeing that psychiatrist who said "paranoia or hearing voices?" and me saying "paranoia," when really it was both.

It doesn't include the medicine changes over and over and over. The overwhelming anxiety and depression and irritation and inability to sit still for days over the summer. Waking up after fourteen hours of sleep and feeling hung over when I hadn't had a drink. Feeling nothing for days and wondering if I had become numb. Losing the ability to feel things after I had just felt so much. Too much.

Was it the drug or was it me?

Would I be allowed to return to school? Would they take me back into the program? Did anyone wonder what had happened to me or how I was? I hadn't heard from anyone. What did they think? What would they say?

* * *

This is a story people do not want to know. It is three stories wrapped into one. It's hard for me to separate them. It's in some ways the unfortunate story of an English Department divided and how those divisions trickle down. It's in some ways a wonderful story of graduate students standing up for their worth and eventually causing a system to change a little. It's in some ways a horrible story of what overworking can do to someone, and how the stress of wanting so desperately to belong can be the breaking point, causing an identity to shatter. A mind to be lost.

There is no conclusion to this story. It does not have an end. I still live this story. Not every day, but some. I still don't have all the pieces. I don't really want them all, anyway. Like you, this is something I'd rather not acknowledge. But ignoring it does not make it go away.

Mental health and self-care in the college environment are important. Everyone should be sure to take good care of themselves. When students need help, there are offices for that. But that's not our job.

Graduate student overwork and exploitation are not new. It's part of how English Departments and universities work. It's part of our culture. It's out of our hands. We need university and national policies that protect graduate students and their labor. Shame on them. But that's not our job.

A good friend once told me some of the nastiest fights happen in English Departments because the stakes are so low. We fight over theoretical perspectives, research methodologies, who gets how many TA lines, who does what kind of work, how release time is determined, what faculty positions are requested and filled, who gets tenure and what for, who teaches what classes and when. These are, no doubt, legitimate issues for any English Department. But how much do they really matter? Really?

Are all the stakes really that low? Maybe we are just missing half the battles.

NOTE

1. During the first couple days of the sit-in (April 3 and 4), there were many reporters interested in telling the story of TFsUnite. Press coverage of the event included *the Chronical of Higher Education, Houstonia, the Houston Chronicle, the Daily Cougar,* and *Overland,* among others.

REFERENCES

American Psychological Association. 2017. "Campus Mental Health." http://www.apa.org/advocacy/higher-education/mental-health/index.aspx.

Babcock, Rebecca Day, and Sharifa Daniels, eds. 2017. *Writing Centers and Disability.* Southlake, TX: Fountainhead.

Evans, Teresa M., Lindsay Bira, Jazmin Beltran Gastelum, L. Todd Weiss, and Nathan L. Vanderford. 2018. "Evidence for a Mental Health Crisis in Graduate Education." *Nature Biotechnology* 36 (3): 282–84.

Kahn, Seth, and Jonghwa Lee. 2010. *Activism and Rhetoric: Theories and Contexts for Political Engagement.* Philadelphia: Routledge.

Kahn, Seth, William B. Lalicker, and Amy Lynch-Biniek, eds. 2017. *Contingency, Exploitation, and Solidarity: Labor and Action in English Composition.* Fort Collins, CO: WAC Clearinghouse and University Press of Colorado.

Levecque, Katia, Frederik Anseel, Alain De Beukelaer, Johan Van der Heyden, and Lydia Gisle. 2017. "Work Organization and Mental Health Problems in PhD Students." *Research Policy* 46 (4): 868–89.

McClure, Randall, Dayna V. Goldstein, and Michael A. Pemberton, eds. 2017. *Labored: The State(ment) and Future of Work in Composition.* Anderson, SC: Parlor.

Miller, Susan. 1991. *Textual Carnivals: The Politics of Composition.* Carbondale: Southern Illinois University Press.

North, Paul. 2012. *The Problem of Distraction.* Stanford, CA: Stanford University Press.

Pettman, Dominic. 2016. *Infinite Distraction.* Hoboken, NJ: John Wiley and Sons.

Price, Margaret, Mark S. Salzer, Amber O'Shea, and Stephanie L. Kerschbaum. 2017. "Disclosure of Mental Disability by College and University Faculty: The Negotiation of Accommodations, Supports, and Barriers." *Disability Studies Quarterly* 37 (2).

Rand, Erin J. 2014. *Reclaiming Queer: Activist and Academic Rhetorics of Resistance.* Tuscaloosa: University of Alabama Press.

Read, Jason. 2014. "Distracted by Attention." The *New Inquiry,* December 18. https://thenewinquiry.com/distracted-by-attention/.

Scott, Tony. 2016. "Subverting Crisis in the Political Economy of Composition." *College Composition and Communication* 68 (1): 10–37.

Tamas, Sophie. 2009. "Writing and Righting Trauma: Troubling the Autoethnographic Voice." *Forum: Qualitative Social Research* 10 (1). http://www.qualitative-research.net/index.php/fqs/article/view/1211/264.

4
CRITICAL PEDAGOGY AND THE COMPOSITION CLASSROOM
Searching for a Middle Ground between Epistemological Despair and "Radical Hope"

Leslie Akst

Within the context of this chapter, I define autoethnography as the study of communities, cultures, institutions, and/or institutional entities and their members in relation to the researcher who situates observations, discoveries, and reflections within a theoretical and methodological framework. Findings are then synthesized with research literature and conveyed through evocative communication including deep description, dramatization, and dialogue in a distinct narrative voice.

The differentiating factor between autoethnography and personal narrative is the depth and breadth of theoretical and methodological engagement. This level of engagement takes the writer/researcher beyond self-actualization—oftentimes the destination of personal narrative—in order to reflect, account for, and problematize their ways of knowing and being in relation to who or what they are studying, even (especially) if they were unaware of such aspects at the study's outset. The researcher then places their discoveries in conversation with a body of research literature in order to arrive at a more expansive sociological understanding of the area of study.

During the fall 2012 semester, I conducted an IRB-approved autoethnographic study in two sections of English composition I taught at a New York City-area community college. My study participants were primarily working-class, first-generation college students, students of color, multilingual students, and first- and second-generation Americans. During the semester, I took in-depth, "thick" notes after every session. I also collected and studied student writing and metacognitive texts. In the following semester, I conducted interviews with consenting students while, again, taking detailed "thick" notes, adding their observations to my body of data in order to triangulate their versions of the semester with mine. Informed by grounded theory, once I was through collecting data, I used open, then axial, coding to identify and refine significant thematic strands to synthesize alongside research literature. I then built chapters, such as this one, around those subject areas.

DOI: 10.7330/9781646421213.c004

On a humid, May afternoon, I met with Alejandra,[1] my former student. It had been nearly five months since I'd seen her. We walked to the back of the English department, where it was particularly stuffy, chatting in the stilted way that happens when I run into students and feel compelled to make small talk. Two weeks earlier, I had emailed her to remind her of the study I conducted in her composition class.

Through autoethnography, I observed myself and my students as I taught a curriculum I designed informed by Paulo Freire's (1970) edict that a self-generated desire to "create knowledge" is far more likely to result in meaningful, holistic learning than simply "banking" information.[2] In the first half of the semester, I instructed students in writing memoir, demonstrating strategies and literary devices of creative nonfiction. In the balance of the semester, I guided them as they analyzed their personal narratives, searching for ways institutionalized systems of power including race, religion, culture, gender, social class, economics, corporatization, and education were woven through their texts. Students then interrogated those systems of power through individualized research projects. My goal was to open a space for students to connect the personal and political by demonstrating how such powerful, yet invisible, institutional determinants affect the ways individuals conceptualize themselves and move through the world. In the process, I thought students' evolving critical awareness might create the promise of social activism, that students' newly acquired knowledge might spur them towards becoming actively informed critical thinkers and writers able to participate in the democratic process (Giroux 2016, 57).

After the semester ended and I submitted grades, I saw that Alejandra signed one of the consent forms locked in a file cabinet in the department chair's office. I hadn't wanted to waste my time talking to her, though. I only sent the interview request out of obligation because that's what I did with the other students who, on the second day of class, checked the box saying they were willing to be interviewed.

Alejandra, a second-generation Ecuadorian American who is pale with dark eyes and hair, began as one of my strongest students. But in the last month of class, with her absences piling up, I dismissed her as an otherwise bright student who bailed on the course. It wouldn't be the first time it had happened during my seven years teaching at this community college. Resting on their As from earlier in the semester, some students seem to overestimate the grade cushion they've created and fail the course just as readily as someone who never turned in an assignment.

At my urging, Alejandra submitted a sparsely researched, hastily written, "Hail Mary" of a final essay on the seemingly random topic of noise-induced hearing loss I pushed her to write. Despite what at the time looked like a reversal of work ethic, however, I liked Alejandra. I appreciated that for three-quarters of the semester, she was one of a handful of talkers in a course filled with enough passive students to induce habitual silence. I didn't want to see her fail the course outright by not submitting a final project.

I was surprised when Alejandra responded to my email, enthusiastically no less, saying, "I would love to help you with your dissertation!" It was nice and all, but I still didn't think she could add anything to my research.

When people asked me how I became a college writing instructor, I used to say *by accident*. After 9/11, six months away from completing a master's degree in journalism at Columbia University, I was laid off from my job as a magazine editor. I spent the next three years alternating between un- and underemployment while tearfully navigating exploitive jobs and the New York City Department of Labor. In my frenzied hustle to find work, I cycled through temporary admin jobs, temporary proofreading jobs, and part-time administrative work at the journalism school. I worked for marketing companies handing out samples at busy Manhattan street corners. I worked as a waitress. I worked as a Jello-shot girl.

Finally, I took the advice of people who said, *you have a master's degree, why don't you teach?* I thought it was ridiculous. I didn't know how to be a teacher. But later, after going on so many interviews and missing out on so many positions, I decided to try. I wrote a CV and academic cover letter based on ones I found online and sent them to community college English departments I could get to on public transportation. At the very least, I reasoned, the project would give me something to do for a week. Then, four days before the fall 2005 semester began, I was hired as an adjunct English instructor. That process consisted of an email from an administrative assistant asking me if I wanted a class, followed by a phone conversation with the same person asking if I could make it on the first day.

Once Alejandra and I sat down at a small conference table, I asked my planned questions intended to solicit her version of the semester. As with my other study participants, we talked about the course readings. She said she liked the excerpt from *Pedagogy of the Oppressed* I assigned in the first week of class[3] because it validated her feelings about her academic struggles in middle school.

"I thought I was the only one who felt that way," she said.

Alejandra also liked that I had assigned a reading critical of my profession, saying, "That surprised me the most."

We also talked about the agency she and some of her fellow bilingual classmates expressed by writing hybridized English/Spanish prose. In her culture assignment, Alejandra wrote about her mentally disabled older brother, Diego, and the part of his background he most readily identifies with. "*Soy Ecuadorian no Americano!*" she quoted him as saying.[4]

"Writing in Spanish was the best way to show my brother," she said. "Some things don't sound the same in English. I tried to write about him in English but I just didn't like it."

As the interview progressed, we talked about her disappointment at attending community college. During my opening monologue on the first day of class, I mentioned the nearby university where I was completing my PhD. After class, she asked me about transferring there when she hadn't even been enrolled at this college for a full week. In the class's first assignment, an introduction letter to me, she wrote that she was accepted to every four-year school she applied to. During our interview, she elaborated, saying that if her parents hadn't accepted some bad financial advice or if she had been awarded enough of a scholarship, she'd be dorming, taking her first steps toward becoming a veterinarian, and otherwise living the "going-away-to-college" life many working-class students aspire to.

"I worked so hard just to come *here*," she said, aware of the institutionalized embarrassment community colleges carry. From what I've observed, even if students don't feel explicitly bad about attending this community college, they aren't especially thrilled about it either. I can't blame them. Media portrays community college as a joke (Tucciarone 2007, 40).

"I had a plan," she lamented. "I wanted to be proud of where I went. I wanted to say the name and have my parents say the name and be proud."

I had a plan too.

As a composition instructor and, later, a PhD candidate, I wasn't necessarily sad my journalism career never really took off. I didn't regret getting an advanced degree in a profession I ultimately abandoned. In spite of the $50K price tag, my master's degree led me to what I believed was my life's work: teaching. My first semesters were definitely a struggle,[5] one that moves too far outside the scope of this chapter to narrate in detail. Eventually though, I did get my bearings. My "accidental" professorship evolved into an intentional, professional practice. For a time, I was happy doing a job I liked, felt had purpose, and, despite a clumsy start, was good at.

However, in the years leading up to meeting Alejandra and especially after, I've felt trapped, suffering from a kind of Stockholm syndrome that almost convinces me at times that as a contingent faculty member, I don't do all that much, nor is my job terribly difficult or important. It didn't occur to me at the time, but the way I was hired pretty much screams it. As a consequence, my time, labor, experience, expertise, and doctoral degree don't merit job security, professional support, or especially a paycheck in keeping with my level of education and the amount of work I actually do. As with most of my adjunct peers, when I divide how much I am paid per course by the actual time it takes to complete the expected parts of my job, I make well below minimum wage (Saccaro 2014).[6]

Since teaching more than two classes at any one institution might necessitate that the institution hire me as a full-time employee, I, like so many of my adjunct peers, work at several campuses, sometimes on the same day, to cobble together a living. Yet, I do much of my work before I am on anyone's payroll. Between semesters, I plan courses, prepare individual lessons, fine-tune existing ones, and create new courses when necessary, often with less than a week's notice. During the semester, I teach too many courses, enrolled with too many students, at too many schools (Saccaro 2014). I work on the lessons I was too resentful to complete or think about when I was working for free in the summer and January, meet with students outside class, answer emails (which I am also unofficially accountable for between semesters, when, again, I am not employed by my respective campuses), write recommendations and, at a campus I recently left, write mandatory individual progress reports at three-week intervals. Missing deadlines for those progress reports got me an automated email threatening my termination and veiled in-person threats by administrators I was unlucky enough to encounter in passing. In recent years, my role has also expanded to include serving as classroom disciplinarian and writing unofficial cover-my-ass dossiers on students who increasingly appeal grades or have any number of issues that might require administrative intervention.

Being an adjunct takes over my life. There is never a day I am not working in one form or another. On the days I teach, due to metro New York City's oftentimes bumper-to-bumper traffic, I am never at one desk at one campus long enough to read more than a handful of assignments or make a few photocopies. And, because I am on the job market, I work to advance my own scholarship, which too often takes a backseat to my students' needs. The sheer volume of writing I must read and meaningfully comment on if I want my students to actually learn feels like a choke chain around my neck. I can't keep up. I can't stay organized. I'm constantly overwhelmed and distracted. I'm short with people. I forget things. The quality of my instruction suffers. It doesn't feel good knowing I could be doing a better job if only I weren't so overextended. Fears about money, job insecurity, insufficient time for my students, and even less time for myself leave me psychologically gutted, able to do little more than stew in my anger and plan my escape.

Like Alejandra, I worked so hard just to end up *here*.

At the conference table in the back of the English department, Alejandra and I continued talking about her brother, Diego. In an early assignment, she described him as her "hero." I asked her to take me through the decision to write about him in her longer personal narrative.

"I took a deep breath and said, 'I can do this.' The piece itself wasn't hard to write, but writing it was hard on me."

In the essay, she explained how she became aware of Diego's condition and what it was like living—and then not living—with him after circumstances required that he move to a facility far away from home. Alejandra elaborated on her disappointment that her brother isn't a part of her daily life when she wrote in her end-of-the semester metatext, "I'm not over the fact that my brother can't be normal and I don't think I ever will."

Finally, I needed to ask, "What happened with your research paper? The last month of class . . . ?"

Because Alejandra wrote so much about Diego, I had suggested for her final project that she research ways the mentally disabled are regarded in the United States and how those narratives affect how society treats them. I asked her to think about how attitudes have changed or not and what she thought needed to be done. Initially, she said it was a great idea. However, midway through the process, she emailed me to say she wanted to write about noise-induced hearing loss.

"I thought [the original topic] would be a good way to finish the semester," she said. "I thought it would be easy and useful . . . and interesting, in a way, to help my mother."

But as she continued, her eyes turned shiny with tears. "I read about places where people got hurt, got raped and this and that. Something like that happened to my brother when he was much younger. I didn't know that people getting abused this way was common."

"I wish you would have told me," I said looking down, feeling terrible, sweat collecting on my lower back. "You didn't have to give me the details, but we could have come up with something that wouldn't have sent you into a tailspin."

Alejandra then revealed that one of the reasons she agreed to my interview request was that she wanted to explain why she didn't complete the paper she was initially excited to write. She followed with a refrain that surfaced intermittently during our discussion: "I didn't want you to feel sorry for me. I didn't want anyone to look at me differently."

When I began writing the Alejandra section of my dissertation, I wished I could go back and conduct my interview with her again. I wanted to ask her exactly what she meant by that. In reading her narrative about Diego, I thought I was reading about the reality of Alejandra's family, not raw confession. Her end-of-semester metatext offered a small hint of insight, saying, "I think what I'm going to remember most about this class is the experience I had when I wrote my memoir. How I opened myself up to a complete stranger but yet felt as if I could trust them with my deepest darkest secrets." I'm still not sure what those "deepest darkest secrets" are. The fact of Diego's disability, which was the result of medical malpractice during his birth? That he could be violent? That once after her father tried to stop Diego from hitting their mother, Diego told a bus driver his father hit him, which caused child-protective services to investigate, and that the case was subsequently dismissed? That as an adult, Diego couldn't be left alone with his family without supervision from the facility where he lived? The catastrophic failings of intersecting institutional powers that resulted in his abuse?

By characterizing these details as "deepest darkest secrets," I imagine Alejandra was revealing she felt a certain amount of shame, but none of that shame belonged to Alejandra, Diego, or her family. There wasn't anything in me that felt pity for Alejandra or changed the way I saw her. But then I'm not sure that matters. Shame doesn't work that way. *She believed* that telling me the real reason she didn't follow through with her original research project would evoke my pity and make me look at her differently.

It's taken long past my dissertation defense to realize my well-intended exercise in critical pedagogy only traveled part of the way. It was missing a crucial ingredient necessary to offset feelings of powerlessness, anger, disillusionment, and cynicism that an understanding of institutional power can engender—emotions I imagine assaulted Alejandra as she conducted her initial research. My curriculum was absent any sense of hope. The preamble of my syllabus brushed against hope for a millisecond when I invoked Freire's (1970) often-quoted line from *Pedagogy of the Oppressed*, "Knowledge emerges only through invention and re-invention, through the restless, impatient, continuing, *hopeful* inquiry human beings pursue in the world, with the world, and with each other" (72; my italics). The *hopeful* never impacted me the way I imagine Freire might have intended. In spite of my admiration for

Freire, *hopeful* was just the quaint fourth in a string of far more compelling adjectives. Reading the sentence out loud during the first session, my voice dipped when I got to "hopeful." In attempting to unpack the sentence, I reiterated "restless, impatient, continuing," ticking off the words with my fingers. I skipped "hopeful" entirely.

Yet, in the preface to *Pedagogy of Hope: Reliving Pedagogy of the Oppressed*, Freire (1994) frames hope as elemental to the human experience. He writes, "Hope is an ontological need. Hopelessness is but hope that has lost its bearings, and become a distortion of that ontological need" (2). At the time, I'd never given the idea of hope that much thought. If anyone had asked me about the *hopeful*, I probably would have said something saccharin for the benefit of the class while internally rolling my eyes. In the throes of my own epistemological despair, it simply didn't occur to me critical pedagogy could—or should—be tethered to the idea of hope, radical or otherwise.

There's a reason that throughout my doctoral program, I felt such a strong pull towards critical pedagogues including Freire, bell hooks, Henry Giroux, and the like. Studying the ways sociocultural narratives of power, privilege, and hierarchy distill into individual lived experience helped me make sense of what I'd experienced in the years leading up to my unwitting career change. During that time, I had been batted around by institutional power a lot. At the same time, I now realize, studying critical pedagogy left me with a small margin for hope that pervasive institutional narratives can be changed.

While scholars contextualize hope in a spectrum of incarnations (Rossatto 2004; Webb 2013), Darren Webb (2013) summarizes Paulo Freire's conception of "radical hope" as "a profound confidence in the transformative capacities of human agency, a confidence that enables real subjects to insert themselves into history and commit themselves to confronting and overcoming the 'limit situations' that face them" (410). Accordingly, it wasn't enough for my students to simply know institutional forces push and pull them in any number of directions, or for me to presume such knowledge alone would inspire them to interrogate, negotiate and challenge institutional power, disrupt faulty narratives, or take up the mantle of a cause in order to change material conditions for the better. In *Pedagogy of Hope* Freire (1994) says, "A more critical understanding of the situation of oppression does not yet liberate the oppressed. But the revelation is a step in the right direction. Now the person who has this new understanding can engage in a political struggle for the transformation of the concrete condition in which the oppression prevails" (24). Knowing, he implies, is where the real work starts. Yet knowing is where my curriculum started and subsequently ended.

However, as Alejandra demonstrated, knowledge can be paralyzing. In *Empowering Education*, Ira Shor (1992) reinforces the false equivalency of understanding one's circumstances and taking action, writing, "Knowledge is only power for those who can use it to change their conditions" (6). I don't know what made me think I could inspire an army of activists through knowledge alone. By the time I met Alejandra, I had plenty of knowledge and arguably more tools, but I wasn't able to substantively change *my* conditions. Because I wasn't able to register my own ambivalence, not constructing even a minimal framework of hope in all likelihood sent the message to some students, *life is shit, kids. Good luck.*

In his article "Overcoming 'Doom and Gloom': Empowering Students in Courses on Social Problems, Injustice, and Inequality," Brett Johnson (2005) surmises that such college courses are flawed when they stop short of demonstrating or even suggesting specific, local ways students can act in the interest of mitigating harmful institutional constructs. He argues that omitting this necessary final step leads to the cynicism and apathy such courses are intended to mitigate. Accordingly, it was necessary for me to contextualize my critical pedagogy curriculum within its aspirational framework where "knowing" and "hope" are recursive points along a continuum facilitated by time (Rossatto 2004). Through my lessons, readings, and assignments, I could have demonstrated that social justice work is an ongoing project comprised of small advances (Johnson 2005). At the same time, I needed to provide students with mechanisms to generate a sense of self-efficacy, or a belief in their potential—as individuals and collectively—to become agents of change (Bandura 1997; Johnson 2005, 46). Johnson (2005) evokes Albert Bandura (1997), saying, "A person with high self-efficacy believes that s/he is capable of accomplishing a goal and is subsequently more willing to pursue the activity and persevere when encountering difficulties. Actual ability to accomplish the goal is secondary to the individual's *perceived* ability to achieve the outcome" (46; italics in original). In other words, students needed some kernel of belief they could effect change in order to prevent or lessen their own epistemological despair. The problem is, in thinking about my own circumstances, I'm not sure how much I believed it—then or now.

Yet, some students' course work was implicitly hopeful. Rochelle Harris (2004) uses the term "emergent moment" to encapsulate instances in which through narrative, students re-envision themselves in relation to a newly acquired understanding of their lived experience

(402–3). Some of my students that semester developed a sense of connectedness with invisible communities they shared experiences with. This was the case with Isabella, whom I met during her second attempt at college. In her end-of-semester metatext, she wrote, "Being a Spanish girl who grew up in the ghetto the only thing to do according to the media is have a ton of kids and stay home while receiving welfare . . . from my research essay I learned that at the time I first went to college I did the best I could and unfortunately what was expected from someone like me, a low income minority." Through her personal narrative and the critical work that followed, she was able to consider and reconsider how the world saw her and place those perceptions in conversation with how she saw herself and who she aspired to be. That intellectual and emotional work seemed to develop into a new understanding of herself that reified her determination to finish college and become a nurse.

Another hopeful "emergent moment" occurred for Ishaan, a Guyanese student, when he began to empathize with his mother, who raised him as a fervent evangelical Christian. In his personal narrative, he described himself as "a miniature advocate for Christ in a tiny suit" who told Hindu children they were going to Hell. "I was horrible," he said during his interview. By the time Ishaan started high school, he replaced Christianity with what he called "a belief in science." It eventually led him to challenge his mother about praying in public before eating during his birthday dinner when he turned fourteen. Consequently, their relationship turned perpetually acrimonious. However, after his research project on the ways organized religion functions in societies, he said he was able to soften his stance towards his mother's religious practice. During his interview he said, "I learned to accept the fact that my mother uses church just to belong to something. I know she's been through a lot. Religion is her way of coping." Ishaan's "emergent moment" allowed him to understand his mother and their relationship in a way that for some adults takes decades.

My pedagogical oversight didn't negatively impact Isabella and Ishaan. Their critical work organically altered their temporality for the better. However, that same inattention caused Alejandra to rip open old wounds—and create new ones. As I planned my study, I thought that if any students struggled with difficult emotions during the course, it would be as they drafted their personal narratives. It was something I'd seen before and was prepared to handle. I didn't anticipate that becoming cognizant of the ways institutional power manifests could precipitate a crisis of knowing in an eighteen-year-old student's life. After all, the assignment was to write a research paper. They are clinical, dispassionate intellectual exercises, or that's what I would have told myself if I had stopped to consider it. Unlike Isabella and Ishaan, Alejandra's research viscerally, painfully connected to the present tense of her life. "The research paper really messed me up," she said during her interview.

Less than a month after I interviewed Alejandra and was done actively collecting data from my study participants, I learned what the phrase *driven to distraction* not only means but feels like—a situation in which you are so emotionally and intellectually traumatized it takes herculean strength and compartmentalization skills to devote mental energy to, well, anything. The Friday before Memorial Day weekend at about 6 p.m., I received a call saying the class I was scheduled to teach starting the following Tuesday was cancelled. Facing almost four months without an income, barred from collecting unemployment,[7] I white-knuckled my way through a protracted, mortifying battle with the New York City Human Resources Administration (HRA) for food stamps.[8] Weeks later, I was rewarded for my rage-fueled perseverance with the feeling of humiliation while handing my EBT card to supermarket cashiers as people in line looked on.

As the summer wore on and the fall 2013 semester finally began, bringing with it a steady, if miniscule, paycheck, I took pains to hide the fact of the food stamps from colleagues and friends outside my immediate circle. In my attempts to participate in adjunct advocacy and teaching about institutional power in subsequent composition courses, I was hyperaware of saying anything that might somehow indicate why I knew so much about dealing with New York City's Human Resources Administration. I didn't want anyone to figure out *my* "deepest darkest secret." Through that experience, I lost something I can't seem to articulate. I feel something broke inside me I still haven't been able to repair.

It's true all this happened after I was no longer in contact with Alejandra and her classmates. I can only guess about how this experience might have informed my study, the curriculum I developed, or my interactions with my students. It has, however, led me to think about the idea of shame as one of critical pedagogy's more embedded tensions. Since shame is at the nucleus of so many of our ways of knowing, maybe it's the most insidious institutional power of all. Like Alejandra, I don't want anyone to feel sorry for me. I don't want anyone to look at me differently. Unlike Alejandra, I don't need to guess. My fears are motivated by my shame, a shame born out of my (former) class privilege—public assistance doesn't happen to people like me—but it's shame nonetheless. I can't help but wonder if it is this particular brand of privilege-laced shame that, in part, keeps more adjuncts from invoking their political voice. Intellectually, at least, I know a sympathetic audience won't see what I've revealed about myself as embarrassing or shameful. That shame rightly belongs to the institutional entities that created the circumstances that left Alejandra and I feeling powerless in the first place. But, like I said earlier, shame doesn't work that way.

Had my food-stamps experience occurred before I met Alejandra, maybe I would have been more equipped to sit with her and her shame instead of inwardly minimizing it by telling myself it wasn't her fault. In terms of my curriculum, maybe a deeper recognition of shame and how it operates as a mechanism of institutional control, maintenance, and reproduction would have allowed me to problematize it with my students. I might have delineated ways shame is weaponized and stratified, not only how it is ascribed onto individuals but also how shame manifests as an ever-present, firmly affixed mechanism for self-policing (Creed et al. 2014), as it was for Alejandra (and me). Imparting these ideas to my students could have served as an initial move towards the middle ground between epistemological despair and the "radical hope" I suggest in my title.

On a more personal, pedagogical level, this understanding of shame might have helped me recognize sooner that while I see myself as a casualty of higher education, to my students, I am also an agent and enforcer of the academy. Therefore, I am capable of ascribing shame, or the perception of shame, to them the way I wrongly did with Alejandra when I projected willful indolence onto her. In the beginning of this chapter, I said I wanted to inspire my students to interrogate, negotiate, and challenge institutional power. In retrospect, Alejandra absolutely did that. In opting out of the research paper she originally intended to write, the institutional power Alejandra was pushing back against was me.

Towards the end of our interview, Alejandra vouched for the fact that the information she gathered about the mentally disabled didn't just disintegrate when she no longer used it for her research paper.

"Doing the research helped me out a lot. I just didn't write about it," she said. Consequently, Alejandra added what she learned to a store of knowledge she'll access in years to come in order to advocate for someone even more vulnerable to institutional power than she was.

That might not be radical, but it is hopeful.

NOTES
1. All names are pseudonyms.
2. For a comprehensive explanation of the "banking concept," see chapter 2 of *Pedagogy of the Oppressed*.

3. Students read an abridged version of chapter 2 of *Pedagogy of the Oppressed*, which, in addition to introducing the "banking" concept, discusses Freire's interpretation of student/teacher power dynamics.
4. Where students' written work is quoted, it appears as it originally did when it was submitted.
5. For a description of common experiences shared by new and inexperienced adjunct faculty, see *Contingent Commitments: Bringing Part-Time Faculty Into Focus: A Special Report from the Center for Community College Student Engagement* (Center for Community College Engagement 2014).
6. According to the AAUP, the average pay for part-time instructors teaching a three-credit course during the 2012–13 academic year, when I collected my data, was $2,700 per class. In the time since, according to the 2018–19 AAUP Faculty Compensation Survey, that average has increased to $3,894, with a vast gap between a low of $2,925 and a high of $5,858.
7. See AAUP.org, newfacultymajority.info.
8. For a parsing of the HRA's systemic dysfunction and institutionally supported culture of disrespecting recipients of public assistance, see Michelle Chen (2014).

REFERENCES

AAUP. "Research: Faculty Compensation Survey." American Association of University Professors. Accessed 6 June 2021. https://www.aaup.org/our-work/research/FCS.

Bandura, Albert. 1997. *Self-Efficacy: The Exercise of Control.* New York: W. H. Freeman.

Center for Community College Student Engagement (CCCSE). 2014. *Contingent Commitments: Bringing Part-Time Faculty into Focus: A Special Report from the Center for Community College Student Engagement.* https://www.ccsse.org/docs/PTF_Special_Report.pdf.

Chen, Michelle. "Can New York City's Welfare System Be Saved?" 2014. *The Nation*, May 29. https://www.thenation.com/article/can-new-york-citys-welfare-system-be-saved/.

Creed, W. E. Douglas, Bryant Ashley Hudson, Gerardo A. Okhuysen, and Kristen Smith-Crowe. 2014. *Swimming in a Sea of Shame: Incorporating Emotion into Explanations of Institutional Reproduction and Change.* College of Business Administration University of Rhode Island William Orme Working Paper Series. http://www.cba.uri.edu/research/workingpapers/documents/2014/WP3_2014.pdf.

Ellis, Carolyn, Tony E. Adams, and Arthur P. Bochner. 2011. "Autoethnography: An Overview." *Qualitative Sozialforschun / Qualitative Social Research* 12 (1): Art. 10. http://www.qualitative-research.net/index.php/fqs/article/view/1589/3095.

Freire, Paulo. 1970. *Pedagogy of the Oppressed: 30th Anniversary Edition.* New York: Continuum.

Freire, Paulo. 1994. *Pedagogy of Hope: Reliving Pedagogy of the Oppressed.* London: Bloomsbury Academic.

Giroux, Henry. 2016. "Beyond Pedagogies of Repression." *Monthly Review* 67 (10): 55–71. ProQuest Central.

Harris, Rochelle. 2004 "Encouraging Emergent Moments: The Personal, Critical, and Rhetorical in the Writing Classroom." *Pedagogy: Critical Approaches to Teaching Literature, Language, Composition and Culture* 4 (3): 401–18. ProQuest Central.

Johnson, Brett. 2005. "Overcoming 'Doom and Gloom': Empowering Students in Courses on Social Problems, Injustice and Inequality." *Teaching Sociology* 33 (1): 44–58. ProQuest Central.

Rossatto, César Augusto. 2004. *Engaging Paulo Freire's Pedagogy of Possibility: From Blind to Transformative Optimism.* Lanham, MD: Rowman & Littlefield.

Saccaro, Matt. 2014. "Professors on Food Stamps: The Shocking True Story of Academia in 2014." Salon.com. September 21. https://www.salon.com/2014/09/21/professors_on_food_stamps_the_shocking_true_story_of_academia_in_2014/.

Shor, Ira. 1992. *Empowering Education: Critical Teaching for Social Change.* Chicago; University of Chicago Press.

Tucciarone, Krista M. 2007. "Community College Image—By Hollywood." *Community College Enterprise* 13 (1): 37–53. ProQuest Central.

Webb, Darren. 2013. "Pedagogies of Hope." *Studies in Philosophy and Education* 32 (4): 397–414. doi:10.1007/s11217-012-9336-1.

5
A WINDOW INTO THE COMPLEX WORLD OF FACTORY-FLOOR WRITING

Elena G. Garcia and Guadalupe Garcia

INTRODUCTION

This chapter is a collaborative autoethnography (CAE) written by a university professor, Elena Garcia, and her father, Guadalupe (Lupe) Garcia, a machine operator for a food manufacturer we are calling Pillar Foods. A decade ago, a conversation took place that has shaped the ways we both see our work.

> ELENA: I was taking a cultural rhetorics graduate course that focused on working-class culture. In it, I mostly read ethnographies written by academics who studied the nonworking lives of the working class. Since working-class culture tends to be defined by the type of work itself, I was surprised at how little information these ethnographies revealed about the workplaces of the participants. I shared this surprise with my dad and started asking about his work experiences.
>
> LUPE: I have been a factory machine operator at Pillar Foods for over forty years. Even though I have talked to Elena about my work in the past, I never imagined she would connect it to her PhD classes. And I definitely didn't imagine I would be writing publications with her.

From that semester, we homed in on the writing at Pillar Foods as our area of focus. Some of our previous studies have examined writing processes, writing and identity, and the consequences to production when writing practices are ineffective.

Our work has been inspired by and draws upon several broad areas of academic study: professional and workplace writing, writing studies, literacy studies, and new working-class studies. Our research examines the ways texts, particularly procedural manuals, are deeply connected to the power struggles between managers and the working-class machine operators. We are taking the opportunity provided by our relationship to look closely at Pillar Foods specifically because such work "needs to focus on the particular" (*Barton and Hamilton 2012*, xiv) and should be studied within its particular context. Finally, by collaboratively writing this document, we are putting a working-class voice at the center of our study. We go beyond the recommendations of John Russo and Sherry Lee Linkon (2005) to collect and study oral histories, songs, poems, and personal narratives of working-class peoples; instead, the working-class voice in question here is front and center as a coauthor of an academic text.

We determined a collaborative autoethnography would be the best way to show readers tensions and conflicts surrounding writing at Pillar Foods. Within this chapter we focus specifically on the ways the unionized, working-class laborers perceive writing as the domain of "the management" and therefore as a tool for management to use against them. The conflict reveals how writing at Pillar Foods is more about people and relationships than it is about organizing words on paper. For writing studies scholars who focus on workplace and professional writing, especially in relation to power and identities, this chapter adds to the pool of local contexts while also including an insider's voice and perspectives.

METHODOLOGY

> ELENA: Nearly a decade ago, I chose Pillar Foods as the research site for my dissertation because of a specific writing project happening at the time that involved machine operators composing the content for procedural manuals (JSMs). I had gotten the okay to observe this writing in action and had visited the factory floor once before the entire manuals project was stopped. In that moment, my direct access to Pillar Foods was cut off. Industrial workplaces are intense about protecting their secrets from outsiders, and I was no longer on "the list" or allowed through security.

> LUPE: At work, I write guides for my trainees to use when they start working on their own. I try to write well, but it's hard for me. I'm not going to write at home because I already work eight, twelve, sixteen-hour days. At work, I don't have access to a computer, so I write by hand. But I only have the chance to write a few thoughts at a time. I have trouble organizing my ideas and end up rewriting things over and over again. I want to share my knowledge with people at work, even with people outside of work, but it's hard enough to write what I need to write. I definitely can't write and publish something like this by myself.

Such issues of access, knowledge, skills, and time have led us to utilize a collaborative autoethnographic (CAE) research methodology as we engage in our research. We spent several years playing around with different research approaches and methods before we chose the CAE methodology for both practical and ethical reasons.

PRACTICAL

Collaborative autoethnography (CAE) allows for collection and examination of autobiographical information to be analyzed and interpreted in teams. Neither of us has access to the world of the other, but together we have everything we need for an autoethnography: "a researcher recount[ing] a story of his or her own personal experience, coupled with an ethnographic analysis of the cultural context and implications of that experience" (Lapadat 2017, 589). We both want to study the cultural tensions related to writing that exist at Pillar Foods, but neither of us can do that on our own.

CAE is also "well suited to community-based research . . . [and] offers a way to broaden the scope of the autobiographic approach beyond university-trained qualitative researchers" (Lapadat 2017, 598). CAE, then, allows us to leverage our differing knowledges (machine operation versus academic research and writing) and our differing access (Pillar Foods versus academia) in order to share our interest in writing at Pillar Foods with others who are likely to find it interesting.

ETHICAL

ELENA: The ethical motivation to conduct a CAE is solely mine. For my dissertation, I had to see my dad as a research participant instead of as a partner. It felt, well, gross. I tried to highlight his voice in that work as much as I could, but he was still a person being studied and examined and analyzed. This is the main drawback, as I see it, in ethnographic work—the "issue of representing, speaking for, or appropriating the voice of others" (Lapadat 2017, 589). When I thought of how I could bring my dad into my academic world as a partner, I landed on autoethnography as a potential approach because it "enables marginalized communities to publish their own cultural experiences in their own voices, resisting the knowledge being constructed about them" (Canagarajah 2012, 115). Yet my dad isn't going to write a book chapter like this. I had to be the one to put this publication together. CAE allows for the ethics of collaborative research and authorship while still having all the benefits of ethnographic methodologies.

BENEFITS OF CAE IN WRITING STUDIES

We see CAE as working exceptionally well for writing studies for several reasons.

1. It can be difficult to study writing in nonacademic workplaces, especially those that strongly protect against industrial espionage. Collaboration with an insider allows for access.

2. CAE allows those in academia to hear voices that might be unfamiliar and to see those voices in writing.

3. CAE allows for nonacademic researchers to gain entrance into the academic world, expanding the ways we see and talk about writing. The responses we have seen for our collaborative conference presentations tell us there is a lot of interest in hearing these voices in an academic context.

4. CAE can ensure academics do not overshadow the analyses of research partners; the findings are coconstructed and can, therefore, reveal a wider variety of findings, interpretations, and perspectives.

5. As argued by A. Suresh Canagarajah (2012), "The more autoethnographies we have, the better. If all knowledge is local and personal, we must all become storytellers—both inside and outside the academy" (123). Since CAE can bring to writing studies even more stories, the disciplinary understanding of how writing functions in various cultures will become more robust.

ELENA: Finally, CAE and other collaborative methods can help those of us in writing studies stay connected with the places we come from. Finding work in academia has taken me far from my family and my entire support system. I have felt isolated and homesick, separated by miles and by experiences. However, by working with my dad on a subject of interest to both of us, I have stayed connected to him. In fact, this work has allowed me to stay connected with my family as well. Many working-class academics lament the fact that their work and their research causes tension, separation, and loss, as evidenced powerfully in *This Fine Place So Far from Home: Voices of Academics from the Working Class* (Dews and Law 1995). My research is familiar to my family and requires me to talk with them and visit them. I believe this, in combination with the five reasons listed above, provides an even stronger reason for me to pursue CAE as a research methodology.

METHODS

Nailing down our methods involved some testing and practice, for both of us. According to Heewon Chang, Faith Wambura Ngunjiri, and Kathy-Ann Hernandez (2013), our data could include personal memory/recollection, archival materials, self-reflection, self-analysis, and interview (74). Canagarajah (2012) adds that methods could take the form of the self-in-the-collective (when each member of a research team gathers their own data before they come together as a group), interaction ("when two or more subjects each become researcher-cum-subject as they interview each other to co-construct the experience" [18]), and self-reflection. Archival materials are automatically not an option for our work because Pillar Foods does not allow employees to take materials out of the workplace.

Our methods of choice ended up being determined largely by constraints of time and distance. Therefore, we ended up with several layers of data collection and development and, later, analysis. We started with Lupe noting events or conversations that connect to our broad research project (anything relating to writing at Pillar Foods). Then, when he had the time, we examined his notes through recorded phone conversations, during which he engaged in self-reflection as a way to develop the kind of thorough data collection necessary for an ethnographic approach. During these conversations, Elena asked him follow-up questions to encourage him to examine his experience or observation further. Later, Elena transcribed all relevant materials.

We returned to our recorded and transcribed conversations when Elena visited home. We set time aside during these visits to engage in an interactive analysis (Canagarajah 2012, 118) in which we each asked each other questions to examine tensions, issues, and points of interest. The comfort of our relationship allowed for these analysis conversations to last hours, and they were audio recorded and the relevant portions transcribed.

> ELENA: I, necessarily, recorded and transcribed each layer of our conversations. I have dedicated research time in my yearly teaching load for just this kind of work. As I listened to our conversations to transcribe them, I also noted themes, questions, and topics we could later discuss and analyze. Dad wrote his observations and reflections while I worked to make sense of it for us.

When our chapter proposal for this collection was accepted for publication, we focused one of Elena's visits home on the conflicts we noted between management and machine operators regarding the writing of procedural documents. We recorded two long analysis conversations, which became the primary content for this chapter. After Elena transcribed these two conversations, again noting themes, questions, and topics of interest, they became the foundation for a phone conversation to determine our core focus.

> ELENA: Once we determined our core focus—the cultural conflicts between the operators and management surrounding writing procedural documents—I organized the transcribed content into a chapter rough draft. Dad's text, his narrative, is written in his voice while my own text reflects thoughts I had while putting the chapter together. Our combined voice is drawn from our transcribed conversations. We analyzed Dad's experiences together, so that analysis is presented in the first-person plural.

At each revision stage, we came together again to discuss the comments we received and how we might adjust our chapter. Elena took the lead in implementing changes we discussed. In the end, even though our research process was slow and broken up into many small pieces, we feel it is a particularly effective methodology to use in writing studies because it utilizes the strengths of scholars, as well as workplace insiders.

Next, we weave together Lupe's narrative and our combined analysis to reveal a window into a world very different from academia. Through this window, you can see some of the struggles Pillar Foods has with composing effective machine-operation guides and manuals, struggles that result from a long history of mistrust between the machine operators and management.

WRITING AS A WEAPON: PERCEPTIONS OF MACHINE OPERATORS

As expected, the workforces within factories tend to be as small as possible, supplementing a great deal of human labor with computer and robotic labor. A small workforce is expected to maintain high levels of productivity across the vastness of a factory (in terms of actual space, as well as the different kinds of work being done). With this, written communication has become increasingly important.

> LUPE: The management at Pillar Foods has been trying to change the workplace culture. The culture of the place used to be "throw people at it." If there was a problem or if production was slow, they just brought more and more people in to fix things. They decided they're not going to "throw people" at the problem anymore. They decided, "We're going to make sure the problems don't exist." It's funny because a lot of delays can happen simply because there aren't clearly written instructions for how to run the machinery effectively, how to troubleshoot when things go wrong, and how to make minor repairs (mechanics make the big repairs).

Given the importance of correctly producing food, a lack of clear and useful communication has an immense impact on Pillar Food's profits. A lack of comprehensive writing and communication is contributing to failures, delays, and wasted product, causing the company to unnecessarily lose profits; typically, lost profit means lost jobs.

Written communication is not only important but is also becoming increasingly prevalent. This trend reflects a broader national phenomenon of substantial workplace writing. Deborah Brandt (2015), in *The Rise of Writing: Redefining Mass Literacy*, writes, "Millions of Americans now engage in creating, processing, and managing written communications as a major aspect of their work. It is not unusual for American adults to spend 50 percent or more of the workday with their hands on keyboards and their minds on audiences. . . . As the nature of work in the United States has changed—toward making and managing information and knowledge in increasingly globalized settings—intense pressure has come to bear on the productive side of literacy, the writing side" (3). School-based writing often focuses on the effectiveness of that communication, the clarity, the strength of the arguments, and so forth. It's difficult to move away from such conversations when discussing writing with other teachers, even with employers who also tend to focus on the same features. But if writing is becoming more prevalent in all workplaces, even on factory floors, then research must focus on how writing is perceived by the marginalized, less powerful workers. Doing so reveals vastly different conflicts and needs than academic writing instruction tends to focus on.

> LUPE: There is a fear of writing at Pillar. Not really a fear of the act of writing but more of a fear about how writing would be used against the hourly employees. The basic thought is, "If I write down what I know about operating my machine, management will fire me, hire someone else at a lower wage, and that person would use what I wrote to do my job." Instead of taking that risk, a lot of workers keep their knowledge to themselves. It's "Don't tell nobody nothing!" One woman who thinks this way even said to me (when I was new to running a machine she used to work on), "I'll tell you how to run this machine because I like you. If I didn't like you, I'd say 'screw it, you can find out for yourself.'" I guess I'm glad she liked me because I didn't know anything! These operators fear the loss of their one job, the loss of their money. They don't look at everything. They don't see that they're screwing everything up for everybody else. The less people know about how to operate a machine, the less profit the company ends up making, which usually means fewer jobs, including their jobs.

Several years ago, a plant-wide project paired senior machine operators with a technical writer to write job-sequence manuals (JSM). The JSMs, when done well, provide operators with exactly what they need because all the content comes from senior operators, written in collaboration with a technical writer. They have pictures and explanations and guidelines for troubleshooting. A lot of money was spent on this project, but unfortunately there are only a few complete JSMs.

> LUPE: What ended up happening is that somebody, somewhere, shut up the operators working on the JSMs, basically by word of mouth. Because the union had agreed to do the project, they weren't the ones keeping operators quiet. Instead, I think it was coming from other

operators, like "Don't tell them shit. We don't want nobody to know our shit." So, after several weeks of an operator working with the technical writer for a new machine I'm working on, all I have is a JSM with some terminology, and that's it. It's three or four pages long.

The thought process of these workers who "don't want nobody to know our shit" is that once detailed operations procedures are put down into writing, any small amount of power machine operators have is taken away.

> LUPE: They tell each other, "Don't do it because management is just trying to steal our jobs. If we go on strike or whatever, they can hire anyone who can come in and read our stuff and be able to operate it." But there is no way for that to actually happen, even if management believes it can work that way, too. The reason I say no is because there is no way somebody can read a book and be a doctor. There's no way you can read an instruction manual on how to put together a car engine and then put together an engine. You can't do it. You have to have training on it. It's the same way with operating our machines. You have to know what it is and how it functions. Maybe someone could do the basic stuff just by reading a manual, but that's not going to work most of the time. Operators need to have more knowledge and experience than you can ever learn from reading. They have testing tasting, so you have little scoops to gather the food. But you have to know what you're feeling, what it's supposed to taste like. When we start up a product, it goes to "feed" first, where you feel it with your hands, and you feel when it's ready. You can say, "This is good granola" just by the way it feels in your hands. Without even tasting it. You can feel it right in your hands. Everything is dependent on experience with temperatures, the ways the machines have changed over time, the characteristics of the ingredients on a particular day, and the type of food you're getting.

Unfortunately, there doesn't seem to be a good way to convince the employees management is not trying to sabotage them. If machine operators take it upon themselves to write guides or manuals as employees who wants to help ensure the factory produces as much as possible, that's more acceptable to their peers. But it is a very slow process since operators aren't provided with time to do that kind of work. Bringing someone from the outside to help with the writing, though, makes the operators think there is sabotage happening. It feels like an impossible situation.

Yet, the operators' perspective is understandable. Factory laborers, with their working-class identities, are "valued—if at all—as requisite labor and service" but not for their "intelligence and knowledge" (Zandy 1995, 2). Because they are perceived as uneducated, they are often perceived as disposable, particularly since "a preference for machines and a prejudice against human beings is heightened in the technical economy" (14). We see such perceptions at play in Pillar Foods. There is a history of mass firings, forced retirement, cutting down on benefits, and other common tactics to create as small and as cheap a workforce as possible. Knowledge of how to run the machines is the only leverage the floor workers believe they have, and they protect that knowledge, hoarding it even. It is their only power.

CONCLUSION

At Pillar Foods, and at many other workplaces, gathering information requires more than reading and citing texts. It is about talking to people who hold that information and can supply it, or not. We can see the effect of the many competing interests within Pillar Foods in the approaches to writing for the JSMs. It seems the JSM project failed in part because there wasn't the kind of knowledge and ability to understand people. Project leaders didn't anticipate machine operators might be reluctant to share their knowledge, and they didn't make any meaningful adjustments once that reality was evident. Now, many machines at Pillar Foods are not being run effectively because there aren't high-quality manuals available.

The culture and history of Pillar Foods contributed to the ways employees acted and reacted. It is an expensive lesson to learn. Brandt (2015) explains, "Because writing unleashes language into the world, it engages people's sense of power and responsibility. . . . The residual impact of writing on the writer surpasses the ostensible purposes of a text. It is an excess that can register as development, satisfaction, and despair" (162). The questions surrounding ownership of knowledge faced by machine operators reveal the residual impact at Pillar Foods: concern for retaining employment. The fear of writing and the fear of being replaced are both linked to the ways "knowledge, text, and social structures are intertwined" (Winsor 2003, 5) because "texts play a role in the way power is created and deployed" (7). To write something about their work, a vulnerable employee must feel they are important, that they have agency in that writing work, and that they are safe. Otherwise they will remain guarded, even hostile.

This CAE is brief and focused on one workplace and one tension between operators and writing. It is a glimpse into a complex workplace impacted by its past and affected by fear for the future. The work of writing studies can contribute to a better understanding of how cultural tensions play out in similar and different workplaces. In addition, writing studies researchers should collaborate with nonacademic partners, insiders in the cultures and places we want to examine, whenever possible. Such collaboration is particularly important when researching people who feel vulnerable and powerless.

The two of us have been examining the writing culture and practices at Pillar Foods for a decade, and it is only because of our personal relationship that we have been able to maintain such a lengthy project, considering the incredibly long hours worked by machine operators at Pillar Foods. Therefore, we encourage those academic researchers in writing studies to connect with the people they know outside academia to form research relationships, each becoming part of the other person's work world. These personal-research relationships allow each party to see their work from a different perspective, leading to a more thorough and nuanced understanding of the interplay among cultures, tensions, and writing.

REFERENCES

Barton, David, and Mary Hamilton. 2012. *Local Literacies: Reading and Writing in One Community*. Abingdon, UK: Routledge.

Brandt, Deborah. 2015. *The Rise of Writing: Redefining Mass Literacy*. Cambridge: Cambridge University Press.

Canagarajah, A. Suresh. 2012. "Autoethnography in the Study of Multilingual Writers." In *Writing Studies Research in Practice: Methods and Methodologies*, edited by Lee Nickoson and Mary P. Sheridan, 113–24. Carbondale: Southern Illinois University Press.

Chang, Heewon, Faith Wambura Ngunjiri, and Kathy-Ann C. Hernandez. 2013. *Collaborative Autoethnography*. Walnut Creek, CA: Left-Coast.

Dews, Carlos L. and Carolyn Leste Law, eds. 1995. *This Fine Place So Far from Home: Voices of Academics from the Working Class*. Philadelphia: Temple University Press.

Lapadat, Judith C. 2017. "Ethics in Autoethnography and Collaborative Autoethnography." *Qualitative Inquiry* 23 (8): 589–603.

Russo, John, and Sherry Lee Linkon, eds. 2005. *New Working-Class Studies*. Ithaca, NY: Cornell University Press.

Winsor, Dorothy A. 2003. *Writing Power: Communication in an Engineering Center*. Albany: SUNY Press.

Zandy, Janet. 1995. Introduction to *Liberating Memory: Our Work and Our Working-Class Consciousness*, edited by Janet Zandy, 1–15. New Brunswick, NJ: Rutgers University Press.

6

CONSTRUCTING A TRANSNATIONAL-MULTILINGUAL TEACHER SUBJECTIVITY IN A FIRST-YEAR WRITING CLASS

An Autoethnography

Soyeon Lee

Using an autoethnographic approach, this chapter traces a transnational-multilingual teacher's subjectivity construction in college writing classrooms. This autoethnographic method analyzes memories and self-reflections based on my teacher-journal entries, which describe my classroom discourses, activities, and dialogs with students in first-year writing. To trace how writing-teacher subjectivities are shaped by and interact with students' discourses, this study also presents parts of students' writings and interview transcripts, particularly focusing on their use of linguistic resources and perceptions of my teaching activities.

Increasing human mobility in the era of globalization and teaching subjectivity has drawn attention in the field of language and writing education (Miller 2009; Zhang 2018). Since the late 1990s, teachers and scholars in the field of teaching English to speakers of other languages (TESOL) have studied nonnative English-speaking (NNES) teachers' identities with a focus on their teaching experiences and unequal professional environment (Braine 1999, 2010; Ellis 2013; Kamhi-Stein 2016; Llurda 2004; Medgyes 1994). Writing scholars, however, have done little research on migrant graduate student instructors (international graduate teaching assistants in an administrative term) who have transnational backgrounds and for whom English is not the first language. I call them *transnational-multilingual graduate student teachers*.[1] Marianne Yee's 1991 article examines how her subjectivity as an English writing teacher and a speaker of other languages was constructed in the writing classroom. More recently, Yuching Yang, Kasie Kiser, and Paul Kei Matsuda (2017) have investigated an international TA's self-perception of her symbolic capital. Todd Ruecker, Stephan Frazier, and Mariya Tseptsura (2018) have examined nonnative English-speaking teachers (NNESTs) and their experiences and self-perceptions by using surveys and interviews. Although the label *nonnative* or *native* itself might not capture the complexity of teachers' identities and experiences and might paradoxically reinforce the nativeness myth these nonnative teachers criticize themselves (Moussu and Llurda 2008, 318), these emerging movements and surveys in writing studies, which extend advocating work for NNESTs in TESOL and language teaching, draw our attention to how teachers' linguistic traits and their own language ideologies play a crucial role in constructing teachers' subjectivities and professional identities. More important, new methodological approaches have emerged in these movements. In discussing the discourses of international composition teachers, Monika Shehi (2017) integrates her personal experiences and reflections. Like Shehi, Louis M. Maraj (2018) describes his experiences as a Black im/migrant graduate student instructor. In Maraj's case, the method is explicitly identified as autoethnography, particularly drawing from existing Black feminist autoethnographic approaches and their "intersectional lens" (215).

Extending Shehi's (2017) discussion on linguistic identities and Maraj's (2018) methodological approaches, this chapter further analyzes the experiences of a graduate teacher who teaches first-year writing (FYW) classes and is a member of "one of the most vulnerable and powerless populations in the university" (McKinney and Chiseri-Strater 2003, 59). Unlike other studies on self-perceptions of NNESTs, which often have used quantitative methods including large-scale surveys, this study adopts an autoethnographic approach, mainly grounded in my personal, thick narratives based on teaching-journal entries,[2] to explore how teachers' use of transnational literacy can establish their subjectivities in a sociohistorical context. In this chapter, I argue that a transnational social-field perspective (Levitt and Glick Schiller 2004, 1006) and a translingual approach (Horner, NeCamp, and Donahue 2011, 287), with which I cross linguistic and cultural borders and negotiate my literacy resources, enabled me to establish my teacher subjectivity. Yet, I contend that my translingual teaching practices are contingent on the material conditions that constitute the context of my migration experiences.

DEFINING AUTOETHNOGRAPHY AS METHODOLOGY

Autoethnography has been understood as "an approach to research and writing that seeks to describe and systematically analyze (graphy) personal experiences (auto) in order to understand cultural experiences (ethno)" (Ellis, Adams, and Bochner 2011, 1). Building on this well-known definition, that is, a study of culture through self, this chapter particularly adopts transcultural and materialist definitions suggested by Mary Louise Pratt (1991) to examine a migrant teacher's subjectivities in writing education in the unevenly networked world. In Pratt's words, autoethnography is an appropriation that speaks back to the dominant narratives of "others": a "text in which people undertake to describe themselves in ways that engage with representations others have made of them" (35). Taking up Pratt's perspectives, I situate autoethnography as a research method of vulnerable subjects particularly in two sociopolitical contexts: a multilingual context and a postcolonial context. As A. Suresh Canagarajah (2012) notes, an autoethnographic approach plays an important role in researching multilingual practices. According to him, autoethnography enables multilingual writers to avoid misrepresentations or "native speaker norms," which are often seen in ethnographies conducted by nonmultilingual researchers (116). Autoethnography thus stands in contrast to "both the quantitative and qualitative traditions that are informed by modernist principles of objectivity, empiricism, rational analysis" (114). More important, it disrupts the binary between self and culture in material environments, the notion of the self that is often assumed to be a unified subject in Anglo-American autobiographical genres. Given an unequal power structure based on English monolingualism, this chapter eventually advocates social justice for multilingual teachers, particularly those who bear postcolonial history or identities, by using an autoethnographic approach and foregrounding its potential powers.

METHODS

This chapter particularly analyzes my teacher journal from fall 2016 to spring 2017, which describes my classroom discourses, activities, and class-related or personal dialogues with students during office hours in the first and second sequence of the FYW program. To trace how my teacher subjectivities are shaped by and interact with students' discourses, I also collected students' writings and interview transcripts, particularly focusing on their use of self-references, multilingual resources, and perceptions of my teaching practices.[3] This study particularly uses writings and interview transcripts of Javier (pseudonym), one of the research participants in the spring of 2017. In the remaining essay, I describe two reflective narratives of my literacy practices: one, my literacy history, which presents my perception of the linguistic hierarchy, and the other, my negotiating practices, which unsettle and rescale the linguistic hierarchy and interactions with student writings.

SELF-PERCEPTIONS OF MY LANGUAGE IDEOLOGIES: AN ENGLISH-LANGUAGE LEARNER IN A NEOLIBERAL REALITY

My literacy development is rooted in the functional and transactional values of learning English. In my formative years, to learn English was predominantly aimed at acquiring a high score on standardized tests, such as the TOEFL (Test of English as a Foreign Language) or the TOEIC (Test of English for International Communication), to be a competitive neoliberal subject. Like most Koreans, I had a belief that English contained an instrumental value that would allow me to continuously "upgrade" myself on an efficient ladder or "a conduit for economic and social advancement" (Park 2011, 443). Since the IMF (International Monetary Fund) restructured financial systems in Korea in 1997 and began to execute downsizing and massive layoffs in corporations, English was regarded as a tool that would help one adapt to a neoliberal reality (Park and Lo 2012, 156–57). This neoliberal reality intensified the deficit model of language and the myth that learning English could provide an opportunity to sustain the status quo or obtain upward mobility. In retrospect, although I was enlightened by critical theories, I held the deficit model that I would forever be a learner of the English language, rather than a user of the English language, no matter how strong my competency in both the academic and communicative domains.

My identity as an English learner is related to my consciousness that I was a *tojong* English learner, born and educated in Seoul, Korea. In the Korean language, the term *tojong* (土種) literally means a "native." *Tojong* English refers to the almost "perfect" English—in a slightly derisive manner—one has learned only through the Korean education system from Korean teachers whose first language is not English.[4] Mostly I learned English through grammar textbooks and reading comprehension practices to prepare myself for highly competitive exams for college admission and job applications. Of course, my professional study of the English language and literature in my undergraduate years and of comparative literature in my MA program inculcated academic writing skills and genre knowledge both in Korean and in English.

After I immigrated to the United States, my English-language skills along with high TOEFL and GRE scores and academic competence proven by my writing samples helped me be admitted into a PhD program in an English department. I started to teach FYW courses as a graduate teaching assistant in my second year in the PhD program. In my first semester of teaching, however, I struggled to establish a professional identity in teaching English writing. Although many novice teachers experience this anxiety, my lack of ownership was a more socially constructed one. While my institution treated US-born TAs and international TAs equally in terms of the training process or assigning classes, people in my ethnic communities often raised questions about the legitimacy of an international TA as a teacher. For example, one of the most frequent questions I have heard from my family or relatives back in Korea and friends in the United States when they come to know I work as a writing teacher is, "Can you compete with native teachers?" This question uncovers not only the deficit model or the myth of the model English teacher people internalize in the postcolonial context but also an implicit social pressure on transnational teachers.[5] I often felt I needed to demonstrate my own legitimacy as a teacher in the United States.

Similarly, my English academic literacy was not well recognized in the context of mainstream FYW courses. In many cases, my communicative competence was considered illegitimate and led my student audience into misrecognition in which my teacher subjectivity was often reduced to linguistic differences. For example, my self-representation as a competent transnational teacher often came into conflict with students' comments on online faculty evaluations. While one student wrote, "She's from a different country and offers a different point of view," another student commented, "I would not recommend this professor unless they can catch things with a different accent. I just felt so overwhelmed in the course with all the papers I had to keep up with for the course." This contrast suggests that although my linguistic difference is evaluated as a strength ("a different point of view") in some cases, it is often stereotyped as or reduced to the discourse of "accent" and nativist ideologies. The dichotomy between native speakers and nonnative speakers, grounded in implicit monolingual language ideology, was dominant in some students' evaluations.

Furthermore, my Korean language was not valued as a global or academic language as is English or a language such as Spanish, a prevalent language other than English in my region in the United States, or Mandarin, a recently emerging global language. In Houston, my hosting location, my ability to speak the Korean language was not appreciated in my institutional discourse communities. Although I valued my own Korean literacy with which I identified culturally, taught the Korean language to my children, and used it in community gatherings, I had few opportunities to transfer my knowledge of Korean into linguistic capital in academic or institutional settings. In other words, my Korean literate resource is not valued as an academic or a business language.

While navigating graduate courses in rhetoric and composition, my teaching experiences gradually came to be built on various theoretical strands from the field of rhetoric and composition and to be reflected in detail through a teaching journal I began in the first semester of teaching. To focus on the nexus of my migration experience and professional identity as a writing teacher, I turned to two theoretical strands. These theoretical lenses helped me theorize my everyday teaching practices during the first academic year. First, Peggy Levitt and Nina Glick Schiller's (2004) anthropological studies of "transnationalism," particularly a "transnational social field perspective," were helpful to understanding my experiences in the new professional environment, given that Levitt and Glick Schiller aim at "understand[ing] the experience of living simultaneously within and beyond the boundaries of a nation-state" (1006). Echoing Pierre Bourdieu's (1985) concept of social field, they define the notion of social field as "a set of multiple interlocking networks of social relationships through which ideas, practices, and resources are unequally exchanged, organized, and transformed" and expand this notion beyond a nation-state, arguing that "national boundaries are not necessarily contiguous with the boundaries of social fields" (Levitt and Glick Schiller 2004, 1009).

Another theoretical strand is the notion of scales. Drawing on the notion of scales in geography and the social sciences, Jan Blommaert (2010) reconfigures language relationships in the vertical and hierarchical dimensions. He argues that scales "offer us a vertical image of space, of space as stratified and therefore power-invested; but they also suggest deep connections between spatial and temporal features" (33–34). While he acknowledges that Blommaert's metaphor of scales is critical to see "how the difference is turned into inequality," Suresh Canagarajah (2013) regards the notion of scales as a more negotiable one (155). Modifying Blommaert's concept of scales, Canagarajah urges us to rethink the concept of scales as two sided. Although Blommaert and Canagarajah differ in approaching scales, they commonly focus on power-laden spaces and the socioeconomic values of linguistic resources, that is, "space as stratified and therefore power-invested"

(Blommaert 2010, 34) and "scalar analysis" as a tool that "make[s] us sensitive to the diversity of communication and language resources in any context" (Canagarajah 2016, 49). In retrospect, these two lenses I encountered in my graduate studies undergirded my teaching practices consciously and unconsciously. My teaching practices in FYW came to center around these two notions: transnational spaces and rescaling linguistic hierarchies. In the remainder, I also use these two theoretical strands as frameworks in which an individual can be "the node through which information, resources, and identities flow" (Levitt and Glick Schiller 2004, 1009) to analyze my further reflections and study how I rearranged my multiple networks in a new professional environment by mobilizing my linguistic and cultural resources.

SITUATING A TRANSNATIONAL SOCIAL-FIELD PERSPECTIVE AND RESCALING PRACTICES IN FYW

It was during my second semester of teaching that I began to practically apply a translingual approach, in which linguistic differences are considered "a resource for producing meaning" rather than "a barrier to overcome or as a problem to manage" (Horner et al. 2011, 303), in my teaching practices. This pedagogical demonstration of my non-Anglophone literate resources led me into building a transnational social field beyond the deficit model of language learning and shaping my teacher subjectivity. My teacher journal reports a day in detail:

February 13, 2017

While introducing the assignment guidelines of a definition argument essay, I brought out an example of the term *citizenship*. To make the term *citizenship* unfamiliar intentionally, I asked my students, "What is citizenship? Who are citizens, who are not citizens?" A student replied, "Legal people who reside in the US," to which, I raised another question, "What do you mean by legal?" Another student said, "A birth certificate?" "Then, how about immigrant people who newly came to the US?" I complicated the notion of citizenship. "What is the difference between citizens and citizenship? And who decides the criteria?" Silence persisted for several minutes. Although it was an improvised intervention, I brought up another idea after the conversation. I started to recite the Pledge of Allegiance to the Flag of South Korea in the Korean language while putting my right hand on my chest. I noticed puzzlement and excitement in students' faces when I recited the pledge naturally as

I had memorized it during my elementary-school years: "[First recitation of the Pledge of Allegiance to the Flag of South Korea in Korean] 나는 자랑스런 태극기 앞에 조국과 민족의 무궁한 영광을 위하여 몸과 마음을 바쳐 충성을 다할 것을 굳게 다짐합니다." After finishing my recitation, I showed a translated version and recited it again in English: "[Second recitation: Translation in English] In front of the national flag, I pledge allegiance to my nation and my people for the eternal glory of the country, with my body and soul." Then I asked them to recite the US pledge. Tim (pseudonym) smirked and said, "No!" Students were hesitant to recite their pledge although they informed me they had participated in this practice recently in their high schools.

Withstanding the increasing tensions, I showed the text of the Pledge of Allegiance of the United States on the screen after a quick Google search. I was a bit embarrassed I was not able to recite it. But I thought it was okay. After some seconds of silence, I read it aloud from the screen: "[Third recitation: the Pledge of Allegiance of the United States] I pledge allegiance to the flag of the United States of America, and to the republic for which it stands, one nation, under God, indivisible, with liberty and justice for all." Then, I carefully compared it to the Pledge of Allegiance to the Flag of South Korea. I had them focus on commonalities and differences between the two pledges. We went on to discuss how everyday institutional practices, including reciting the pledge of allegiance, have constructed the notion of citizenship in the modern nation-state. We discussed the gap between the literal definition of citizenship and the experienced definition through this institutional practice.

I further explained my spatiotemporal context, resulting from my migration experience. I narrated the first response I had when I witnessed the practice of the Pledge of Allegiance in the United States. "Every morning, I dropped off my four-year-old child at preschool. When I first observed that my son and other preschoolers gathered in a circle and recited together the Pledge of Allegiance, I was a little bit shocked. I thought America was a country of individualism. My preconceived thought was that the Pledge to the Flag that was done in Korea would never be found in the United States. But it was exactly the opposite. In the 1980s and 1990s, Koreans had to recite the pledge whenever they heard the pledge at a school or on a street. Now, it is rarely done except at an exceptional national event. But I learned that every morning American children recite a similar pledge at their schools."

At the moment of this classroom discussion, I felt I had formed an ownership of teaching writing in the United States for the first time and even benefited from a privileged condition as a migrant woman while

Table 6.1. Translation and recitation activities

The Pledge of Allegiance to the Flag of South Korea	The Pledge of Allegiance of the United States
[First recitation in Korean] "나는 자랑스런 태극기 앞에 조국과 민족의 무궁한 영광을 위하여 몸과 마음을 바쳐 충성을 다할 것을 굳게 다짐합니다."	[Third recitation] "I pledge allegiance to the flag of the United States of America, and to the republic for which it stands, one Nation, under God, indivisible, with liberty and justice for all."
[Second recitation: Translation in English] In front of the national flag, I pledge allegiance to my nation and my people for the eternal glory of the country, with my body and soul	

sharing other literate resources with my students, who I realized also came from a wide range of diverse backgrounds. Further, I took a cue about how to strategically shape a professional identity as a transnational writing teacher. (These translation and recitation activities are displayed in table 6.1.) In retrospect, these activities did create a rescaled space in which my students and I collaborated in rethinking ideologies and hierarchies behind a certain term, such as citizenship, with each one's different knowledge and experience. This rescaled space can be understood as a social field because its boundaries are "fluid" and "this field itself is created by the participants who are joined in a struggle for social position" (Levitt and Glick Schiller 2004, 1008). In this transnational social field, linguistic or cultural differences served as a source of critical consciousness.

This rescaling practice through relocalizing my linguistic resources can be interpreted as moments of what Catherine Prendergast (2014) refers to as "upending cross-languaging," or "moments of accidental and purposeful comprehension—and, more crucially, incomprehension—that result in some upending of the established linguistic order" (232). Although I added my translation, in that moment of pledging in Korean I intentionally used intranslatability, or what Prendergast terms "incomprehension," generated from my linguistic difference and act of cross-languaging. This incomprehension might help students to be sensitized to the tacit English-only environment in writing classes and promote their critical-thinking abilities. Furthermore, it overturned not only the linguistic hierarchy but also the cultural or ideological hierarchy in which people assume US social and institutional systems first and foremost advocate individual freedom over national or collective values.

My transnational teaching practices seemed to spark my students' critical thinking and affect their writing practices further. In their first assignments, students used their own various linguistic repertoires including dialects, slang, or their international experiences, which students often do not perceive as appropriate materials for academic writing. My transnational pedagogy seemed to particularly influence those who use languages other than English at home. For instance, Javier, a second-generation Mexican American and first-generation college student, revealed his interconnection with my transnationally mediated multilingual approach in his writing.[6] Although in his interview he said my use of transnational experiences did not directly influence his writing, Javier seemed to take a similar personal and transnational approach to social issues in his research paper. He wrote in his introductory paragraphs,

> Ever since the day I was born, there have been countless times where I have been put in second [place] for not being of American descent. I have been looked down on, mistrusted and I have been displaced as well. Even at a young age, I was kept in ESL classes (English as a Second Language). . . . The faculty just assumed that it would be better to place me there because of my descent. (Javier's final paper, May 2017)

Javier's narrative suggests he started from his own experiences in educational institutions and reflected on how linguistic cultural practices are "unequally" networked. His critical consciousness of his linguistic identity seemed to help him undertake this research paper topic, that is, immigrant minority workers in the business field. Although he did not explicitly use his Spanish repertoire in his paper, what scholars term *code switching* (Young et al. 2014) or *code meshing* (Canagarajah 2006; Young, Barrett, and Young-Rivera 2014), Javier demonstrates meta-awareness of translingual practices between "formal and informative writing," required in his high-school classrooms, and self-writing, to which he can bring topics and languages close to himself. His writing can be triangulated with self-perception of his multilingual repertoires in his interview data. In his interview, he informed me that he regarded his Spanish abilities as "resources" and "another branch," particularly when he conducted research on various subjects, such as "animals" or "famous peoples' biographies," to obtain a more enriched description. He said:

> While the other students were limited to just English resources, I could look through Spanish resources for information as well. Many times, this would work. For example, with researching animals, or famous peoples' biographies, I had another branch for me to reach for instead of just one. (interview on July 8, 2017)

In his paper, he traced how he came to value his Mexican heritage and his father's immigrant history as academic evidence. Although he concluded his argument with somewhat moralistic lessons based on his father's successful immigration history, Javier seemed to have gained enough confidence to employ his social and local networks, such as ESL experiences in his school, for critical thinking in his academic writing and rescaling the linguistic hierarchy.[7] His writing suggests my demonstration of "upending cross-languaging" might create a space in which students can explore their multilingual repertoires beyond national, linguistic, and cultural borders and speak back to the dominant narrative with their own stories. More important, their narratives in class discussions and writing in turn affected my construction of teacher subjectivity and helped me further develop my teaching ability in a translingual approach in which all language activities are envisioned as an act of "translation," and "blending of languages" is a normative act (Horner, NeCamp, and Donahue 2011, 287).

NEGOTIATING TEACHER SUBJECTIVITY

These two narratives may show a shift from the English-language-learner framework or the deficit model of language to the transnational framework in which one negotiates linguistic and cultural resources in US-based higher education institutions. Yet I do not present these two stories as linear or overcoming narratives because I still experience frictions or discordances in my transnational social fields (e.g., students' monolingual attitudes toward my linguistic difference shown in online faculty evaluations and their effects on my teacher subjectivity). Rather, it would be more appropriate to contend that these two narratives still coexist and contradict each other in my everyday literacy and teaching practices. My transnational teaching practice that values global-local dynamics is still fraught with the deficit model around which cultural perceptions toward NNES teachers are interwoven.

Therefore, it is important to note that constructing teacher subjectivity, particularly of migrant teachers, based on cultural and linguistic resources might unintentionally result in flattening their lived and mobile experiences into an abstract exchange of values of resources. As Rebecca Lorimer Leonard (2017) notes, the resources of multilinguals are "contingently" valued in various contexts, not "unchanging, always on call, reliably valuable" (171). Echoing her nuanced approach, I add that negotiating my teacher subjectivity based on leveraging multiple resources is highly contingent on my material conditions. For instance, there is no guarantee students will accept my pedagogical approach, going beyond the moment of intranslatability or incomprehensibility. They might shy away if incomprehensibility of an undervalued language, Korean, deters them from participating in a class discussion. Scholars thus should be wary of the utopian understanding or emancipatory vision of transnational subjectivity, which might assume linguistic or cultural hierarchies can be unlimitedly rescaled or multiple resources can be freely or equally exchanged.

Another material condition can be invisible surveillance and regulative institutional policies around international teaching assistants. For instance, I was not completely without fear that the use of my linguistic and cultural resources, such as my knowledge of the Korean language or global experiences across nations, might be considered by students or supervisors in my institutions as an irrelevant activity in students' writing outcomes. Institutional apparatuses, such as the evaluation process by students and supervisory systems, are more constraining to migrant transnational graduate teachers who are under the constant threat of deportation, control of the state, and strict institutional surveillance.

Nevertheless, I argue that the teacher subjectivity of transnational teachers is porous and negotiable beyond predetermined scales. As my two narratives show, a transnational social field perspective can help us see our writing classroom as a rescaled space in which a migrant teacher can tactically speak back to the dominant stereotypes and shape teacher subjectivity. Also, this approach is not limited to teacher subjectivity. In this teaching practice, even monolingual students can engage in transnational social fields and border-crossing experiences across nation-states, as we can see at the moment of comparing the two different pledges of Korea and the United States. My lived experiences of cross-languaging in an FYW class suggest we must value migrant teachers' transnational perspectives and reconsider their teacher subjectivity in a more dynamic and fluid framework, yet with a nuanced understanding of the material and unequal conditions of the lives of migrant subjects.

DISCUSSION AND CONCLUSION

In this chapter, I present two different narratives, self-perceptions of language ideologies, and reflections on my rescaling teaching activities and interactions with student writing. However, it should be noted that multilingual writers' autoethnographies do not necessarily assume a unified self as an individual. Citing Doris Sommer's (1991) reading of *I, Rigoberta Menchu*, Susan Jarratt (2004) discusses differences between autobiography and *testimonio* (113). Jarratt explains how Sommer differentiates the genre of testimonial from "standard Western autobiography, a centuries-old locus for individuality" (125). According to Sommer (1991), "While the autobiography strains to produce a personal and distinctive style as part of the individuation process, the testimonial strives to preserve or to renew an interpersonal rhetoric" (65). I argue that this differentiation is also crucial in understanding how self-representation in autoethnography by multilingual writers/researchers often demonstrates interpersonal collectiveness, the hidden *we* along with *I*. Although the genre of *testimonio* relies more on the oral tradition, this category helps us grasp how this autoethnographic self-writing performs collective movements among marginalized postcolonial populations, including language-minority groups, rather than the category of autobiography that often assumes Western modernist notions such as private/public, individual/social binaries. In other words, testimonials disrupt the notion of "the individual" by "self-division" (111). Similarly, autoethnographies by multilinguals or language minorities, I argue, complicate the notion of the self and add another layer of an "interpersonal" or "collective" relation with other multilingual teachers and students, as shown in my interaction with Javier's voice. By the term *autoethnography*, I refer to this postcolonial, interpersonal, collective dimension of self-representation, which resists the Western autobiography tradition and its assumption of the unified self.

Furthermore, I illustrate that this autoethnographic method can vitalize performative and transformative subjectivity construction. Revisiting my teacher journals and student writings helps me not only reconstruct my identity as a translingual teacher but also transform my static self-perception of my teacher identity into a fluid, malleable, and collective one. This performing of subjectivity by engaging in autoethnography can offer insights into the professional development of NNES teachers and of NNES students. As Shirley Wilson Logan (2014) notes, transnational graduate students who teach FYW students can be agents who can make changes, as their attitudes affect the "language ownership of first-year students" (188). My autoethnography demonstrates concrete evidence of this potential change. To unsettle the monolingual paradigm, translingual practices must be performed in our FYW classes not only by students or learners but also by teachers themselves.

NOTES

1. In this chapter, I deliberately use the term *transnational* to refer to those who have migrant experiences across national, cultural, or linguistic borders. Transnational graduate students thus include migrant or international graduate students who have crossed physical borders across different nations and local students who were born and have grown up in the United States and have experiences in crossing any cultural or linguistic borders. Therefore, transnational students include both "native" English-speaking people and "nonnative" English-speaking people, albeit that the notion of nativity is contested. It should be noted that local US students can often self-identify or have been categorized as those whose home language is a language other than English. So, the term *transnational students* debunks the myth that people in the United States are supposedly native English-speaking people. Here, in this chapter, the term *transnational-multilingual graduate student teachers* particularly refers to transnational students who crossed physical borders (migrant students) and came from non-English-speaking countries or institutions, so those who have multicommunicative repertoires across languages. Rather than the term *international*, the term *transnational* is implicated in the sociopolitical context and connotes agentive practices. By the prefix *trans*, I do not simply refer to going between two nations but demonstrate an attempt to disrupt a monolithic national and linguistic paradigm through localized practices. The stem of this term, *national*, also implies that this attempt is still contingent on territorial governance including textual bureaucratic regulation (Vieira 2016, 108), implicit or explicit inequality in labor markets, or language policy by a nation-state.
2. My approach also nods to existing methods in writing studies, such as teacher-research that synthesize practices and theories (Ray 1993, 52).
3. This study is part of IRB-approved classroom-based research that explores connections between my teaching practices based on my transnational-multilingual identities and students' uses of self-references in FYW. Five students in a first-year class, for which I was the instructor of record, provided consents, and all participants were self-reportedly multilinguals.
4. In Korean, the term *native seonsangnim* refers to a native English-speaking teacher, who is often perceived as superior, whereas *tojong seonsangnim* refers to a native Korean-speaking English teacher, who is regarded as less qualified. Although *tojong* itself is an equivalent term for "native," it is often used as a derisive term connoting that a *tojong* can never be equal to US- or other English-speaking-country-born natives in terms of proficiency.
5. As Alastair Pennycook (1998) notes, English language teaching (ELT) and colonialism have had an intricate connection. In colonial and postcolonial governance, English has been constructed as a global language, while assumptions about other languages and cultures have been discursively conceptualized. While investigating the relations between ELT and colonialism, he states that ELT should be reconfigured not just as "a tool in service of Empire but also as a *product* of Empire" (19; emphasis added). As he notes, English-language teaching is governed by "popular discourses on language and education that do not seem—at least on the surface—to be so current within the rarefied thinking of applied linguistics" (22). Pennycook's analysis on ELT and discourses of colonialism can be applied in English writing education, in which culturally constructed beliefs about learning English and discourses on NES and NNES teachers are being circulated. Here, I define the postcolonial context as a paradoxical space where these discursive colonial legacies still exist and where postcolonial resistance or appropriation takes place at the same time. It should be noted that Koreans suffered hardships under Japanese

imperialism from 1910 to 1945. After emancipation from Japan in 1945, however, South Korea has been under the influence of explicit or implicit US imperialism. English-language/writing teaching in Korea is still being operated by constructed discourses that bear the history of Western colonialism. As a migrant teacher who came from South Korea to the United States, I notice that discourses on English writing teaching in the academy and the ethnic communities have affected my multilingual-postcolonial identities.

6. This approach can be connected to the notion of "decoding" in Freirean pedagogy (Freire 2012, 105). In decoding, teachers encourage students to get involved in dialogic conversation and unveil the reality. Describing decoding as a "movement of flux and reflux from the abstract to the concrete," Freire argues that it leads to the "supersedence of the abstraction by the critical perception of the concrete, which has already ceased to be a dense, impenetrable reality" (105).

7. In his interview, he explained how the rhetorical use of self-references in my writing class, which was foregrounded as a lesson point in each writing assignment, promoted his rhetorical agency as a translingual writer: "In my high school when given a paper to write, unless instructed to do so, we were not allowed to use the first person. They said our papers were supposed to be 'formal' and 'informative.' It would be difficult at times, but eventually we all got the hang of it. So, when I came into ENGL 1303 and 1304 using it was very confusing at first but as the year went on, it became easier and easier because it connects the writer to the topic and paper" (Javier's interview excerpts, July 8, 2017).

REFERENCES

Blommaert, Jan. 2010. *The Sociolinguistics of Globalization*. Cambridge: Cambridge University Press.

Bourdieu, Pierre. 1985. "The Social Space and the Genesis of Groups." *Theory and Society* 14 (6): 723–44.

Braine, George, ed. 1999. *Non-Native Educators in English Language Teaching*. Mahwah, NJ: Erlbaum.

Braine, George. 2010. *Nonnative Speaker English Teachers: Research, Pedagogy and Professional Growth*. New York: Routledge.

Canagarajah, A. Suresh. 2006. "The Place of World Englishes in Composition: Pluralization Continued." *College Composition and Communication* 57 (4): 586–19.

Canagarajah, A. Suresh. 2012. "Autoethnography in the Study of Multilingual Writers." In *Writing Studies Research in Practice: Methods and Methodologies*, edited by Lee Nickoson and Mary P. Sheridan, 113–24. Carbondale: Southern Illinois University Press.

Canagarajah, Suresh. 2013. *Translingual Practice: Global Englishes and Cosmopolitan Relations*. New York: Routledge.

Canagarajah, Suresh. 2016. "Shuttling Between Scales in the Workplace: Reexamining Policies and Pedagogies for Migrant Professionals." *Linguistics and Education* 34: 47–57.

Ellis, Carolyn S., Tony E. Adams, and Arthur P. Bochner. 2011. "Autoethnography: An Overview." *Historical Social Research/Historische Sozialforschung* 12 (1): Art. 10.

Ellis, Elizabeth. 2013. "The ESL Teacher as Plurilingual: An Australian Perspective." *TESOL Quarterly* 47 (3): 446–71.

Freire, Paulo. 2012. *Pedagogy of the Oppressed*. New York: Continuum.

Horner, Bruce, Min-Zhan Lu, Jacqueline Jones Royster, and John Trimbur. 2011. "Language Difference in Writing: Toward a Translingual Approach." *College English* 73 (3): 303–21.

Horner, Bruce, Samantha NeCamp, and Christiane Donahue. 2011. "Toward a Multilingual Composition Scholarship: From English Only to a Translingual Norm." *College Composition and Communication* 63 (2): 269–300.

Jarratt, Susan C. 2004. "Beside Ourselves: Rhetoric and Representation in Postcolonial Feminist Writing." In *Crossing Borderlands: Composition and Postcolonial Studies*, edited by Andrea A. Lunsford and Lahoucine Ouzgane, 110–28. Pittsburgh, PA: University of Pittsburgh Press.

Kamhi-Stein, Lía D. 2016. "The Non-Native English Speaker Teachers in TESOL Movement." *ELT Journal* 70 (2): 180–89.

Levitt, Peggy, and Nina Glick Schiller. 2004. "Conceptualizing Simultaneity: A Transnational Social Field Perspective on Society." *International Migration Review* 38 (3): 1002–39.

Llurda, Enric. 2004. "Non-native-speaker Teachers and English as an International Language." *International Journal of Applied Linguistics* 14 (3): 314–23.

Logan, Shirley Wilson. 2014. "Ownership of Language and the Teaching of Writing." In *Cross-Language Relations in Composition*, edited by Bruce Horner, Min-Zhan Lu, and Paul Kei Matsuda, 183–88. Carbondale: Southern Illinois University Press.

Lorimer Leonard, Rebecca. 2017. "Literate Resources and the Contingent Value of Language." In *Economies of Writing: Revaluations in Rhetoric and Composition*, edited by Bruce Horner, Brice Nordquist, and Susan M. Ryan, 161–71. Logan: Utah State University Press.

Maraj, Louis M. 2018. "'Are You Black, Though?': Black Autoethnography and Racing the Graduate Student/Instructor." In *Precarious Rhetorics*, edited by Wendy S. Hesford, Adela C. Licona, and Christa Teston, 212–33. Columbus: The Ohio State University Press.

McKinney, Jackie Grutsch, and Elizabeth Chiseri-Strater. 2003. "Inventing a Teacherly Self: Positioning Journals in the TA Seminar." *WPA: Writing Program Administration* 27 (1/2): 59–74.

Medgyes, Peter. 1994. *The Non-Native Teacher*. London: Macmillan.

Miller, Jennifer. 2009. "Teacher Identity." In *The Cambridge Guide to Second Language Teacher Education*, edited by Anne Burns and Jack C. Richards, 172–81. Cambridge: Cambridge University Press.

Moussu, Lucie, and Enric Llurda, E. 2008. "Non-native English-speaking English Language Teachers: History and Research." *Language Teaching* 41 (3): 315–38.

Park, Joseph Sung-Yul. 2011. "The Promise of English: Linguistic Capital and the Neoliberal Worker in the South Korean Job Market." *International Journal of Bilingual Education and Bilingualism* 14 (4): 443–55.

Park, Joseph Sung-Yul, and Adrienne Lo. 2012. "Transnational South Korea as a Site for a Sociolinguistics of Globalization: Markets, Timescales, Neoliberalism." *Journal of Sociolinguistics* 16 (2): 147–64.

Pennycook, Alastair. 1998. "The Right to Language: Towards a Situated Ethics of Language Possibilities." *Language Sciences* 20 (1): 73–87.

Pratt, Mary Louise. 1991. "Arts of the Contact Zone." *Profession* 33–40.

Prendergast, Catherine. 2014. "In Praise of Incomprehension." In *Cross-Language Relations in Composition*, edited by Bruce Horner, Min-Zhan Lu, and Paul Kei Matsuda, 230–35. Carbondale: Southern Illinois University Press.

Ray, Ruth E., 1993. *The Practice of Theory: Teacher Research in Composition*. Urbana, IL: NCTE.

Ruecker, Todd, Stefan Frazier, and Mariya Tseptsura. 2018. "Language Difference Can Be an Asset: Exploring the Experiences of Nonnative English-Speaking Teachers of Writing." *College Composition and Communication* 69 (4): 612–41.

Shehi, Monika. 2017. "Why Is My English Teacher a Foreigner? Re-authoring the Story of International Composition Teachers." *Teaching English in the Two Year College* 44 (3): 260–75.

Sommer, Dorris. 1991. "No Secrets: Rigoberta's Guarded Truth." *Women's Studies* 20 (1): 51–72.

Yang, Yuching Jill, Kacie Kiser, and Paul Kei Matsuda. 2017. "Symbolic Capital in the First-Year Composition Classroom." In *Economies of Writing: Revaluations in Rhetoric and*

Composition, edited by Bruce Horner, Brice Nordquist, and Susan M. Ryan, 99–111. Logan: Utah State University Press.

Yee, Marianne. 1991. "Are You the Teacher?" In *Composition and Resistance*, edited by C. Mark Hurlbert and Michael Blitz, 24–31. Portsmouth, NH: Heinemann.

Vieira, Kate. 2016. *American by Paper: How Documents Matter in Immigrant Literacy*. Minneapolis: University of Minnesota Press.

Young, Vershawn Ashanti, Rusty Barrett, and Y'Shanda Young-Rivera. 2014. *Other People's English: Code-Meshing, Code-Switching, and African American Literacy*. New York: Teachers College Press.

Zhang, Yufeng. 2018. "English Teacher Identity Development through a Cross-Border Writing Activity." In *Transnational Writing Education: Theory, History, and Practice*, edited by. Xiaoye You, 187–202. New York: Routledge.

PART TWO

Teaching Writing Studies Autoethnography

7
EMPOWERING AUTOETHNOGRAPHY IN TWO-YEAR COLLEGE REFORM

Kirsten Higgins, Anthony Warnke, and Marcie Sims

In the past decade, efforts to reform developmental education at two-year colleges have gained widespread traction. Empirical research on the underplacement of many students into developmental courses has dovetailed with longstanding basic writing scholarship detailing the barriers to access constructed for students labeled as *basic* or *developmental*. Projects such as the Community College of Baltimore County's accelerated learning program have streamlined students' progression through college-level English courses while offering noncognitive and academic support. As a result, colleges across the country have seen substantial increases in success rates for students passing "gatekeeper" courses such as English 101. Because students who place into developmental courses often come from underserved and underrepresented student populations, developmental reform has begun to address equity gaps for students of color and first-generation college students. The work of acceleration and reform is, intrinsically, social justice work, increasing the likelihood of retention, persistence, and completion for the most marginalized students.

To truly meet the needs of our students, structural reform isn't enough. In most permutations we've seen, ALP and other acceleration frameworks take up the work of mainstreaming in a way that principally draws on an assimilationist paradigm—one that asks students to draw on a static, monolithic notion of academic discourse. Many reform efforts, although placing students into college-level courses, implicitly reify their liminal status by categorizing the courses as remediation in terms of course numbering, content, and approach. Such partial approaches to reform still position students as outsiders to the academy who need to leave their domains of knowledge, experiences, and language practices at the college door. Students facing structural barriers often face barriers in the language ideology, content, and ways of knowing writing

DOI: 10.7330/9781646421213.c007

instructors typically conceptualize as college ready or academic. We wonder how, in our efforts to reform developmental English, we can also more critically conceive of academic writing and academic knowledge.

At Green River College, we have implemented our own version of the accelerated learning program (ALP) with these social justice objectives in mind. At an institution with an increasingly diverse student body, we sought to address the equity gap exacerbated by structural inequities. Our reformulated ALP seeks to help students become rhetorically attuned to norms of academic writing while we also seek to become more rhetorically attuned to our own dynamic student population. As Rebecca Lorimer Leonard (2014) explains, "Rhetorical attunement is a kind of hearing that treats language difference as an element 'at the heart' of rhetoric" (230). Rather than eliminating difference in pursuit of homogeneous standards, we ask how we can invite and value difference as integral to the college writing experience. We hope to build an institutional and classroom culture that treats students as insiders to whom the academy should continually attune.

Often progressively oriented writing course content centers on exploring issues of cultural plurality and Otherness while ironically adopting a discourse of exclusion around questions of Otherness. For us, autoethnography, especially evocative autoethnography, as a genre and social practice, allows students to write themselves into, and also reshape, academic discourse. Autoethnography assignments can help writing instructors rhetorically attune our classrooms and our writing programs, and perhaps even our campuses, by disrupting the status quo ecology to invite students on the margins into knowledge creation. We want the autoethnography to bridge, and perhaps collapse, the distance from academia to students' real lives by providing room for heterogeneity rather than a focus on Otherness that must be translated into the language of power. As Deborah Mutnick (1998) puts it in "Rethinking the Personal Narrative: Life Writing and Composition Pedagogy," an autoethnography might make space for "students on the social margins" to give them "the opportunity to articulate a perspective in writing in their own life experiences [that] can be a bridge between their communities and the academy" (84). With this assignment, we wonder, How can we better give space to the literacies, language practices, and experiences of our students? How can we position their real, lived experiences as legitimate academic inquiry? And how can we use the assignment as a strategy for challenging exclusionary assessment practices that unintentionally contribute to disparate impact? How can the autoethnography help us reframe the value of two-year college students' abilities and our own instructional practices?

Much of what we liked about ALP was its potential to focus on learning as not only cognitive but also the noncognitive, acknowledging the role of the affective and emotional. The autoethnography refutes this dichotomy between the cognitive and affective, acknowledging that the false separation of students into discrete parts is inherently reductive, and sees affective work as merely instrumental for assimilation into the academic discourse students are consistently positioned as underprepared for. This positioning has the unintended consequence of instantiating a narrative in our writing programs of students as deficient (Adler-Kassner and Estrem 2009). We suggest this kind of redesign work can form the nexus for a larger rethinking and reframing of the way we construct our writing programs and how they value the whole student.

THE AUTOETHNOGRAPHY ASSIGNMENT IN A CO-REQUISITE STRUCTURE

In our equity-focused ALP pilot, we assign the autoethnography as the second major essay of the quarter. Different instructors have tailored the assignment to their own needs; overall, however, the assignment asks students to produce an autoethnography that reflects how they construct their self or selves within certain social and narrative ecologies. As the second major essay assignment, the autoethnography builds on the first assignment, a researched argumentative essay, precipitating a sophisticated rhetorical positioning within the course itself. In some ways an uncanny turn—which students recognize as both "about me" and "not about me"—its placement as the second assignment suggests the autoethnography is the more challenging of the two major essay assignments. Students produce about twelve hundred words in which they discuss the stories they tell about their identities, as well as the origins, limits, and possibilities of their story making. The autoethnography specifically emphasizes creativity, self-study, and narrative techniques and becomes a tool for our students to explore their identities in tension with the cultural narratives that contribute to the self or perception of the self.

The assignment effectively blends and bends both personal and academic lines of inquiry. Furthermore, this blending happens not only on the level of subject matter but also when we encourage students to incorporate linguistic diversity. Seeking to take a translingual approach (Horner et al. 2011), we strive to release students from mandates to replicate academic voice and achieve grammatical perfection. Finally, students integrate sources that help them conceptualize their relationships to the larger structures of knowledge that have been built around their identities. As Mutnick (1998) notes, "The articulation of 'I' and the autobiographical impulse, in this sense, are never purely individual acts in that they insert the writer into public discourse, creating new social spaces for all group members" (82). The student's self is a site of both inquiry and meaning making, both explored and performed in the process. This move reflects autoethnography's synthesis of the academic and the personal and its generic, disciplinary prerogative to challenge objectivity. As Leon Anderson (2006) writes, "By virtue of the autoethnographer's dual role as a member in the social world under study and as a researcher of that world, autoethnography demands enhanced textual visibility of the researcher's self. . . . Autoethnographers should expect to be involved in the construction of meaning and values in the social worlds they investigate" (383).

To frame course conversations concerning identity, students' reading assignments include an excerpt from bell hooks's *Talking Back*, Chimamanda Ngozi Adichie's TED talk "The Danger of a Single Story," Beverly Daniel Tatum's "The Complexity of Identity: 'Who Am I?,'" Paul Gorski's "The Trouble with the 'Culture of Poverty' and Other Stereotypes about People in Poverty," and narrative psychologists Andrea Breen and Kate McLean's "Selves in a World of Stories During Emerging Adulthood." Concepts of narrative and story help students understand identity as emergent, in process, and existing in a larger narrative ecology and within larger personal, classroom, institutional, and/or societal constraints.

Our prompt includes some of the following lines of inquiry for students to reflect on and shape their autoethnographic essays. Students are not limited to these questions; rather, they provide a starting point. As they explore these questions, students are asked to consider how their personal experiences reflect and represent the theoretical frameworks about identity we have been studying in class.

1. Performance and Perception Questions: When have you found yourself performing a part of your identity? In what ways have you performed a certain identity in order to achieve a goal or "play the game," even if you didn't necessarily believe in that identity? When did your perception of your own identity conflict with someone else's perception? How did you negotiate this difference? How do certain settings or contexts alter your identity?

2. Change Questions: What's a big moment in which you felt your identity change or shift? Was the change permanent? To what extent were you in control of that change? When did you discover a part of your identity

that surprised you? Have you consciously worked to develop a part of your identity or downplay another part?

3. Influence and Cultural Narrative Questions: What have you modeled your identity on? How have you compared your identity to others? Have you formed your identity in relationship to others? In what ways do the cultural narratives about categories of identity such as gender identity, racial identity, or sexuality impact your own view of your identity? How are parts of your identity made invisible or obfuscated? How do cultural narratives, such as the redemption story or other master narratives, relate to your own way of telling about your identity?

These lines of inquiry have generated some of the following essay topics. We have loosely categorized them here to demonstrate the complexity and variety of student responses. First, some have written about perceived versus lived identities, such as introversion and religious expectations of the expression of sexuality. Others have framed this work in terms of trauma, especially war refugees. Many students emphasize the ways they encounter—and often counter—representations of their identities in media, such as Latina pop stars and feminine confidence or furries' experiences of media misrepresentations. Other students have grappled with materiality and the everyday work of identity construction, such as the signifier of the sneaker as indicative of obsession with consumer culture. Students have run the gamut, from family identity to intersectionality, always exerting their own control over the topics in ways that have surprised and moved us.

Throughout this work, we recognize our institutional authority and the dangers of soliciting students to self-disclose. However, we see structural promises of access as parallel to pedagogical and curricular moves allowing students to access aspects of their identity many other academic courses marginalize. With this balance of opportunity and risk in mind, we hope to give students a wide berth and set of resources for reflecting on their identities, letting them choose and refuse what feels appropriate for them in terms of subject matter. The writing itself, and the process of writing, becomes a way of making space for a variety of subjectivities in which students are "composing words, composing selves" (Mutnick 1998, 85). Students engage in a dialogue between personal identity and public identity, where intersections of selves never end in one, fixed place or become easily reduced to one category. In a sense, students assume spaces designed for performance and fluidity, allowing them to inhabit momentary "figurations" that fulfill the assignment and, perhaps, provide some provisional sites of agency or at least positive self-regard (Braidotti 2001; Guerra 2004).

Our autoethnography assignment becomes multimodal when students "remix" it into a 1.5 to 2.5-minute podcast. The podcast requires students to record themselves reading short sections of their papers, post the recordings in a Canvas discussion forum, and listen to and comment on each other's recordings. Students frequently remark on the power of hearing each other's voices in the podcast. It is the material, the time bound—the utterance-as-act—that students comment upon. The way they receive each other's podcasts emphasizes the embodied, affective element. "I could really hear their real emotions," they write, more or less repeatedly, many of them noting they "couldn't hear them" when they'd peer reviewed each other's papers. Students acknowledge the power of each other's voices to compel them to reimagine classmates they "thought they knew," as well as the necessity of reframing their own struggles in the context of this reimagined classroom community. Through the material voice, students' experiences become imbricated in the academic work, melding the affective with the disciplinary knowledge. Knowing the community, knowing the selves that create that community, acknowledging and valuing their self-representations—all this powerfully reconfigures the relationships among students, as well as our own notions of the stories our students carry and their emotional labor. This is a turn beyond critique, beyond "They Say, I Say" and static notions of academic discourse, and it enables us as instructors to recognize the tellability of students' stories we haven't encountered before.

Some have theorized autoethnography as inherently liberatory, and we resist this theorization due to the complexity associated with our own positions. Whether autoethnographies are considered as written or spoken performances, we must acknowledge the very real dynamics of teacher/student, institutional/individual hierarchies no utopic curriculum or assignment can ever circumvent, including the bind of our own cultural privileges, namely white privilege and relative economic privilege. Juan Guerra's 2004 critique of pedagogies of critical literacy cautions us of "critical literacy's tendency to situate the teacher as hero, as the only individual in the classroom who has achieved critical consciousness and whose job it now is to enlighten his or her students so that they can be transformed and emancipated" (6). Critical pedagogy's professed aim of emancipation, especially when taken up by instructors with various markers of privilege, can, in fact, reinforce the Otherness of our students, requiring our recognition of their legitimacy.

AUTOETHNOGRAPHY AND LOCALLY VALID ASSESSMENT

As two-year college instructors navigating competing imperatives for how to teach our students in effective but also socially just ways, we are increasingly aware of assessment's impact on our work. In the two-year college, assessment work often boils down to a few afternoons' labor in a hectic race to satisfactorily justify our work to outside audiences, such as accreditation bodies. Yet assessment work is one of our most powerful tools for adequately responding to the pressures associated with the "accountability narrative," as well as, more significantly, a way to grapple with the equity gap resulting from disparate impact—the "unintended racial differences resulting from policies or practices intended to be neutral and that on the surface appear to lack bias" (White, Elliot, and Peckham 2015, 172). Pamela Moss has argued for an assessment paradigm that "honors the purposes teachers and students bring to their work" (quoted in Broad et al. 2009, 3). Because the autoethnography begins with the local and particular experiences of individual students, it demands assessment practices—at both the classroom level and program level—sensitive to the local and highly attuned to students' experiences. It demands of us that we attempt to meet them, to "be there" (Gallagher 2011) with them in the classroom. We argue, further, that we must be in alliance with students when we assess their work and assess our programs. Autoethnography supports assessment practices that humanize the practice itself, attends to the questions of power so carefully elided by most assessment practices, and, most important, honors the affective, embodied student who produces the work.

Two-year college students always lose when we apply idealized, standardized (read: white, middle-class) notions of the college ready and academic. These idealized standards neglect local actors and local contexts in order to say "your students have to be like X," "your students need to write like X," or "your students need to write about X" in order to be valued. In addition, idealized standards bracket out the lived experience, linguistic heterogeneity, and embodied selves autoethnography may open space for. It attends to students' experiences and literacies, and it allows for deeply local exploration and assessment. By refusing to take them out of time and place, or see their histories as incidental or besides the academic point, the autoethnography resists the reductive narrative of two-year college students. The autoethnography, and the process of writing it, are the point, and our assessment practices, at both the classroom level and program level, must attend to the entire local, organic landscape.

Centering students' experiences, access, and resources leads to reimagining assessment practices at the larger, program level. Using autoethnography for student empowerment and voice asks community college instructors to rethink paradigms that understand two-year college students as always already deficient. Instead, we reimagine our communities as those comprising our various, intersectional students; indeed, we reimagine our communities in terms of their larger ecologies. In the first chapter of Bob Broad's 2009 *Organic Writing Assessment: Dynamic Criteria Mapping in Action*, "Organic Matters: In Praise of Locally Grown Writing Assessment," Broad pauses to unpack the metaphor from which the title of the book is drawn. He considers the various, complex definitions of organic and turns to Henry Brockman's 2001 work complicating and enriching the term *organic*. Brockman relates his desire to know the full story of a commercially grown tomato before he consumes it, listing a series of questions as to its provenance and its role in a larger ecology. Though perhaps too easily paralleled by Portlandia's free-range chicken sketch, Brockman's sincere questions, adeptly unpacked by Broad, provide a robust framing for an informed decision about whether to eat the tomato: Brockman must know more than whether it has been labelled *organic* or not. He must know what soil it was grown in, under what conditions it was harvested, and so on. In a similar way, opening space for students' work demands we assess the work with deep, careful consideration of their lived experience, as well as the writing program and institutional ecology.

To assess the autoethnography requires eschewing standardized metanarratives of "good assessment," or, at the very least, making the kind of tactical move described by Linda Adler-Kassner and Heidi Estrem (2009) in their "The Journey Is the Destination: The Place of Assessment in an Activist Writing Program" that draws from both external standards of good writing and local concerns that impact that campus's narrative about student writing. Furthermore, as Edward M. White, Norbert Elliot, and Irvin Peckham's (2015) *Very Like a Whale: The Assessment of Writing Programs* suggests, the classroom assessment that is "usually a private transaction between the teacher and the student" is typically a building block of program assessment (23–24). When we hold space for students within our program assessments, as well as within our classroom assessments, we've begun to do the radical work required to remake the community college as a space that more fully opens access to students and their lived experiences.

In order to facilitate the greatest institutional change, we wonder how two-year college faculty can complement structural reform that counters disparate impact with assessment practices that share the same ethos and political commitment. The time has come for a multidimensional view of equity that asserts the importance of the whole student at the level of writing program and within the classroom. Situating autoethnography as a method for opening space for students, especially students marginalized or reduced by institutional actors, may allow it to function as the sort of tactical move endorsed by Adler-Kassner and Estrem (2009) in the context of rich, localized assessment practices. We suggest autoethnography is part of a strategic turn in repositioning assessment within two-year colleges, one that is key in terms of attending to complex local landscapes.

OPENING SPACE, REMAKING INSTITUTIONS: WE ARE NOT THE KINGS OF SPAIN

We suggest that, at the two-year college, the autoethnography helps open up compelling but fraught intersections and contradictions, ones that map onto larger disciplinary debates about the extent to which we are asking students to assimilate into academic norms, critically appropriate academic norms, resist academic norms, and/or transform them. Holding space for students requires us to acknowledge that they often grapple with systemic and epistemic conflicts we don't fully understand and that our autoethnography assignment certainly will not resolve. In her work "Arts of the Contact Zone," Mary Louise Pratt (1991) situates colonized subjects' resistance in approaches related to the autoethnography, arguing that it opens a space in which those distanced from the metropole and its attendant hierarchical relations can speak back to those at the centers of power. She demonstrates how an Andean subject schools the King of Spain and, in so doing, adapts the communication tools and strategies of the colonizing Spaniards yet demands an interrogation of hierarchical practices, including the racist dismissal and denigration of Andean culture and history.

We are community college writing instructors, not the kings of Spain. Yet we come armed with our own dismissive ideological tools: you must adapt to the institution, we tell students. You must demonstrate grit, adopt a growth mindset, learn to reason in the ways we recognize as reasoning, adopt academic discourse, decommission much of your linguistic repertoire, and navigate institutional and systemic barriers without missing a beat. Yet we may choose this as the pedagogical moment to break from our allegiance to narratives of assimilation that, as Vershawn Ashanti Young (2009) notes, have long been offered to students of color and other marginalized students as tickets to their socioeconomic mobility, despite little empirical evidence that supports such claims. We extend this critique to the implicit promise of mobility in order to question why students must fulfill alien expectations for promises we, as writing instructors within two-year colleges, cannot keep. Instead, we wonder, how we can ally ourselves deeply, and in every institutional step we take, with our students, imagining them as centrally located in our communities (Anderson 1998). Autoethnography helps us, as teacher allies, hold a space from which students may decide how to speak, how to act, how to tactically engage or even circumnavigate certain kinds of engagement. Autoethnography, in the context of programmatic work and assessment, allows us to value students' utterances, as well as their refusal to reveal, to tell, to utter—it allows us to value their not-knowing or not-telling without denigrating it as deficit.

While this is all aspirational, we hope autoethnography in accelerated course structures acts as a microcosm of a larger progressive ethos towards developmental reform and two-year colleges. We hope the spirit of the assignment reflects a larger move towards eliminating the dominant, largely unquestioned deficit thinking that hinders how we conceive of and teach our students. We hope that beginning hyperlocally, literally with our students' individual experiences and forms of meaning making, speaks to a humility towards the vast array of experiences, literacies, and identities our students bring into our classrooms. It also allows them to engage in certain refusals—refusing, perhaps, to disclose or faithfully "report" what can be very personal aspects of their identities, refusing to conform to prepackaged, preconceived identity categories and the assumptions that come along with them. Rather than understanding them as data points in generalized identity categories, we hope including the autoethnography as part of our assessment practice provides nuance to the quantitative data and default representations that often circumscribe our perceptions and expectations of two-year college students. Instead, to remake the two-year college as an aspirational space of linguistic heterogeneity and contact zones doesn't require romanticization; rather, it requires humility, rhetorical attunement, and rhetorical listening that reposition our pedagogical and assessment practices—a willingness to learn as much as to teach.

REFERENCES

Adams, Tony E., Stacy Holman Jones, and Carolyn Ellis. 2015. *Autoethnography*. Oxford: Oxford University Press.

Adler-Kassner, Linda, and Heidi Estrem. 2009. "The Journey Is the Destination: The Place of Assessment in an Activist Writing Program." In *Organic Writing Assessment: Dynamic Criteria Mapping in Action*, edited by Bob Broad, 14–35. Logan: Utah State University Press.

Anderson, Benedict. 1998. *Imagined Communities: Reflections on the Origin and Spread of Nationalism*. Rev. ed. New York: Verso.

Anderson, Leon. 2006. "Analytic Autoethnography." *Journal of Contemporary Ethnography* (35) 4: 373–95.

Braidotti, Rosi. 2001. "Toward a New Nomadism." In *Deleuze and Guattari: Critical Assessments of Leading Philosophers*, edited by Gary Genosco, 1414–39. Abingdon, UK: Routledge.

Broad, Bob, Linda Adler Kassner, Barry Alford, and Jane Detweiler. 2009. *Organic Writing Assessment: Dynamic Criteria Mapping in Action*. Logan: Utah State University Press.

Brockman, Henry. 2001. *Organic Matters*. Congerville, IL: Terra Books.

Gallagher, Chris W. 2011. "Being There: (Re)making the Assessment Scene." *College Composition and Communication* 62 (3): 450–76.

Guerra, Juan C. 2004. "Putting Literacy in Its Place: Nomadic Consciousness and the Practice of Transcultural Repositioning." Chicano Studies Institute, UC Santa Barbara. https://escholarship.org/uc/item/52q817fq.

Horner, Bruce, Min-Zhan Lu, Jacqueline Jones Royster, and John Trimbur. 2011. "Language Difference in Writing: Toward a Translingual Approach." *College English* 73 (3): 303–21.

Lorimer Leonard, Rebecca. 2014. "Multilingual Writing as Rhetorical Attunement." *College English* 76 (3): 227–47.

Mutnick, Deborah. 1998. "Rethinking the Personal Narrative: Life-Writing and Composition Pedagogy." In *Under Construction: Working at the Intersections of Composition Theory, Research, and Practice*, edited by Christine Farris and Chris M. Anson, 79–92. Logan: Utah State University Press.

Pratt, Mary Louise. 1991. "Arts of the Contact Zone." *Profession*: 33–40.

White, Edward M., Norbert Elliot, and Irvin Peckham. 2015. *Very Like a Whale*. Logan: Utah State University Press.

Young, Vershawn Ashanti. 2009. " 'Nah, We Straight': An Argument Against Code Switching." *JAC* 29 (1/2): 49–76.

8
"SAY WHAT YOU WANT TO SAY!"
Teaching Literacy Autoethnography to Resist Linguistic Prejudice

Amanda Sladek

Mary Louise Pratt's "Arts of the Contact Zone" (1991) defines autoethnography as "a text in which people undertake to describe themselves in ways that engage with representations others have made of them" (35). This self-representation is a powerful tool for marginalized people to grapple with the misrepresentation, discord, and "highly asymmetrical relations of power" (34) present in contact zones, social spheres characterized by cultural contact and conflict. Pratt's metaphor of the contact zone has been used to characterize writing classrooms where students from diverse ethnic and linguistic backgrounds grapple with the constraints and demands of the academy (Canagarajah 1997; Kells 2002). In this context, autoethnography can provide marginalized student writers with an opportunity to work through their relationships with the English language, writing, the academy, and the culture at large "in their own voices, resisting the knowledge constructed about them" (Canagarajah 2012, 115) in dominant academic discourses.

This chapter explores the power of autoethnography in classrooms with multilingual writers, illustrated by the literacy autoethnographies of four international, multilingual students studying in the United States. A close reading of their essays reveals that, rather than forcing these students into Western discourse conventions, the literacy autoethnography allowed them to explore their communities through their own lenses and using their own Englishes, giving them an opportunity to advocate for their own linguistic agency and encouraging linguistic and cultural tolerance among all students in the contact zone of the US writing classroom. First, though, it is necessary to clarify what literacy autoethnography means in first-year writing.

DOI: 10.7330/9781646421213.c008

DEFINING LITERACY AUTOETHNOGRAPHY IN FIRST-YEAR WRITING

As the introduction to this volume notes, the definition of autoethnography is contested. Rebecca Jackson and Jackie Grutsch McKinney conclude in this introduction that, in order to be considered an autoethnography in writing studies, a text should be written from personal experience, utilize qualitative analysis, and be written "in conversation with other texts" to make a point about/talk back to a culture/cultural narrative. A literacy autoethnography, then, uses qualitative methods to analyze the author's literacy experiences in conversation with other texts (broadly defined) in a way that makes some sort of cultural point. Or, using Pratt's above quoted definition of autoethnography, the literacy autoethnography puts the author's representation of their literacy acquisition into dialogue with the ways their literacy is represented by the dominant culture. It is this engagement with culture I believe distinguishes the literacy autoethnography from a closely related genre, the literacy narrative.

A literacy narrative is an autobiographical narrative explaining the author's reading, writing, and language development. At first glance, this can read like a simplified version of the definition of literacy autoethnography. As Alison Cardinal, Melissa Atienza, and Aliyah Jones point out in chapter 14 of this volume, several writing studies texts traditionally considered literacy narratives can be more productively thought of as literacy autoethnographies. However, the distinction between literacy narrative and literacy autoethnography is an important one. Our editors caution in the introduction that "autoethnography should not be used to rebrand an existing genre" and that "if it's a literacy narrative, it's a literacy narrative." While I agree to an extent and accept their larger point, I argue that the relationship (and the distinction) between literacy narrative and literacy autoethnography is more complex. A. Suresh Canagarajah (2012) specifically addresses this relationship, asserting that "the extent to which the authors consider their literacy trajectory and practices in relation to social and cultural influences will help us decide if they are autoethnography" (113). With this in mind, one can view the literacy narrative and literacy autoethnography at opposite ends of a continuum, with greater cultural and social engagement pushing a text closer to autoethnography. This continuum must also be adaptable to different contexts; what I would consider sufficient cultural engagement for an autoethnography from a beginning writing student would not necessarily equal the level of cultural critique I would expect from an advanced scholar's autoethnography.

When differentiating between narrative and autoethnography in the classroom, then, it is important to consider not only the texts students produce but also our teaching contexts and goals. The pedagogical purposes of some literacy-narrative assignments focus more on the writers themselves than the cultures in which they write. Such goals include transitioning beginning students to college-level writing (Hall and Minnix 2012), introducing them to the literary-essay genre (Beaufort 2007), and ascertaining their attitudes toward reading and writing (Williams 2003/2004). Narratives like these are not intended to be autoethnographies; thus, they do not demonstrate the critical engagement with cultural context that characterizes autoethnography. The texts students produce in response to these assignments are clearly literacy narratives.

Yet, some literacy narrative assignments do seek the kind of social engagement typically seen in autoethnography. For example, in their *Writing about Writing* reader (2014), Elizabeth Wardle and Doug Downs provide a literacy narrative prompt that asks students to analyze cultural aspects of their literacy stories (206). I myself, reasoning that *narrative* is a less intimidating term than *autoethnography*, have been guilty of assigning both literacy narratives and literacy autoethnographies with more or less the same goal. Assignments like these complicate the distinction between narrative and autoethnography. If the genres represent opposite ends of a continuum, it can be difficult to determine how much cultural engagement is necessary to warrant the *autoethnography* label.

What I am suggesting, then, is not that we use autoethnography to "rebrand an existing" assignment but that we acknowledge and even celebrate the messiness of the relationship between literacy narrative and literacy autoethnography. This means working with the inevitable problem with continuums: the fact that what falls in the middle is difficult to label. The most interesting, rhetorically effective literacy narratives inevitably engage with culture in some way, and narrative is a defining feature of the most interesting, rhetorically effective autoethnographies. We can consider the two genres separately while honoring the contributions they simultaneously make to each other. The students discussed in the next section, who use their personal stories to speak to larger cultural forces and representations of their literacy, demonstrate the rhetorical force resulting from the foregrounding of narrative in literacy autoethnography.

LINGUISTIC AND CULTURAL EMPOWERMENT IN STUDENTS' LITERACY AUTOETHNOGRAPHIES

The four students discussed in this chapter wrote their literacy autoethnographies in an introductory writing course at a large public research university in the midwestern United States.[1] This course is the first in a two-semester sequence intended to lay the foundation for college-level writing. Each student was enrolled in a different section taught by an instructor participating in a study of the assignment. Though the instructors adapted the literacy autoethnography to their own curricula, they each devoted an entire unit to the project and worked from a common assignment prompt that asked students to "examine [themselves] as . . . reader[s] and writer[s] of texts (written or otherwise) in multiple contexts" and reflect critically on "how [they] have been a member of, or influenced by, various communities and contexts." The work leading up to this assignment prompted students to examine the social construction of literacy and analyze the relationship between literacies and cultures. Of the 111 students who participated in the larger study, only the 4 profiled here self-identified in their submissions as second language (L2) English speakers, and they used this assignment as an opportunity to describe their experiences learning English and/or adjusting to US culture.[2]

Hui framed her autoethnography around learning English at school in her native China. Her essay is, in many ways, a literacy narrative. Of the four writers discussed here, she spends the least time reflecting on culture and the most time narrating her literacy experiences. Yet, her autoethnography does illuminate how learning English in China is complicated by issues of geography, economics, and access. She writes that she began her English education in the rural elementary school where she spent her early childhood, but she felt that education was inadequate: "It was so basic that I did not seem to grasp anything. As a result, I was not able to read in English until the last two years of my elementary education when my father was transferred for his job from the small town near our village to the city of Shanghai."[3] This reflects a broader trend: despite the Chinese government's efforts to improve English teaching in rural areas, many small villages lack the financial resources and qualified teachers necessary for effective English education (Bing 2016). Hui goes on to describe how, with the help of her teachers and a private tutor in Shanghai, she was able to become proficient in English.

Though her autoethnography may lack the cultural analysis we expect from the genre, Hui still challenges dominant representations of L2 speakers and finds linguistic empowerment in telling her story: "Today . . . I owe my reading and writing skills to my father, my private English tutor in elementary school, my English teachers in junior and high school and more importantly my own hard work and determination." She doesn't approach her English usage from a deficit perspective; rather, she owns her "reading and writing skills." Moreover, she credits those skills not only to her own initiative but also to the people who helped her in China. While she does not identify the cultural backgrounds of her teachers, by situating her literacy autoethnography primarily in China, she challenges the belief that English can only be learned in the West or when taught by native speakers. She resists the representation of speakers of East Asian Englishes as deficient; rather, the English spoken by Hui, her family, and her instructors in China is valid and skilled. US writing teachers, myself included, are often guilty of focusing on multilingual students' deviations from standardized academic English. Hui's positive representation of herself and her culture is essential in English classrooms and writing studies more broadly, as it emphasizes the need to approach the writing of multilingual students from a perspective that honors their linguistic strengths.

Jianguo, also from China, focused his literacy autoethnography on the period after he learned English and moved to the United States. His essay, entitled "Why Chinese Students Like Hang Out Together?," explores the dynamics of social interactions between Chinese international students and US-born students at the university. The title is inspired by a question asked by one of Jianguo's American friends, who was disappointed that few Chinese students seemed interested in befriending Americans. Jianguo's answer to this question is one of the most direct instances in this sample of a student author challenging dominant representations of their cultural group. He rejects the notion that Chinese students are uninterested in developing friendships with Americans; instead, he explains his friendships with other Chinese students are established through their common linguistic and cultural backgrounds, while his friendships with US students are marked by linguistic insecurity. While he emphasizes the need to build relationships with people from many cultures, he indicates this is only possible when members of the dominant culture allow him to communicate in his own English.

He illustrates by detailing a conversation in which he introduced himself to an American classmate. Inquiring about his classmate's progress in his degree program, Jianguo asked, "What years do you?" Despite Jianguo's embarrassment, his new friend was understanding and encouraged him to speak without hesitation or fear of mistakes. Jianguo agreed: "Yeah. You are right. Say what you want to say!" Though Jianguo expresses more linguistic insecurity than Hui even at the end of his narrative, he still claims his right to the English language. Moreover, he directly confronts the Othering of international students in academia, where they are judged for their linguistic and cultural differences. He then explains how he was able to adjust to the university's culture by attending events such as parties and football games. Jianguo's essay identifies not only the factors that lead to international students' cultural isolation but also their positive integration into the university. In doing so, he gives his monolingual classmates an opportunity to consider the difficulties of learning a foreign country's norms and asks them to reflect on their own representations of international students, correcting their own potentially intolerant attitudes and behaviors.

Unlike Hui and Jianguo, James had lived in the United States for roughly a decade before writing his autoethnography. Born in the United States to a Chinese Olympic athlete, he moved to Germany when he was a year old, then to China to live with his grandparents when he was two. The majority of his autoethnography centers on his experience learning English after moving back to the United States when he was seven, as well as his negotiation of his Chinese and US identities. He explains that while it was initially difficult for him to learn English and connect with his classmates, he eventually caught up, to the point that he lost his Chinese accent and much of the Chinese language. At this point, his mother made him take Chinese classes and complete written exercises to retain his first language.

In his autoethnography, James complicates the notion of the native speaker. The native versus nonnative distinction is problematic for several reasons, including its failure to account for proficiency level (Canagarajah 2006) and speaker identity (Higgins 2003). Though James self-identifies as an L2 speaker, he had been living and studying in the United States for most of his life when he enrolled in college. He was born in the United States and, by his estimate, communicates without an accent or any L2 features. He likely passes as a native speaker in many situations, and it is possible he does so in the classroom. Of the four students profiled here, he is seemingly the one who assimilated the most into US culture; he notes it wasn't until he lost his accent and graduated from his school's ELL program that he "finally felt normal and just like everyone else." His connection to China and his identification as an L2 speaker demonstrates the diversity of multilingual or "nonnative" English speakers, challenging the common representations held by many in US education and in US culture at large.

On the other end of the spectrum, Kim's literacy autoethnography explores a somewhat adversarial relationship with English and the United States. It centers on her experiences learning English in her native Vietnam and illustrates how the fraught relationship between Vietnam and the United States informed her early experiences learning English. She opens with, "I hated English. . . . I only saw English as something that I was forced to learn. After the Vietnam War, or as we call it the 'Resistance Against the US,' ended, children were taught that Americans tried to take our land and to never trust these outsiders. Yet, many of us are sent overseas to an American institution by our parents and elementary students in Vietnam are taught English so they can have, as my dad usually put it, a 'brighter future.'" Kim's provocative opening paragraph complicates the assumption that English is always viewed positively by those who learn it (an assumption Soyeon Lee explores in more depth in chapter 6 of this volume).

As instructors, we often presume the multilingual students in our classes view English literacy in a positive light as a tool for social advancement. Nhan Trong Nguyen (2017) notes that "English has become a fever gripping [Vietnam]," with 98% of students learning English "to expand overseas study options, to look for well-paid jobs and to enhance job promotion prospects" (33). While Kim acknowledges the role English is seen to play in Vietnamese students' success, she paints a more complex picture of English in Vietnam. She reveals that English is taught almost as a necessary evil, colored by the troubled history between Vietnam and the United States.

Kim's literacy autoethnography is also a bold statement of cultural and linguistic pride. Despite cultural assumptions that "nonnative" Englishes are deficient (Higgins 2003), Kim claims her ownership of the language. She uses her experiences learning English as a framing device for an exploration of her Vietnamese culture and its relationship with the Western world. She ends with this thought: "English is . . . a communication tool for me to connect with the other part of the world, understand a different culture, and use it to tell true stories of Vietnam." This statement reflects Pratt's (1991) observation that autoethnographic texts "involve a selective collaboration and appropriation of idioms of the metropolis or the conqueror . . . to create self-representations intended to intervene in metropolitan modes of understanding" (35). Rather than conforming to US cultural and linguistic values, Kim is appropriating the language of the untrusted "outsiders"—or, as Kim characterizes in her narrative, the literal conquerors—in support of Vietnamese culture. She self-represents as a proud Vietnamese citizen using the oppressor's tools to advance her own representation of her culture, challenging the assumption that English-language learners have the goal of communicating like a "native" speaker. Moreover, autoethnographies such as Kim's interrogate the imperialist aspects of the spread of English, a perspective most Americans have been socialized to ignore (or celebrate). Like the autoethnographies of Hui, Jianguo, and James, Kim's autoethnography forces monolingual, US-born English speakers to challenge their perspectives on the English language and the diversity of its speakers.

THE LITERACY AUTOETHNOGRAPHY AND THE WRITING CLASSROOM

Literacy autoethnography acknowledges student writers' agency to be analysts, storytellers, and advocates for their own communities. This exercise is valuable for both multilingual and monolingual students, as it increases their critical awareness of the relationship among language, literacy, and culture. Sharing their work with classmates can aid in this process. Cardinal, Atienza, and Jones (chapter 14 of this collection) point to the power of students sharing their literacy autoethnographies with their peers, explaining that it validates the experiences of students from marginalized groups and helps everyone understand the group's diverse literacy experiences. The same principle applies to language in linguistically diverse classes. English speakers from the traditional "home bases" of English (such as the United States and England) often feel they "own" the language, a perspective quickly becoming irrelevant. Canagarajah (2006), drawing on David Graddol, explains that L2 English speakers have outnumbered "native" speakers since the 1970s and that the number of L2 speakers is growing more quickly than that of "native" speakers (589). Thus, the idea that US or British speech and writing is correct does not reflect the reality of English today. Christina Higgins (2003) suggests that exposure to different models of linguistic "correctness" (as often experienced in non-Western countries) increases language tolerance (640). Hence, exposure to other perspectives through classmates' literacy autoethnographies (through peer review, posting to a common discussion board, or another method) can force monolingual English speakers to reconsider their relationship to a language they often misguidedly view as theirs.

On an individual level, the autoethnographies of Hui, Jianguo, James, Kim, and other multilingual student writers force me to examine my own linguistic privilege. While I try my best to model linguistic tolerance and interrogate standardized English in the contact zone of my classroom, my efforts are complicated by my position as the (white, American, "native"-speaking) gatekeeper of academic literacy. It is one thing for me to lead discussions on multiliteracies or explain the concept of World Englishes to my students, but the message necessarily changes when presented through my filter. While I don't want to tokenize my multilingual students or force them to represent their culture to their US classmates, it is imperative to allow students to speak for themselves using their own words. While there is no easy or perfect resolution here, the literacy autoethnography can serve as one step to providing all students a space to speak as the authority on their language without being put on the spot in class.

Knowing our students' literacy histories also, as Bronwyn Williams (2003/2004) notes, helps us craft our instructional methods to best meet our students' needs. For example, had I been Hui's instructor, we could have discussed the teaching methods she appreciated in China and her expectations for her current English classes. In the case of multilingual students, autoethnographies can also help us avoid the deficit perspective that plagues much of the discourse around English-language-learner (ELL) pedagogy, "whereby students' deficiencies are foregrounded" in an "essentialist view of language in which language is understood to be a decontextualized skill that can be taught in isolation from the production of meaning" (Zamel 1994, 510). The literacy-autoethnography genre itself works against this assumption, particularly when considering the essays of students with a range of languages and literacies. Similar to Pratt's (1991) observation that autoethnography can serve as "a marginalized group's point of entry into the dominant circuits of print culture" (35), the literacy autoethnography can be an effective point of entry into the university's discourse for linguistically marginalized students.

The work of Hui, Jianguo, James, and Kim demonstrates the power of literacy autoethnography in the contact zones of the writing classroom and the discipline of writing studies. It gave them an opportunity to explore and self-represent their literacy histories in relation to the social and academic expectations of the university and to articulate those connections to their instructors and peers. In examining their experiences with the English language and US culture, they claimed the language as their own and asserted their rights to it, defying deficit-oriented representations of L2 speakers in US culture and education. The literacy autoethnography can thus make a positive contribution to individual writing classrooms and writing studies more broadly, making room at the table for marginalized and linguistically diverse voices.

NOTES

1. All students are referred to by pseudonyms. Each participant provided written consent for their work to be used. The study has been approved by the university's IRB and English Department.

2. Though my classes were part of the larger study, none of my students self-identified in their narratives as L2 speakers; therefore, none of my students are included here.
3. In order to preserve students' unique voices and Englishes, I present passages from their essays without editing their usage to conform to standardized academic English.

REFERENCES

Beaufort, Anne. 2007. *College Writing and Beyond: A New Framework for University Writing Instruction.* Logan: Utah State University Press.

Bing, Wang. 2016. "The English Education in Primary Schools in Minor Ethnic Areas in Western China—Taking Leshan City as an Example." *English Language Teaching* 9 (8): 152–55.

Canagarajah, A. Suresh. 1997. "Safe Houses in the Contact Zone: Coping Strategies of African-American Students in the Academy." *College Composition and Communication* 48 (2): 173–96.

Canagarajah, A. Suresh. 2006. "The Place of World Englishes in Composition Studies: Pluralization Continued." *College Composition and Communication* 57 (4): 586–619.

Canagarajah, A. Suresh. 2012. "Autoethnography in the Study of Multilingual Writers." In *Writing Studies Research in Practice: Methods and Methodologies,* edited by Mary P. Sheridan and Lee Nickoson, 113–24. Carbondale: Southern Illinois University Press.

Hall, Anne-Marie, and Christopher Minnix. 2012. "Beyond the Bridge Metaphor: Rethinking the Place of the Literacy Narrative in the Basic Writing Curriculum." *Journal of Basic Writing* 31 (2): 57–82.

Higgins, Christina. 2003. "'Ownership' of English in the Outer Circle: An Alternative to the NS-NNS Dichotomy." *TESOL Quarterly* 37 (4): 615–44.

Kells, Michelle Hall. 2002. "Linguistic Contact Zones in the College Writing Classroom: An Examination of Ethnolinguistic Identity and Language Attitudes." *Written Communication* 19 (1): 5–43.

Nguyen, Nhan Trong. 2017. "Thirty Years of English Language and English Education in Vietnam." *English Today* 33 (1): 33–35.

Pratt, Mary Louise. 1991. "Arts of the Contact Zone." *Profession:* 33–40.

Wardle, Elizabeth, and Doug Downs. 2014. *Writing about Writing: A College Reader.* 2nd ed. Boston: Bedford/St. Martin's.

Williams, Bronwyn T. 2003/4. "Heroes, Rebels, and Victims: Student Identities in Literacy Narratives." *Journal of Adolescent and Adult Literacy* 47 (4): 342–45.

Zamel, Vivian. 1994. "Strangers in Academia: The Experiences of Faculty and ESL Students across the Curriculum." *College Composition and Communication* 46 (4): 506–21.

9
WHAT THE STUDENTS TAUGHT THE TEACHER IN A GRADUATE AUTOETHNOGRAPHY CLASS

Sue Doe, Kira Marshall-McKelvey, Ross Atkinson, Caleb Gonzalez, Lilly Halboth, and Jennifer Owen

In this autoethnographic account of a graduate course in autoethnography, offered from the perspectives of the course instructor and several students, we aim for the enactment of both the analytic and evocative ends of the autoethnographic spectrum, as well as the critical and political purposes imagined by theorists. In Leon Anderson's (2006) analytic terms, this inquiry employs complete member-researcher status of its authors, analytic reflexivity of those authors, narrative visibility of our author-researcher selves, inclusion of external informants, and a commitment to analytic purposes (373). In Carolyn Ellis's terms, we aspire to demonstrate "struggle, passion, embodied life, and the collaborative creation of sense-making" (Ellis and Bochner 2006, 433). In Mary Louise Pratt's (1991) terms, we seek to engage in political, collaborative authorship "intended to intervene in metropolitan modes of understanding" rather than "autochthonous forms of expression or self-representation" (35). Inspired as well by the work of Ruth Behar (1993), we set out to create an unruly text from the "academic borderlands" where we, as professor and students, write together "both courageously and outrageously." Indeed, together we found we had a story to "smuggle across the border," a border that exists right in our own backyard in the context of resource-constrained writing studies, a border many readers may share (234). Our aim is to represent and empower voices of graduate students who worked alongside a faculty member and informed that faculty member of the experiences of those on the margins (and beginnings) of disciplinary identity development. As coauthors, even as we describe the course we shared, we also set out to explore autoethnography as a rich area of inquiry and revelation and as a form of writing that entails significant challenges due to its interrogation of traditional hierarchies.

DOI: 10.7330/9781646421213.c009

We arrived at this project when Sue, a tenured faculty member, was preparing to write a chapter proposal for this collection about a graduate course in autoethnography even as she was also getting ready to teach a graduate class in autoethnography for a third time. For Sue, this writing opportunity seemed like a good chance to take her own autoethnographic self-reflexivity to a new level by inviting students from the class to coauthor and represent their experiences and insights, informing her along the way about factors her own positionality made her oblivious to. Invitations were made to the whole class, and five graduate students chose to participate in coauthorship, most of which took place after the close of the semester. Among the coauthors only Sue is fully visible in the text. The other coauthors, all graduate students, chose to be identified by pseudonyms in order to avoid potential repercussions from their disclosures. Coauthors Kira, Ross, Lilly, Jen, and Caleb are identified as Michael, Louise, Kailey, Gabriel, and Alaina, although not necessarily in that order and with identities deliberately blurred. Together, the graduate student coauthors offer perspectives that reflect their varying concentrations and disciplinary focuses from a writing studies context; as with the class as a whole, the coauthors represent creative writers, compositionists, public school teachers, linguists, and students of literature.

Our autoethnographic account enacts an inquiry from the disciplinary location of the graduate seminar, which William Duffy argues in chapter 10 of this collection is a site that's "especially conducive to such autoethnographic inquiry," particularly since autoethnography involves practices that can "encourage novice voices to account for the beliefs and values with which they perceive the discipline" (153). Among the values writing studies has had to contend with and has had much to say about is labor justice in the academic setting. As a brief sample, consider Eileen Schell (Schell and Stock 2001), Tony Scott (2009), Doe et al. (2011), Seth Kahn, William Lalicker, and Amy Lynch-Biniek (2017), as well as position statements from the Conference on College Composition and Communication (2016), the National Council of Teachers of English (2010), and the Modern Language Association (2020). Indeed, in chapter 3 of this collection, Rebecca Hallman Martini takes up the economic violence experienced by graduate students, as they often subsist at a poverty level. Hallman Martini's chapter shows the price paid, the pound of flesh demanded, when graduate students talk back to exploitive labor practices, a story Hallman Martini explores through an account autoethnographic writing practices animate. For our examination here, we take up a different autoethnographic project and consider the toll on graduate students when assistantship and fellowship opportunities in writing studies are doled out parsimoniously. In the case we report, dimensions of stress and labor-induced health issues among graduate students as reported by Hallman Martini are less visible, although they are similarly experienced and lie just beneath the surface. In our chapter, we look at the differences in graduate experience that are created, the injuries caused, when some graduate students obtain funding through teaching assistantships and others do not. At some risk of romanticizing the teaching assistantship, we explore that dimension of graduate school life in which the consequences of precious teaching assistantships become an internalized message of worth. Perhaps most tellingly for this chapter, we found, as Duffy suggests, that the ability to discuss such manifestations of disciplinary politics is made substantially more possible when examined through autoethnographic research and writing, perhaps especially when such an investigation is done across rank.

In the following sections we briefly outline major components of the course and focus on a particular assignment that became emblematic for us of the potential benefits of a graduate course in autoethnography. We discovered, among other things, that our extended commitment to our topic beyond the constraints of the semester, ensured due to coauthorship of this chapter, not only deepened our understanding of an important query but demonstrated autoethnography's affordances. Because we were able to continue our inquiry beyond the end of the semester, we, instructor and students alike, gained insights that might not otherwise have been possible. The topic was graduate student life, and the focus quickly became funding and the hierarchies of opportunity afforded graduate students, an economy in which faculty like Sue are generally complicit but around which they are too often self-protectively naïve or dismissive. The writing of this autoethnographic reflection allowed us to carry forward the commitments of the autoethnographic genre, ultimately offering us a critical assessment of the equity dimensions of graduate school funding and the advocacy responsibilities of faculty like Sue. This project began as an assignment completed in week four of the course and grew in depth and detail throughout the course and beyond as we worked together as coauthors.

COMPONENTS AND CHRONOLOGY OF THE COURSE[1]

The course was offered as a special topics course in a traditional sixteen-week format. One of Sue's goals as instructor was to invite a capacious interpretation of autoethnography's applications. As a result, one creative writer examined autoethnography's potential as a repertoire expander. A graduate student from English Education examined action-research projects in the public school context. A literature concentrator studied autoethnography as an opportunity for literary theory's application to politics of representation. A student from the rhetoric and composition program critically studied the autoethnographic features of her interest in the crime-story genre. This variety of autoethnographic interests reflected the varied disciplinary approaches of the people in the room, all of whom identify as graduate students in writing studies. From a pragmatic point of view, given concerns about declining enrollment in the arts and humanities, the popularity and flexibility of the autoethnographic course topic reported here may make it especially valuable in other locations.

As central features of the course, and prior to the designation of specific areas of inquiry by each student, we interrogated autoethnography's potential to

- study historic and current representations in popular culture of marginalized and underrepresented populations;
- consider salient problems associated with efforts at representation of the self and Other;
- explore strategies associated with autoethnographic research and performance/writing.

Although cognizant of the fact that autoethnographic texts challenge and enlarge dominant, mainstream, and official narratives, we were constrained, of course, by the conventions of traditional grading and the length of the semester. Course objectives had to be declared up front rather than allowed to emerge, and research projects had to reach a level of completion by the end of sixteen weeks. Nonetheless, Sue set the learning objectives in terms as broad as possible:

- articulate theories about autoethnography and relevant precursors;
- explain the relevance of positionality, liminality, intersectionality, self-reflexivity, and opacity;
- demonstrate practical knowledge of autoethnographic research methods, especially field methods associated with autoethnographic purposes;
- identify and discuss the characteristics of sample autoethnographic texts, distinguishing autoethnographic approaches from full autoethnography;
- write autoethnographically, especially through demonstration of critical self-reflexivity and increased understanding of positionality as a central component of research and its writing.

Reflecting these objectives, the course's main assignments included entries to the weekly discussion forums in the online learning-management system, analysis and oral introduction of book-length autoethnographies to the class,[2] an independently researched and presented autoethnographic project, and an autoethnographic exploration of life as a graduate student. The project mentioned last is the one we focus on for much of our discussion in this chapter.

A WORKING DEFINITION OF AUTOETHNOGRAPHY

By one month in, after reading selections from Zora Neal Hurston's (1991) *Dust Tracks on a Road,* Ruth Behar's (1993) *Translated Woman,* Laurel Richardson's (1997) *Fields of Play: Constructing an Academic Life,* Deborah E. Reed-Danahay's (1997) *Auto/Ethnography: Rewriting the Self and the Social,* Heewon Chang's (2008) *Autoethnography As Method,* and Allen Hancock, Ayana Allen, and Chance W. Lewis's (2015) *Autoethnography as a Lighthouse,* we had derived some preliminary definitions of autoethnography:

- a reflexive performance of the self as immersed in a given culture and/or community of which the researcher is a part; an acknowledgment of invisible forces around individuals and communities that shape not only what is experienced but what is written/disclosed;
- a purposeful construction of narratives and characterizations that disrupt dominant discourse, mainstream ways of understanding phenomena, and generalizable findings; a recognition of the humanity or human dimension behind, contained within, and often obscured by broad conversations about trends and issues;
- a strategy for inquiry in which the researcher is positioned as a participant-observer but may also choose to include member cross-checking obtained through observation, interview, and data collected from others; a method of writing and researching to subjectively explore the cultures people are part of; a tool to dismantle oppressive forces;
- a form of writing that often includes personal narrative and asserts the personal and the narrated as legitimate forms of scholarship; a way of illuminating areas of marginalized identity best described by members of community possessing direct experience and insight; a reaction to other forms of research writing that tend to sever writers from their bodies; a layering of the academic and the creative.

DISCUSSION FORUMS

We responded in online discussions to assigned reading and the book-length autoethnographies selected by classmates. Our weekly discussion topics ranged from matters of representation to topical areas of interest such as travel narratives. We treated the forum entries as semiformal writing. Class members were expected to contribute one main entry and respond to at least one other person each week for a total of at least ten weekly submissions. Here are a few examples of discussion prompts:

1. During a week on travel: Think about a journey you have undertaken (outward, inward, or local). Create a visual travel autoethnography using PowerPoint. Your submission should consist of at least five slides that represent the elements that demonstrate your positionality as a traveler within a specific culture.

2. During a week on genre: Discuss an autoethnographic genre we haven't talked about so we might derive a catalog of examples, such as trauma narrative, confession, prayer, encyclical, benediction, manifesto.

3. During a week on embodiment: Review a number of theoretical sources including excerpts from Glissant on opacity, Foucault on biopower and biopolitics, and Collins on intersectionality. How do you see these theories applying to the topic for this week—illness, disease, and aging: caring when bodies betray?

CRITICAL DISCOVERIES: THE AUTOETHNOGRAPHIC EXPLORATION OF GRADUATE SCHOOL LIFE

The key project of the semester, which we focus on for the remainder of our chapter, asked students to query their graduate student experience. The assignment read as follows:

> Conduct an autoethnographic exploration of your graduate academic life, applying methods such as interview, observation, document analysis, and critical reflection to analyze information about your life as a graduate student. Consider this an "anthropological dig" into your life as a grad student.

Initial discoveries included the following statement by Louise, who seemed to capture the feelings of alienation experienced by several of the graduate students in this course:

> LOUISE: We're grad students, so, by Anderson's standard, we have Complete Member Researcher status when analyzing graduate students as a demographic; it's deceptively simple. But how can you analyze your positionality within research about a particular group when a core struggle of your identity is your uncertain ability to define yourself as a true member of that group? In simpler terms, an autoethnography about your identity as a grad student forces you, in its premise, to accept yourself as a member of the community you're studying. It means accepting that you belong. This is easier said than done.

IDENTITY WORK IN THE AUTOETHNOGRAPHY COURSE

Our autoethnographic explorations of graduate school experiences in the local setting called for us to explore questions of identity in order to consider the ways both privilege and marginalization were functioning in our classroom space. These efforts contributed to the rising awareness of funding as a form of graduate school privilege. To understand the notion of positionalities better, we focused on the scholarship of Kathy Obear (2017) and Elsie Cross (2000). Drawing on Obear's (2017) work, we considered identity memberships across a spectrum of areas and applied an equity lens to our increasingly careful examination of our university environment. A side benefit was that we got to know one another better in the process. Drawing on the work of Cross (2000), we also began to PAN, an acronym for pay attention now, which allowed us to look critically at environmental cues that consciously or unconsciously communicate bias. Each of us also took three Harvard Implicit Association Tests, all of us completing the race survey and each of us selecting two other surveys such as ones relating to class, gender, age, and ableism (Harvard Implicit Bias Tests 2011).

Here we discuss how our investigations into identity, and particularly membership in privileged and marginalized groups, interacted with our experiences in the academy and descriptions of life as a graduate student:

> KAILEY: Each student brought three objects that they felt best represented their identities: I brought an eyeshadow palette, a book titled "How to Be a Person in the World," and a pair of earrings in Penn State's colors. While I thought that each object represented something that was uniquely mine, I realized that each piece demonstrated my social and financial privilege. I had deemed my financial privilege in graduate school socially acceptable, as it derived in large part from the assistantship which was merit-based, rather than situational. However, the course and our identity work challenged me to question how merit-based this financial security really was. Had I not had support through college, I may not have succeeded. I may not have been given access to opportunities that afforded later experiences in graduate school.
>
> ALAINA: I now have a better understanding of how my positionality is entirely relevant to my research. I understand that I have areas where I am more privileged than others. There's a certain responsibility that comes with understanding this. As a GTA, I realize that even though I come from humble beginnings, I am in a position of privilege now. As a married, heterosexual woman with two children and a paying if not quite living wage, I am in a position of power.

BRINGING IDENTITY AND POSITIONALITY TOGETHER: GRADUATE TEACHING ASSISTANT STATUS

As the excerpts suggest, graduate students in the course critically considered their stories, stances, and positionalities, grounding their points in a deepening awareness of the multiple and sometimes competing positionalities of peers and colleagues in the same classroom. During the coauthorship phase of this project, we began to discuss more directly the power and opportunity differences in our local setting. Specifically, we discussed the degree to which GTAs enjoy many forms of privilege and opportunity that masquerade as the norm yet do not reflect the context of most of the graduate students in our department. Of the one hundred or so admitted graduate students in any given year, only a fraction, twenty or so, are awarded teaching assistantships that continue on for a second year or in some cases a third year for the MFA. In this context, non-GTAs often feel alienated and are also subjected to sleights, including classroom references that assume they are all graduate teaching assistants and balancing graduate work with the teaching of first-year composition. Yet material conditions vary greatly based on whether a graduate student is a GTA or not. For instance, GTAs have mailboxes in the same room as the faculty; they have offices that provide official space on campus for their work; they have direct opportunity to liaise with faculty who teach writing. Additionally, they are paid a not-quite-living wage and gain at least two years of teaching experience with associated professional development, including significant training in uses of the library and its databases. They have opportunities for funded travel to conferences, have access to professionalizing uses of emergent writing technologies, and are provided career guidance in regard to college teaching. Perhaps most obviously, they have the opportunity to try out theories of writing studies in classrooms of their own. In the following section we explore how GTA and non-GTA positionality became increasingly important and politicized in our graduate cohort as result of the autoethnography classroom.

> ALAINA: I am fully aware of the role I play as both a graduate student and as a graduate teaching assistant. Over the past two years, as a graduate teaching assistant, I have developed close relationships with certain members of the teaching community, while other groups have remained clearly separated from it. This in-group, out-group phenomenon was not something I had initially noticed, but as I completed an autoethnography of my graduate school experience, I realized how similar my experiences as a marginalized undergraduate had been to many of my fellow students in the graduate program.

GABRIEL: Having a Graduate Teaching Assistantship has provided me with a tremendous advantage in advancing my academic and professional career, and I have come to realize that this opportunity was not offered to everyone. Without the GTA, I would neither be at this university nor have the opportunity to grow as a teaching professional. This has allowed me to reflect on the financial struggles and feelings of alienation that graduate students without an assistantship face every semester. Additionally, when I began the GTA, my work was steeped in Creative Writing pedagogy, and I was not keen on challenging myself in other areas of scholarship. I was complicit in being consumed by a culture of scholarship division amongst all graduate students and the GTAs, especially. As I navigate myself through the assistantship, I am motivated to expand my area of study to encompass writing studies that is not only creative but academic. Part of this comes directly from the first-year writing classes that I am privileged to teach. I recognize that these are small experiences and advantages that are not offered to everyone.

LOUISE: Competition stands in a toxic lake between us. Grad students can't get subsidized federal loans and there are limited GTAs to offer. I didn't receive one coming into grad school, and that reality has haunted my lungs before class, during, after—everyone I know is a GTA and I wasn't good enough to be counted amongst them. From the outside, the GTA cohort appears strong, their conversations dwelling in a sphere I can never visit. Professors spend entire class periods speaking to GTAs about GTA duties, and I have felt cut from conversations I didn't feel I could join. Without the GTA, I found work in the Writing Center. The Writing Center was where I belonged, where I shined; but the Writing Center was also a source of shame, because I was clearly below my peers: the GTAs, the friends who already had a solid bond, who had experience, who were better than me in all the ways we're taught to value: financially, professionally, and socially.

MICHAEL: Painted by the bright lie of collaboration, the spaces of the university are a breeding ground for competition between peers for specific academic positions, one of which is the position of GTA, a position that I do not hold. Those students offered the position of GTA, from the outset, are placed in a special group that worries less about funding, collaborates together, and is often explicitly referenced by professors during class: "GTAs, what could we take from this to better instruct your students in CO150?"

As a result of these insights, some of the greatest discoveries of the course and from the research and writing of this chapter belonged to the person at the front of the room, which is to say Sue, who, as instructor of record for this course and as director of composition and supervisor to GTAs, reflected this way:

SUE: I have been guilty of the very statement Michael refers to above where the professor asks the class what might be learned for "our" classrooms, as if everyone were a GTA. As Director of Composition, my daily life is consumed by oversight of first-year, developmental, and advanced composition. Student complaints and integrity issues, teaching challenges, equipment breakdowns, registration and enrollment issues, transfer evaluations, and state-wide articulations make up my days. I have been casual about referring to these ongoing perturbations as distractions and annoyances without consideration of who might find such characterizations an exhibition of indulgent self-service and a reminder of exclusion. I recognize that we forget at our own risk that one person's workaday challenges represent unrealized opportunity to others. Ironically, or perhaps inevitably, as we wrote this article, I was engaged in the annual ritual of GTA selection, which is set up to obtain balance among programs across the English Department while maintaining the pretense of selecting the most promising teachers. From among over 100 applicants, we would choose 19. These 19 would be selected from seven distinct programs and programs were free to advance the names of those they chose while as Director of Composition, my job was to review the files for red flags. While the system was efficient, it did nothing to reduce my awareness of the dozens of graduate students whose strong files did not advance and whose futures would be affected. Prompted largely by the insights of my co-authors for this article, I found myself compelled to make more visible the importance of financial support for our graduate students and to review files carefully, even or perhaps especially for students who were not selected for assistantships.

MOVING FORWARD

Examining the graduate school context was not the only preoccupation of our course, as earlier descriptions clarify. In the final weeks of the class, graduate students wrote and briefed the class on their independent autoethnographic projects, which included the following topics:

1. "A Military Spouse's Search for Home"
2. "The Myth of the Student-Veteran"
3. "Autoethnographic Critique of an LGBTQIA Resource Center"
4. "Surviving Social Justice After 10 Years of Activist Theater"
5. "To List or Not to List: Reflections on How and Why We Bird"
6. "Needing Introversion: Opaque Spaces for Student Learning"
7. "An Autoethnographic Exploration of My Body in the Video Game Industry"
8. "Straight-Up Confused: An Autoethnographic Exploration of Sexuality on YouTube"

9. "Silence as Communicative Act in Family Culture"
10. "Deconstructing Certainty in Evangelicalism"
11. "Not Your Average Soccer Mom"
12. "Contemplative Learning in the Active Classroom"
13. "Audience Motives for True Crime Podcasts"

As these topics suggest, autoethnographic research and writing opened up topics that might otherwise have stayed in the shadows of graduate student interest due to their connections to the intersection of personal story and cultural critique. But we return here at the end to the class project that shed light on the graduate experience. Our shared autoethnographic discovery was that funding is the clearest way to signal we value graduate students. As result of this course and our coauthorship of this autoethnographic account of an autoethnography course, Sue recommitted herself to finding new revenue sources so her department commits to coming closer to the goal of providing funding to every graduate student who is admitted. She credits her coauthors for bringing her to new levels of autoethnographic self-reflexivity and recognition of her responsibility. This point suggests how much we learn not just by assigning autoethnography but by engaging in it beside our students, learning as autoethnographers do to be grateful for the knowledge others bring to us from the other side, Behar's (1993) *el otro lado*. For we who coauthored in this project, this is what autoethnography clarified—that through autoethnography some offer the gift of their stories of struggle; they risk sharing those stories with others. Others, like Sue, who function from a position of power and privilege, have an autoethnographic task as well; it involves an obligation to approach our learning from others with a grateful heart, not a dismissive or judgmental one, no matter how difficult the message that has been brought to us. Autoethnography testifies even as it also calls to action. Those who testify have no obligation to do so; those who are called to action bear full responsibility to listen, to hear, and to act.

NOTES

1. Syllabus available upon request. Contact Sue Doe at sue.doe@colostate.edu.
2. Book-length autoethnographic discussions and examples included Pico Iyer, *Tropical Classical: Essays from Several Directions* (1997); Marjane Satrapi, *Persepolis* (2008); Julie Serrano, *Whipping Girl: A Transsexual Woman on Sexism and the Scapegoating of Femininity* (2007); Stella Suberman, *The GI Bill Boys: A Memoir* (2012); Aziz Ansari and Eric Klinenberg, *Modern Romance: An Investigation* (2015); Janet M. Alger and Steven F. Alger, *Cat Culture: The Social World of a Cat Shelter* (2003).

REFERENCES

Alger, Janet M., and Steven F. Alger. 2003. *Cat Culture: The Social World of a Cat Shelter*. Philadelphia: Temple University Press.
Anderson, Leon. 2006. "Analytic Autoethnography." *Journal of Contemporary Ethnography* 35 (4): 373–95.
Ansari, Aziz, and Eric Klinenberg. 2015. *Modern Romance: An Investigation*. New York: Penguin.
Behar, Ruth. 1993. *Translated Woman: Crossing the Border with Esperanza's Story*. Boston: Beacon.
Chang, Heewon. 2008. *Autoethnography as Method: Developing Qualitative Inquiry*. Walnut Creek, CA: Left Coast.
Conference on College Composition and Communication. 2016. "CCCC Statement of Best Practices in Faculty Hiring for Tenure-Track and Non-Tenure-Track Positions in Rhetoric and Composition/Writing Studies." https://cccc.ncte.org/cccc/resources/positions/faculty-hiring.
Collins, Patricia Hill. 2015. "Intersectionality's Definitional Dilemmas." *Annual Review of Sociology* 41: 1–20.
Cross, Elsie Y. 2000. *Managing Diversity—the Courage to Lead*. Westport, CT: Quorum Books.
Doe, Sue, Natalie Barnes, David Bowen, David Gilkey, David Smoak, Ginger Guardiola, Sarah Ryan, Kirk Sarell, Laura H. Thomas, Lucy J. Troup, and Mike Palmquist. 2011. "Discourse of the Firetenders: Considering Contingent Faculty through the Lens of Activity Theory." *College English* 73 (4): 428–49.
Ellis, Carolyn S., and Arthur P. Bochner. 2006. "Analyzing Analytic Autoethnography: An Autopsy." *Journal of Contemporary Ethnography* 35 (4): 429–49.
Glissant, Edouard. 1997. *Poetics of Relation*. Translated by Betsy Wing. Ann Arbor: University of Michigan Press.
Hancock, Stephen, Ayana Allen, and Chance W. Lewis. 2015. *Autoethnography as a Lighthouse: Illuminating Race, Research, and the Politics of Schooling*. Charlotte, NC: Information Age.
"Harvard Implicit Bias Test." 2011. *Project Implicit*. Last modified 2011. https://implicit.harvard.edu/implicit/takeatest.html.
Hurston, Zora Neale. 1991. *Dust Tracks on a Road*. 1st ed. New York: Harper Perennial Olive Editions.
Iyer, Pico. 1997. *Tropical Classical: Essays from Several Directions*. 1st ed. New York: Random House.
Kahn, Seth, William B. Lalicker, and Amy Lynch-Biniek. 2017. *Contingency, Exploitation, and Solidarity: Labor and Action in English Composition*. Fort Collins, CO: WAC Clearinghouse.
Modern Language Association. 2020. "Recommendation on Minimum Per-Course Compensation for Part-Time Faculty Members." https://www.mla.org/Resources/Research/Surveys-Reports-and-Other-Documents/Staffing-Salaries-and-Other-Professional-Issues/MLA-Recommendation-on-Minimum-Per-Course-Compensation-for-Part-Time-Faculty-Members.
National Council of Teachers of English. 2010. "NCTE Statement on the Status and Working Conditions of Contingent Faculty." Position Statements. http://www2.ncte.org/statement/contingent_faculty/.
Obear, Kathy. 2017. *But I'm Not Racist!: Tools for Well Meaning Whites*. McLean, VA: The Difference Press.
Pratt, Mary Louise. 1991. "Arts of the Contact Zones." *Profession*: 33–40.
Reed-Danahay, Deborah E., ed. 1997. *Auto/Ethnography: Rewriting the Self and the Social*. New York: Berg.
Richardson, Laurel. 1997. *Fields of Play: Constructing an Academic Life*. New Brunswick, NJ: Rutgers University Press.

Satrapi, Marjane. 2008. *Persepolis*. London: Vintage.
Schell, Eileen E., and Patricia L. Stock. 2001. *Moving a Mountain: Transforming the Role of Contingent Faculty in Composition Studies and Higher Education* Urbana, IL: NCTE.
Scott, Tony. 2009. *Dangerous Writing: Understanding the Political Economy of Composition*. Logan: Utah State University Press.
Serrano, Julie. 2007. *Whipping Girl: A Transsexual Woman on Sexism and the Scapegoating of Femininity*. Emery, CA: Seal.
Suberman, Stella. 2012. *The GI Bill Boys: A Memoir*. 1st ed. Knoxville: University of Tennessee Press.

10
AGENTIC DISCORD IN WRITING STUDIES
Toward Autoethnographic Accounts of Disciplinary Lore

William Duffy

> *I have come to understand the politics of writing by learning that power is, at its root, telling our own stories. Without "good" stories to rely on, no minority or marginalized majority has a chance to change its status, or, more importantly, to identify and question the "bad" tales that create it.*
> —Susan Miller

The purpose of this chapter is to examine how the tools of autoethnography can help us reconcile our localized experiences as writing studies professionals with the disciplinary identifications we use to navigate the field. For instance, when I accepted my current faculty position and began to teach graduate seminars for the first time, I realized my own conception of the discipline was very different from the one my graduate students recognized. I work in an English department that arranges itself into specific concentrations that operate independently of one another. I'm a member of the Composition Studies and Professional Writing concentration. Besides being clunky and inelegant, this concentration moniker is also quite specific, almost to a fault. In fact, the graduate students I first encountered here tended to identify with only one of these areas, composition studies or professional writing.[1] This was a challenge for me on several fronts. Not only did many of these students tend to express indifference about the "other" area of their concentration, but they also failed to recognize how this divide reflected the local history of this specific program more than it did the generalized terrain of these areas as academic disciplines.

I came to writing studies by way of a generalist doctoral program that required me to follow what at the time was a fairly rigid curriculum. While I was able to specialize in rhetoric and composition, it was harder for me to locate this specialized area of study as something completely separate from the other areas in which I took coursework. With that said, I did experience to a certain degree the felt pressures that come with claiming a disciplinary identity, especially as it concerned which part of rhetoric and composition deserved the most allegiance, the more classroom-oriented work of teaching writing or the more theory-oriented work of rhetorical studies. This is a false dichotomy, of course, one that writing studies practitioners have long debunked.[2] I bring this up, however, because a tacit component of my enculturation into the field of writing studies focused on developing an understanding of and appreciation for the politics of disciplinarity and how they manifest in various professional settings. This is not a seamless process, of course, nor is it one that happens all at once. In fact, the more I have come to shape a professional identity in writing studies, the more I have come to appreciate the ways such identifications do and do not matter in the local contexts where I do the work of a writing studies specialist day in and day out. When I arrived at my current institution and met a group of graduate students who had a limited vision of what Composition Studies and Professional Writing is and could be, I was thus reminded how challenging it can be to distinguish one's understanding of a discipline from one's experience of it.

Such a challenge doesn't just apply to graduate students, of course, it also affects anyone who claims writing studies (or whatever moniker one chooses to name this field) as a disciplinary home. As a case in point, I followed with great interest a discussion on the Writing Program Administrators Listserv (WPA-L) in April 2018 about the status of non-tenure-track (NTT) jobs for composition specialists. At the time of this writing, there have been nearly sixty responses to this discussion thread, which was initiated by someone who posed a straightforward observation about seeing an increase in advertisements on the listserv for NTT positions. Some respondents quickly connected this observation to larger trends concerning the casualization of labor in postsecondary education, while others made explicit claims about the ethical responsibilities of writing program administrators (WPAs) who hire and oversee NTT and adjunct instructors. Another group of respondents pushed back at those who were generalizing about NTT positions and pointed to their own institutions where such positions come with fair contracts, equal benefits, and a voice in shared governance, which is to say these latter respondents evoked their own experiences to reject the narrative that NTT positions are "lesser" and should thus be avoided.

Go back and review this discussion thread, however, and you'll see how many topics get taken up that go beyond the one raised in the original post. Moreover, many of these other discussions tangentially engage issues we find ourselves always debating to one extent or another when we come together as a group of professionals to talk about what we do. What is the status of composition, or writing studies, as an academic field? Are we primarily a "service" discipline? Who should be teaching composition courses, and how should they be trained? Are English departments the right fit for us? Should nontenured faculty serve as WPAs? There are no straightforward answers to these questions, of course, which is one reason they are so frequently posed. But another reason is that such discussions almost always beg questions of disciplinary lore, commonplaces that can be invoked to bypass what would otherwise be the need for laborious contextualization. We can think of disciplinary lore as narrative fragments that can be put together in any variety of contexts to serve any variety of needs depending on the topic under discussion. For instance, it's a commonplace to say the field of composition struggles to define itself; it's also a commonplace to suggest composition lacks legitimacy in most academic bureaucracies. To take the example from my own graduate school experience, it's a commonplace that as an intellectual enterprise composition is given short shrift compared to rhetoric. While it's certainly possible to historicize these claims by tracing how writing studies has developed as an academic discipline, the function of these claims as pieces of disciplinary lore is less historical than it is epideictic. The veracity of disciplinary lore is often inconsequential, that is, because what matters for those who invoke it is how these narratives allow us to create a shared experience of the discipline itself, even if our lived experiences of the field are substantially different from one person to the next. It could thus be argued that disciplinary lore is foundational to disciplinarity itself; it collects narratives, beliefs, and values, the knowledge of which gives us the reference points needed to navigate the discipline's discourse.

But my defense of disciplinary lore is not without qualification.[3] These fragments of narrative can and often do contribute to the "bad" stories about composition Susan Miller (1991) mentions at the beginning of *Textual Carnivals*. Following Miller, we might ask how disciplinary lore contributes to the power differentials she goes on to document in her rendering of composition as "cacophonous, anarchic, and trivial" but also "always in a state of becoming, of reinventing itself to compensate for its perceived lack of fixed goals and methods" (12). The agentic discord manifested in the discussion of NTT faculty on the WPA-L serves as a case in point. But disciplinary lore might also stand in for narratives rooted in more nuanced beliefs about the profession, pieces of doxa that have a localized origin or sphere of influence. Accordingly, trying to assess whether a piece of lore is "good" or "bad" might be less important than trying to comprehend its relevance for a particular group of people. For this reason, I agree with Debra Journet (2012), who invokes a piece of disciplinary lore (although she doesn't call it that) when she discusses the politics of narrative research: "Though claims are often made that narratives of personal experience are inherently more authentic accounts, I argue instead that such narratives are, at least in part, conventionalized ways of representing disciplinary knowledge" (13). Disciplinary lore should thus be considered through a pragmatic rather than epistemic lens; that is, asking questions about the meaning of these commonplaces might not be as useful or interesting as thinking about what we do with them as practitioners.

What might such inquiry look like? A handful of writing studies scholars have produced versions of what Richard Miller (2005) calls "institutional autobiography" in his *Writing at the End of the World*, a book that serves as an example of such a genre. Miller blends carefully crafted autobiographical accounts alongside explication and analysis of literary texts, pedagogical scenarios, and current events to probe "the seemingly opposed worlds of the personal—where one is unique, free, and outside of history—and the institutional—where one is constrained, anonymous, and imprisoned by the accretion of past practices" (138). Such writing harkens to what two years earlier Jane Hindman (2003) described as a need for more "embodied personal writing"; Hindman points to scholars such as Patricia Bizzell, Jacqueline Jones Royster, Andrea Lunsford, and Lynn Worsham, who also call for related, more autobiographically informed "alternative discourse(s)" of professional practice (10, 11). These proposals suggest the value of scholarship that explicitly draws on personal experience as a site of inquiry for understanding disciplinary knowledge. However, the majority of field narratives available to writing studies professionals that interrogate the discipline's identifications through such personal lenses tend to resemble what Lester Faigley (2000) describes in his appropriately titled "Veterans' Stories on the Porch," autobiographical accounts of an individual's career that also stand in as retrospective histories of the discipline.[4] As the editors write in their introduction to *History, Reflection, and Narrative: The Professionalization of Composition, 1963–1983*, in which Faigley's piece appears, these narratives are "constructions based on the writer's choices—ideological, epistemological, aesthetic—about what constitutes significance" (Journet, Boehm, and Rosner 2000, xiv). Unless they are well-known senior scholars, few writing studies professionals have the opportunity to inscribe such personal accounts. As useful as these narratives are for historical reasons, in other words, certainly we stand to benefit from learning about the disciplinary significations newcomers to the field embrace as they pursue professionalization.

As I've developed an appreciation for such newcomer perspectives, I've come to believe the qualitative methods associated with autoethnography offer a useful roadmap for systematically narrating personal and professional experience side by side. I echo the editors of this collection who define autoethnography as narratives of experience from within a culture, narratives whose purpose is to interrogate or better understand that culture. With that said, the educational anthropologist Heewon Chang (2008) notes that when discussing autoethnography, it's important to recognize competing approaches to this method that highlight the different values researchers bring to it. The approach she promotes "combines cultural analysis and interpretation with narrative details," which is to say she prefers autoethnography that is more "social scientific inquiry" than "performative storytelling"; or as she explains, "I expect the stories of autoethnographers to be reflected upon, analyzed, and interpreted within their broader sociocultural context" (46). Insofar as the discipline of writing studies might be able to better interrogate and understand the values and beliefs novice members of the field bring to their experiences as teachers, researchers, and administrators of composition, I agree with Chang that autoethnographic inquiry in such contexts must be reflected upon and interpreted alongside the more obvious sociocultural elements of the field. As I detail above, the field's disciplinary lore represents just such an element because these are the narratives compositionists learn as they are initiated into the discipline.

In the remainder of this chapter, I suggest how autoethnographic inquiry, in particular what Leon Anderson (2006) calls "analytic autoethnography," offers writing studies professionals a guide for not only naming specific iterations of disciplinary lore but also accounting for the significations of this lore in our experiences of the discipline. While such autoethnographic accounts of the discipline already exist, rather than elaborate on various examples, I want to sketch a vision for how Anderson's approach can be used in settings like graduate seminars, for example, to encourage novice voices to account for the beliefs and values with which they perceive the discipline.

Anderson's approach to analytic autoethnography is of particular value because it reflects Chang's (2008) concern that "autoethnography should be ethnographic in its methodological orientation, cultural in its interpretative orientation, and autobiographical in its content orientation" (48).⁵ Analytic autoethnography requires its writers to define contexts, collect data, and explain their interpretative choices as they render autobiographical experiences into text. Moreover, analytic autoethnography is useful because Anderson (2006) developed it to help initiate newcomers like "current graduate students and other novices in field research who are contending with the pull of various approaches to qualitative inquiry" (374). Specifically, Anderson outlines five features that define analytic autoethnography: "(1) complete member researcher (CMR) status, (2) analytic reflexivity, (3) narrative visibility of the researcher's self, (4) dialogue with informants beyond the self, and (5) commitment to theoretical analysis" (378). Anderson is careful to note these criteria are flexible—how one determines CMR status will vary from one case to the next, for instance—but considered together they suggest how autoethnographic inquiry should grow out of and speak back to specific communities of practice.

One disciplinary site especially conducive to such autoethnographic inquiry is the graduate seminar. Whether one is an advanced doctoral candidate or a first-year graduate student, being enrolled in a graduate seminar offers something akin to CMR status, even if that status is partial and provisional. In chapter 9 of this collection, Sue Doe, Kira Marshall-McKelvey, Lilly Halboth, Ross Atkinson, Caleb Gonzalez, and Jennifer Owen use Anderson's model to offer a collective analytic autoethnography that takes a graduate seminar as its focus of study in order to identify, name, and interrogate how graduate students navigate disciplinary hierarchies in ways that aren't always obvious to their mentors and other full-time faculty.

In explaining "analytic reflexivity," Anderson (2006) writes that it "entails self-conscious introspection guided by a desire to better understand both self and others through examining one's actions and perceptions in reference to and dialogue with those of others" (382). In other words, the autoethnographer doesn't probe their experiences alone in a garret, so to speak, but is engaged with others who share CMR status in that particular subculture. A graduate seminar provides just such a community, one in which novice practitioners can discuss beliefs, values, and practices they bring to that space. Anderson's third criterion, narrative visibility of the researcher's self, simply implies the writer is willing to foreground their experience through narrative. However, it's the fourth and fifth criteria that round out why the space of a graduate seminar is ideal for analytic autoethnography. To be engaged in dialogue with informants beyond the self is what many of us require of our graduate students when we assign reading responses and lead class discussions; it is to practice the work of listening to others' ideas and then speaking back to those ideas in ways that mimic the kinds of professional dialogues that maintain the discipline. And what better space to practice theoretical analysis? Indeed, most graduate seminars require students to apply the theories and methods under discussion, if not in a capstone paper then through other assignments.[6]

To conclude, I detail how I've started to incorporate analytic autoethnography into my graduate seminars as a way for students to identify and speak back to the disciplinary lore that informs how they perceive the fields of study in which most of them envision building careers. Accordingly, I begin most of the seminars I teach by asking students to compose what I call a *positioning essay*, the details of which vary from one course to the next but always require students to render observations and experiences just as researchers collect data in the field. For example, in a recent seminar that introduced students to scholarly writing and publishing in composition and professional writing, I asked students to read an essay by Marcy Taylor and Jennifer Holberg (1999) about how students get positioned in writing studies graduate programs, but instead of asking students to compose a response to this reading, I gave them the prompt for a positioning essay that opens with the following excerpt from Taylor and Holberg's article:

> In the case of the field of composition studies, the ways in which graduate students are named helps to define their position in relation to the institutions in which they work, the students whom they teach, and the "colleagues" (other faculty and administrators) who are often responsible for determining the shape of their work, identity and status. At the same time, the ways graduate students name themselves perpetuate these determinations. (610)

Next came this pair of questions: Who are you? And why are you here? I qualified these questions in the prompt by pointing to how Taylor and Holberg explain there is often a stymieing contradiction that results when the question of who you are converges with the question of what you do because graduate students are often boxed into hybrid identities. They are not considered faculty, but many of them are instructors of record; they aren't credentialed experts, but many of them pursue professional activities; they haven't graduated, but many of them are already employed in the field. The remainder of the prompt introduced Anderson's conception of analytic autoethnography and its five criteria and instructed students to compose an autoethnographic essay that documented the beliefs and assumptions they were bringing to this course about their prospective areas of study.

At various points over the next twelve weeks, I developed in-class writing assignments shaped around questions that functioned heuristically to engage the kinds of inquiry promoted by analytic autoethnography. For example, after reading various essays from two edited collections, *Just Being Difficult: Academic Writing in the Public Arena* (Culler and Lamb 2003) and *Publishing in Rhetoric and Composition* (Olson and Taylor 1997), students had to document responses to the following:

What are 2–3 of the most important values you associate with scholarly publishing?

Where and how did you come to learn about these values?

What evidence can you point us to where you see these values articulated or enacted?

To what extent do these values align with your own interest in writing for publication?

As students developed responses to prompts like these, I asked them to take notes comparing those answers to what they wrote in their initial positioning essay. By the end of the semester, students accumulated close to a dozen pages of autoethnographic data that could then be used to compose a revised positioning essay, one that inevitably engaged and reflected a wider range of voices and levels of theoretical analysis to which Anderson stipulates analytic autoethnography should aspire.

What has been the consequence of asking students to experiment with analytic autoethnography in these ways? Besides the obvious value that comes with taking stock of one's professional identity, such writing tends to boost the confidence of graduate students, many of whom have never been invited to assert, following Miller (1991), their own stories about the discipline, however provisional and speculative. For my part, I'm less confounded by the range of beliefs and assumptions I see graduate students bring to their work. I'm also more aware of the situatedness of writing studies as a discipline and how apart from our direct experiences in the specific institutional contexts we inhabit, everything else we say about writing studies is disciplinary lore.

Autoethnographic inquiry allows us to develop these nuanced accounts, and in the end, these are the only accounts that really matter because they speak out of and to our lived experiences of the discipline. To be sure, requiring students to experiment with autoethnography won't resolve the agentic discord that is part and partial of navigating the paradoxical positions they must assume as they progress on their professional paths. Still, my graduate students are teaching me much about the field, not the least of which is what it means to be a compositionist in my department. Rather than hoping they will come to adopt the habitus from which I perceive the field, I see how much more useful it is to embrace my position as a member of a community of compositionists—expert, novice, and many in between—who mutually determine what constitutes the field as it exists in this specific place.

NOTES

1. Our concentration has since reorganized itself into a unitary program that better reflects the intersections of writing studies, rhetoric, and professional/technical writing. Our new program name is Writing, Rhetoric, and Technical Communication, which aims to better reflect the overlapping disciplinary positions of our faculty and the multiple areas in which students can specialize.
2. I discuss the politics of this division in my recent review (Duffy 2016) of Paul Lynch's *After Pedagogy* (2013), a book in which Lynch considers the value of foregoing debate about theory and practice altogether by focusing on John Dewey's understanding of experience.
3. Since I have limited space, I will forego discussion of how the concept of lore has been problematized by scholars in writing studies. Most readers will no doubt be reminded of Stephen North's (1987) definition of lore as "the accumulated body of traditions, practices, and beliefs in terms of which Practitioners [i.e., teachers of writing] understand how writing is done, learned, and taught" (22). What I'm calling *disciplinary lore* in this essay overlaps with North's definition to a certain extent, but I don't see such lore as fodder only for "practitioners," as North calls those in the field who primarily teach.
4. Prime examples of these texts are collected in *Living Rhetoric and Composition*, edited by Duane Roen, Stuart Brown, and Theresa Enos (1999). As I mention in the body of this essay, these autobiographical accounts tend to be written by veteran members of the field who have a national profile. It can thus be argued that such narratives represent a privileged genre most compositionists don't (and won't) have access to as a publication platform.
5. Anderson (2006) explicitly situates analytic autoethnography as an alternative to "evocative autoethnography" (374), which is an approach that relies heavily on experimentation with form, narrative, voice, and style, which is to say evocative autoethnographies are often positioned as hybrid texts that draw on conventions from both the social sciences and the humanities, especially creative writing. While Anderson doesn't criticize evocative autoethnography, like Chang he is cognizant that these more creative texts have met with resistance by more traditional ethnographers. For more on evocative autoethnography, see Arthur Bochner and Carolyn Ellis (2016).
6. In the previous chapter, Doe and her graduate students use the various assignments they completed in the seminar as an organizational map for their autoethnography, one that gives their piece chronological structure.

REFERENCES

Anderson, Leon. 2006. "Analytic Autoethnography." *Journal of Contemporary Ethnography* 35 (4): 373–95.

Bochner, Arthur, and Carolyn Ellis. 2016. *Evocative Autoethnography: Writing Lives and Telling Stories*. New York: Routledge.

Chang, Heewon. 2008. *Autoethnography as Method*. Walnut Creek, CA: Left Coast.
Culler, Jonathan, and Kevin Lamb, eds. 2003. *Just Being Difficult? Academic Writing in the Public Arena*. Stanford: Stanford University Press.
Duffy, William. 2016. Review of *After Pedagogy: The Experience of Teaching* by Paul Lynch. *Journal of Teaching Writing* 31 (2): 89–95.
Faigley, Lester. 2000. "Veterans' Stories on the Porch." In *History, Reflection, and Narrative: The Professionalization of Composition, 1963–1983*, edited by Mary Rosner, Beth Boehm, and Debra Journet, 23–37. Stamford, CT: Ablex.
Hindman, Jane E. 2003. "Thoughts on Reading 'the Personal': Toward a Discursive Ethics of Professional Critical Literacy." *College English* 66 (1): 9–20.
Journet, Debra. 2012. "Narrative Turns in Writing Studies Research." In *Writing Studies Research in Practice*, edited by Lee Nickoson and Mary P. Sheridan. Carbondale: Southern Illinois University Press.
Journet, Debra, Beth Boehm, and Mary Rosner. 2000. Introduction to *History, Reflection, and Narrative: The Professionalization of Composition, 1963–1983*, edited by Mary Rosner, Beth Boehm, and Debra Journet, xiii–xxiii. Stamford, CT: Ablex.
Lynch, Paul. 2013. *After Pedagogy: The Experience of Teaching*. CCCC Studies in Writing and Rhetoric. Urbana, IL: CCCC/NCTE.
Miller, Richard. 2005. *Writing at the End of the World*. Pittsburgh, PA: University of Pittsburgh Press.
Miller, Susan. 1991. *Textual Carnivals: The Politics of Composition*. Carbondale: Southern Illinois University Press.
North, Stephen. 1987. *The Making of Knowledge in Composition: Portrait of an Emerging Field*. Upper Montclair, NJ: Boynton.
Olson, Gary, and Todd Taylor. 1997. *Publishing in Rhetoric and Composition*. Albany: SUNY Press.
Roen, Duane, Stuart Brown, and Theresa Enos, eds. 1999. *Living Rhetoric and Composition: Stories of the Discipline*. Mahwah, NJ: Lawrence Erlbaum.
Taylor, March, and Jennifer Holberg. 1999. "'Tales of Neglect and Sadism': Disciplinarity and the Figuring of the Graduate Student in Composition." *College Composition and Communication* 50 (4): 607–25.

11
COLLAGING THE CLASSROOM, THE PERSONAL, AND THE CRITICAL
Autoethnographic Writing in the National Writing Project

Trixie G. Smith

This collage essay argues through example, story, and theory that the practice of autoethnography has always been alive and well in National Writing Project sites. NWP has three goals for teachers: to see themselves as writers, to see themselves as teachers of writing (no matter the discipline or age of students), and to see themselves as teacher leaders and professionals who (can/do) theorize their writing and their work with students and in the greater world. The Invitational Summer Institute is a key moment in which participants are invited to write and think and make connections. As autoethnography does, NWP Teacher Consultants (TCs) use their personal composing as methodology to interrogate their writing skills, their critical standpoint as teachers/writers/humans, and their reflections on experiences both within and outside the classroom with the aim of making connections they can/do share with others at various levels.

Writing about themselves is never really just writing about themselves; it's also about politics, social issues, and family dynamics.

It Just Is
I am fifty-one, queer, and female
Born in the Southern Baptist Church where they don't believe in that same-sex stuff
But their disbelief doesn't erase my desire or my love for my wife
Their label of sin doesn't make my marriage license less legal or somehow different
It just is

I believe in a God who is love and light and truthfulness
I don't believe she sits around judging and disclaiming; she has better things to do
But my disbelief doesn't make these Christians more loving or understanding

My label of sin doesn't stop their exclusion or hate speech or political drive
I suppose, it just is

My daughter is three, bi-racial, with two mommies
Born in abandonment, but chosen through love and thankfulness
She's the belief, the hope, that bridges this gap—making opposing forces
    deal with each other and move forward
A lot of weight for one little girl, but she carries it with lightness and grace
For her, love just is.

The summer of 2016 was my first year back facilitating an Invitational Summer Institute (ISI), the heart of the National Writing Project (NWP) model. I had spent the past nine months getting to know the Red Cedar Writing Project (RCWP), which I became director of in 2015 after the founding director retired. I had cofounded my own site more than ten years earlier and was eager to get back to NWP work, particularly the writing time it afforded leaders and participants.

That summer, having just married my partner less than a year after it became legal to do so, all my writing seemed to revolve around my daughter and our newly formed family. But my daughter, wife, and family were a source of happiness and celebration for me; why were my writings so serious? Depressing even? I continued to reflect on this conundrum as I moved into the fall term teaching queer rhetorics to graduate students with their own personal and theoretical tensions, compounded by the outcome of the presidential election that fall. The outrage and protests that moved us into 2017 were accompanied by the teaching of Cultural Rhetorics, a course I teach as methodology, which includes critical autoethnography as an influence.[1] We spent several weeks reading and analyzing autoethnography, dissecting methods of writing it and the arguments embedded in the stories, and reflecting on the theoretical stances revealed through narrative.[2]

It was this moment in Cultural Rhetorics when it all crystallized for me. In the ISI, we weren't just asking teachers to write about their classrooms and theorize about their teaching. We were asking them to analyze and theorize their experiences, their beliefs, their lives. The happiness I experienced with my nontraditional family was a queer reflection of the heteronormative social/cultural expectations that surrounded us, as well as the policies and laws that governed our lives. It also highlighted for me the struggles that still remained for so many others, our trans kin for example, as well as the fear of new rights being taken away under a new political regime. Not a binary but a full continuum of emotions and reactions that came with just living our queer lives.

Writing about themselves is never really just writing about themselves; it's also about struggle, pain, and embodied experiences.

* * *

In their introduction to *Critical Autoethnography: Intersecting Cultural Identities in Everyday Life*, Robin M. Boylorn and Mark P. Orbe (2014) note that their edited collection "benefits from the foundations of autoethnography and intersectionality . . . making the link between our heads and hearts possible" (11). They further explain that for them the goal of autoethnography is to invite readers into the lived experience of others, especially those presumed to be "Other." They want readers to understand, experience viscerally, the embodied experiences of their authors, and consequently they do not distinguish doing research from living life (15).

That same claim is made and showcased throughout this essay, which combines personal experiences and writings with reflections and writings from RCWP ISI participants, arguments from NWP teacher-researchers and sometimes their research participants, writing advice from authors we read in the ISI, and autoethnographic authors and theorizers. It is my hope you will see the presence of the NWP teachers/researchers/leaders/participants in this personal-professional collection of snapshots from the work of RCWP.

* * *

In *Teachers at the Center: A Memoir of the Early Years of the National Writing Project*, James Gray (2000), founding director of the National Writing Project, describes the writing projects the facilitators asked teachers to do in the first few summer institutes and the value the projects had for the teachers. He admits to being "surprised and a bit bewildered when they would rate their own experience with writing as the most important part of the summer institute" (84). Gray explains that while giving teachers the freedom to write whatever they want, "we do suggest a structure that includes four major pieces of writing, the first three on a topic of personal choice with no two pieces alike, an assignment that typically moves the writer from a personal experience to an essay about some idea inherent in the initial experience. . . . The fourth and final assignment could be either a policy statement on the teaching of writing that expresses the teacher's current thinking, an article on teaching writing to be submitted for publication, or a working draft of a school writing policy that could be presented to colleagues for their reactions and contributions" (85). What soon occurred was a developmental linking of the four assignments.

Fred Zook, an early participant, exemplifies this process. He first wrote a set of short descriptive pieces about the small town in Kansas he left behind when he moved to California. He then recreated letters from his family's past that described Kansas when it was still a territory. His third piece was a one-act play about a farmer and his wife recalling their move from being struggling family-farmers to wealthy landowners. His final piece was a personal essay about the changes and growth in the agricultural industry (Gray 2000, 85–86). Another participant turned her personal story about the tragic shooting of her brother-in-law policeman, as well as other shooting stories shared in her writing group, to an argument for gun control. Yet another participant turned her reflection about journal usage in her class into a position paper for her school about the rationale for using classroom journals, complete with strategies and pedagogical effectiveness (87).

The process Gray illustrates in his text and in his coaching of other NWP directors/leaders exemplifies many of the autoethnographic characteristics described by Cheryl Le Roux (2017) and Laurel Richardson (2000) and presented in appendix A of the introduction to this collection. While autoethnography was not a named method or product in the 70s and 80s when the National Writing Project was establishing itself, the moves of autoethnography as codified in this text were certainly being enacted by the project as a whole and by the teachers who were experiencing the summer institute.

Writing about themselves is never really just writing about themselves; it's also about public policies and fights for change, it's about trauma and dreams for a better life.

A MOMENT THAT MATTERS
by Caitlin Pebble, RCWP ISI 2016 participant

"I took her out and that bitch wouldn't sleep with me," Sam, one of my boyfriend's best friends, grumbled with an air of self-pity. His shaggy, dark hair showed all the signs of bedhead; his pale cheeks and dark under-eye circles told me he was hungover. The maroon athletic shorts and Spartan green t-shirt that fit loosely around his stocky frame reminded me of his sloth-like manner. They reminded me of how little effort he seemed to put into his appearance and life's obstacles in general.

"Wait, why is she a bitch? Just because she didn't want to sleep with you on the first date?" my hostile inquiry was out in the open.

"Well, she could have told me that before I wasted time and money." Sam looked me right in the eye. His voice carried the boisterous tone of one who was performing a monologue. "I could have fucked Kelsey instead." Why was there a sense of sympathy for Sam in the room around me? Why were these guys nodding along empathetically, like they all had been there too? Poor Sam. He didn't get any last night. Instead of vomiting my hot, hateful words, I swallowed them.

Later, driving home with Jack in my passenger seat, I couldn't pretend what I had witnessed wasn't still replaying in my mind. I had wanted my 6'3" knight in shining armor to ride in on his white horse and save me. He hadn't shown up. "Jack, why didn't you SAY anything?!" I demanded as I braked at the flashing red light before turning left.

"What do you mean?" he questioned defensively. He pretended like he didn't know what I was talking about. How could he not remember?

"Do you guys really sit around and talk like that when I'm not there? Do you really think it's okay for Sam to say things like that about girls? Do you agree with him?" I crescendoed with each accusation. I stole a glance at Jack's face and saw a shadow of annoyance darken his eyes.

Jack stated sourly, "Caitlin, Sam was joking. He's not like that. You should know better."

"Well, if he's 'not like that,' then why did he decide to act like that? You can't just sit there and let him speak that way. If you don't stand up and tell Sam it's wrong, he's never going to think that anything he said was wrong!" I was incredulous. How could my boyfriend, the man I entrusted with my very soul, not understand? An angry tear escaped the corner of my eye. How dare it give me away.

"Jesus, Caitlin! Stop overreacting. It was a joke. Get over it." He was done with the conversation. He was done with me.

That night, I stared at my reflection in the bathroom mirror. I looked the same as I had that morning. The same as I had four years ago, before my virginity was stolen. I wish I could stop reacting. I wish I could command that I get over it. I wish declaring myself cured would make it so. I wish the same for thousands of other girls. But we can't. Because it's not a joke. It's rape.

* * *

NWP Core Principles

The core principles at the foundation of the National Writing Project's national program (2018) model are:

- Teachers at every level—from kindergarten through college—are the agents of reform; . . .
- Writing can and should be taught, not just assigned, at every grade level. Professional development programs should provide

- opportunities for teachers to work together to understand the full spectrum of writing development across grades and across subject areas.
- Knowledge about the teaching of writing comes from many sources: theory and research, the analysis of practice, and the experience of writing. . . .
- There is no single right approach to teaching writing; however, . . . a reflective and informed community of practice is in the best position to design and develop comprehensive writing programs.
- Teachers who are well informed and effective in their practice can be successful teachers of other teachers as well as partners in educational research, development, and implementation. Collectively, teacher-leaders are our greatest resource for educational reform.

* * *

Writing about themselves is never really just writing about themselves; it's also about teaching, challenges, celebrations, learning, growth.

* * *

The social practices embedded in NWP professional development not only build community but also encourage intellectual development. What might seem simple at first glance turns out to be a complex intertwining of process and content, the personal and the professional, the individual and the collective, the intellectual and the social, the short term and the long haul (Lieberman and Wood 2003, 100).

Sue Doe, Kira Marshall-McKelvey, Lilly Halboth, Ross Atkinson, Caleb Gonzalez, and Jennifer Owen (this collection, chapter 9) explain that "through autoethnography some offer the gift of their stories of struggle; they risk sharing those stories with others" (146) and thus it is our responsibility to respond to these stories in concrete ways. She and her graduate students saw autoethnography as a method for crossing borderlands, bringing the personal into the professional domain, pushing against traditional research methods and standard academic genres. Similarly, writing project teachers bring "critical self-reflexivity and increased understanding of positionality as a central component of research and its writing" as well as its application in their own lives and teaching jobs.

* * *

Troy Hicks, Anne Elrod Whitney, James Fredricksen, and Leah Zuidema (2017), all writing project teacher consultants and teacher-leaders, describe teacher-writers as "reflective practitioners" who use their writing to do things for their students and their own teaching, as well as the field of teaching, or perhaps even the world. They are "skillful, intentional, creative, thoughtful, curious, and passionate" (1). These are teacher-writers who have things "they want to write and say to others in forums and forms that are often new to them" (13).[3]

Christine Dawson (2017), also an NWP teacher-leader, likewise writes about teacher-writers. She explains that much of the writing that occurred in the writing groups she studied began with personal narratives and poetry: "We are experts, after all, on our own experiences, so generating personal content sometimes comes more easily" (53). The writing rarely stops there though. She goes on to show how teacher-writers find ideas for writing all around them while also expanding their ideas of what it means to be a writer, expanding ideas of the writing they actually do on a regular basis, reclaiming, for example, professional documents and tasks. Over time, the two become integrated, and then true autoethnography begins: the personal becomes the professional and vice versa; one is used to argue for and illustrate the other.

* * *

Writing about themselves is never really just writing about themselves; it's also about reflections, connections, belief.

* * *

Linda was an interview participant in an NWP study conducted by Ann Lieberman and Diane Wood (2003). During her interview, Linda claimed that "learning to write, learning to teach others to write, and learning to teach teachers all required the same processes" (75). When pressed to be more specific she had three points:

1. All learners come with different experiences and abilities but must "be treated as if they have something of value to say to others" (75).

2. Learning requires reflection: through NWP she "came across teacher lore, that is, teachers writing about experiences in the classroom" (75). She believed "this practice deepens teachers' capacities for self-critique" (76).

3. "Learners need to take ownership over their own learning. If teachers are really going to engage in professional learning, she contended, then they need to 'own' both what they already know and what they have yet to know in order to be better teachers" (76).

Linda embodies the call for autoethnographic writing in the NWP. She moves back and forth between the personal and professional, with both her students and teaching colleagues, and she uses both to sustain her teaching and writing, as well as her relationships with colleagues. As

NWP instructs through its core principals, she uses her personal writing and reflection to move towards reform, starting in her own classroom and moving outward. Lieberman and Wood (2003) note, "Writing produces occasions to foreground and clarify thinking; to record, shape, and analyze experiences; to express internal lives; to explore ideas learned from others. Writers have opportunities to discern both what they understand and what they have yet to learn" (19).

* * *

RCWP ISI 2017 REFLECTION
by high-school teacher Melanie Lounds
I am open to sharing very personal material and feel refreshed through giving my time to writing. I want feedback and want to be able to touch people's lives. One way I hope to do that is through my writing, writing short pieces that my neighbors will appreciate. I imagine that if I touch one person's soul in a positive way then I am in fact living a true life, one I can be proud of at the end of my days. . . . As a teacher and a writer, my voice is active in education.

* * *

Writing about themselves is never really just writing about themselves; it's also about reflections, connections, belief.

* * *

THIS I BELIEVE/SACRED WRITING MASH
by Wonderful Faison, RCWP participant, ISI 2017
I believe I should not have to constantly state my beliefs. I live in an academic world where positionality, who and why and why should we care must constantly be articulated. I don't state my beliefs, I am busy. Above all: know thine self. And had I not known myself (or enough of myself) by 30, no amount of elitist academic rhetorical positioning of the self will help me know myself.

THIS: I believe

I believe in stating the obvious: Racism, sexism, homophobia, xenophobia, transphobia (and the like) are a thing. A thing that I need not articulate. A thing that when I have to (positionality bullshit [need a thesis for the thesis asshole reviewer rhetoric]) articulate the obvious I am flung into a fury. The academy is maddening

I interject

As I sit here in another academic meeting that really shoulda been an email, I begin to think about rat races. And *how every damn job in the*

capitalist system is a rat race. Academic life is a race. In grad school, faculty tell you it's a marathon, not a sprint
  Rather, Trixie tells me this, but she knows I do not believe her.
In the meeting we are discussing how to better serve the needs of POC.
  But I'm here wondering why I'm the only Person of Color in the room. And why does the only Person of Color in the room have to be Black? Is that that weird and problematic Black/White binary shit? Get America's MOST oppressed body to sit in the room while you theorize your good intentions around her? I'm done
We talk about how we should "value" and learn from culture. And how do we show our students of color that we value their experience?
  I swear fo' God if I hear value one more goddamned time—
  I interject
What have the students of color said their issues were?
Well, the data
  Ah damn, here we go with some fuckin retention data bout colored folk not excelling in a class
suggests that our students of Color are not achieving
  God no, please don't say it
"to the same standards as their peers"
  You ass. God damn it, I subliminally messaged you to tell you NOT to say what you thinking. I'm finna to go off, now.
  I interject
While I understand your numbers, what's going on in the syllabus?
Why do you have Black people reading Harry Potter? I mean, some Black person somewhere might like Harry Potter
  who this Black person is I do not know but I will quickly introduce said person to Ms. Sophia, Celie, Shaft, Foxxy Brown, and Dolimite, but not Blackula, Blackula was just horrible. I continue
But I think the real issue here is so much of the syllabus content shows a clear catering to the interests of the dominant culture.
Ah, so we should add more texts from and by POC in the syllabus.
  No numb nuts, well, yes numb nut, but no. Gooooooooood, stop being reductive.
  I interject
Well, that's a good start for sure.
Oh good. Because we have a plan and this [random white male faculty member] is working on racial diversity in this course, so this will help.
  What the actual fuck? How will that help. U sending Howdy Doody to solve this? Dear God—
  I interject
I suggest we find a Critical Race Theorist for this; they may be able to give him far more resources than I can.

Critical Race Theorists? I dunno if we have one of those in the department

Oh, we got a few in the department and on campus, *like me muthafucka*

Well who do u suggest?

I do not interject

THIS: I also believe

I believe in education. I always have. I believe education traumatizes people. It always has. I believe we cannot educate without trauma—because we must indoctrinate (er—socialize, I mean). I believe I am indoctrinated into a doctrine of which I am not sure I concur. PhD

Doctor of Philosophy

Doctorate, Doctrine, Indoctrinate—these are the root words

THIS: I believe

* * *

In any case, the bottom line is that if you want to write, you get to, but you probably won't be able to get very far if you don't start trying to get over your perfectionism. . . . What people somehow (inadvertently, I'm sure) forgot to mention when we were children was that we need to make messes in order to find out who we are and why we are here—and, by extension, what we're supposed to be writing (Lamott 1994, 31–32).

William Duffy explains in chapter 10 of this collection that inviting graduate students to assert their own positions and identities in the field through autoethnography is a method of building confidence and, over time, of developing more nuanced accounts of their experiences in the field of writing studies. They are invited to work through the messiness of their day-to-day as they write and revise. The same is true of teachers in the NWP, professionals who have often been silenced in their jobs, particularly about their own expertise in the classroom and their experiences with students. Inviting them to write through their day-to-day both in and out of the classroom also builds these teachers' confidence levels and helps them better understand and theorize their practice(s) as teacher-writers and teacher-leaders.

PER- (A FOUND POEM FROM "PERFECTIONISM," A CHAPTER IN *BIRD BY BIRD* BY ANNE LAMOTT)

Amy Cottrill, RCWP ISI 2017 participant

You set out to tell a story
To tell the truth as you feel it

Something is calling you
Go ahead

Perfectionism

Find out who we are
Why we are here
We need to make messes
Messes are the artist's true friend

Perfectionism

Held breath
Suspended animation
Clutter and mess
Will ruin your writing

Perfectionism

I needed
A prescription for painkillers
A little mixed grill of drugs
For experiencing life in a naked and immediate way

Perfectionism

Uptight, judgmental, perfectionist
Run carefully
Hitting each steppingstone just right
Will only drive you mad
The aromatic smoke crooks its finger
I notice a life force
I begin to chew it
With great hostility and skepticism

Perseverance

Get a grip

* * *

Writing about themselves is never really just writing about themselves; it's also about process, identity, anger, secrets revealed, lessons.

* * *

I AM FROM INK
Tania de Sostoa-McCue, RCWP ISI 2017 participant

I am the browning thistle patch,
An overabundance of forsythia,

The white home without personality.
I am chrysanthemums and lilies
Colors clenched tight from spring to fall.

I am from ink

From compressed anger
From "your mother is sick" to exposure,
Exposure to the breaking apart of lies.

I am from alcoholism,
I am from Catholicism.

I held death in my fingers
His hand in mine, his last breath indelible
His death holding on so tight.

I am the ink

I am agnosticism.
I don't trust belief.

I am boxes of 100-year-old letters from Shanghai and Argentina
Spain and South Africa
I am superstition, salt over the shoulder.
Arepa Sundays, trips to Mexican town
For the perfect queso blanco

I am from São Paulo and Spain
churrascaria, the remembrance
Of six-year-old fingers and feet, a wooden
floor and Xucha, pão de queijo pilfered from the table
As I danced.

I am the ink

I am stolen pictures hidden under my mother's table
I am unrecorded stories
Women's invisible lives,
Lifelines unmarked.

I will be the ink.

Edie's escape, isolation,
drowning in Popov and bitterness
Monica's stories of the Blitz, of faux stockings during times of ration.
I am from Eloise without knowing,
Margaret's secret mental breakdown at seventeen.

I am women whose stories I may never know
I am from the ink.

I will be the ink.
I am the ink.
The storyteller.

* * *

Anne Lamott (1994) advises writers to put themselves and their beliefs at the core of their writing: "The core, ethical concepts in which you most passionately believe are the language in which you are writing" (103). She also advises that this writing takes time and space: "Your whole piece is the truth, not just one shining epigrammatic moment in it. There will need to be some kind of unfolding in order to contain it, and there will need to be layers. We are dealing with the ineffable here—we're out there somewhere between the known and the unknown" (104).

* * *

In *Evocative Autoethnography: Writing Lives and Telling Stories*, Arthur P. Bochner and Carolyn Ellis (2016) "teach" a workshop on how to do and write autoethnography. The narrator Art has this to say in the end, referring to the collage or mosaic art that graces the cover of their book: "Donald Kuspit refers to collage as 'a demonstration of the many becoming the one, with the one never fully resolved because of the many that continue to impinge upon it' (Kuspit 2000, 128). As we've indicated through-out the workshop, evocative autoethnography keeps the possibilities of connection between the one and the many in play, highlighting the never finished, continually becoming, qualities of means in motion. What we see, think, and feel about what we've lived through continues to evolve rather than resolve" (268).

"Collage also shares a feeling kind of truth with autoethnography," Bochner continues. "It invites viewers to rearrange the fragmented materials. Those observing participate by giving form to connections they themselves make among and with the materials. The result is a kind of subjective concreteness activated by viewers, which also is what we seek from readers of autoethnography" (Bochner and Ellis 2016, 268).

* * *

Writing about themselves is never really just writing about themselves; and reading is never just about the text.

NOTES

1. In particular, we read multiple selections from *Critical Autoethnography: Intersecting Cultural Identities in Everyday Life, edited by* Robin M. Boylorn, and Mark P. Orbe (2014), a superb selection that showcases a wide variety of writing styles and topics for discussion and emulation. I also recommend *Evocative Autoethnography: Writing Lives and Telling Stories* by Arthur P. Bochner and Carolyn Ellis (2016).
2. We were also reading texts like Thomas King's *The Truth about Stories: A Native Narrative* (University of 2003) and Shawn Wilson's *Research Is Ceremony: Indigenous Research Methods* (2008), both of which helped us look at a constellation of theories, perspectives, and stories in order to provide and/or get at the bigger, more complete, but never whole, picture.
3. Hicks et al. (2017) are also intentional about the term *teacher-writer*, building out from the traditional NWP vision of teacher as writer. "We see the 'teachers as writers' construction as limiting. Teachers as writers puts our colleagues smack in the middle of a simile, as if teachers can pretend to be writers, or can be writers only in some contexts" (xii). They also see the teachers-as-writers image as grounded in the process-oriented pedagogy of the 1970s and 80s. This writing-workshop model was important at the launch of the NWP. Soon, however, the 1990s and 2000s saw the push for teacher-researchers who wrote about inquiry and research as forms of professional development for the field and themselves. Hicks et al. now argue for a third phase, which is in place today and gaining momentum—advocacy. Educational reform, mostly in the form of privatization and testing in the 2000s and 2010s, has created a context where "teachers write as a form of activism and resistance," which also means they are writing for a much broader and more diverse audience (7–8).

REFERENCES

Bochner, Arthur P., and Carolyn Ellis. 2016. *Evocative Autoethnography: Writing Lives and Telling Stories*. New York: Routledge.

Boylorn, Robin M., and Mark P. Orbe, eds. 2014. *Critical Autoethnography: Intersecting Cultural Identities in Everyday Life*. New York: Routledge.

Dawson, Christine M. 2017. *The Teacher-Writer: Creating Writing Groups for Personal and Professional Growth*. New York: Teachers College Press.

Gray, James. 2000. *Teachers at the Center: A Memoir of the Early Years of the National Writing Project*. Berkeley, CA: National Writing Project.

Hicks, Troy, Anne Elrod Whitney, James Fredricksen, and Leah Zuidema. 2017. *Coaching Teacher-Writers: Practical Steps to Nurture Professional Writing*. New York: Teachers College Press.

Lamott, Anne. 1994. *Bird by Bird: Some Instructions on Writing and Life*. New York: Random House.

Lieberman, Ann, and Diane R. Wood. 2003. *Inside the National Writing Project: Connecting Network Learning and Classroom Teaching*. New York: Teachers College Press.

National Writing Project. 2018. "Core Principles." https://archive.nwp.org/cs/public/print/doc/about.csp.

Powell, Malea, Daisy Levy, Andrea Riley-Muskavetz, Marilee Brooks-Gillies, Maria Novotny, and Jennifer Fisch-Ferguson. 2014. "Our Story Begins Here: Constellating Cultural Rhetorics." *Enculturation: A Journal of Rhetoric, Writing, and Culture*, October 2014. http://enculturation.net/our-story-begins-here.

Richardson, Laurel. 2000. "Evaluating Ethnography." *Qualitative Inquiry* 6 (2): 253–55.

PART THREE

Extending Writing Studies Autoethnography

12
YOU CAN'T DO THAT HERE
Black/Feminist Autoethnography and Histories of Intellectual Exclusion

Louis M. Maraj

It's fall 2017, and while prepping for the onslaught of the academic job market and finishing my dissertation, I'm advised to shop my Black im/migrant autoethnography chapter to journals.[1] My advisor enthusiastically prompts me to aim for top venues in rhetoric and writing studies. Autoethnography could "sell" my project. My stories on being confronted by questions of racial legibility and institutional violence are ready for sharing. I review journals, research fits for the project, and settle on a largely traditional writing studies venue. My advisor believes the journal should welcome something radically different from its usual fare. I send off my essay that not only tells various stories about im/migrant Blackness but also carefully plots a Black/feminist tradition of autoethnographic work in rhetoric, writing, and literacy studies. The response, which comes quickly, details the very aspects of disciplinary anti-Blackness the essay pushes against.

The editor of this journal sends a desk rejection of the essay, but it's not just the usual boilerplate letter. No, this white woman editor defensively spends a lengthy parenthetical paragraph to explain just why my autoethnography is, in fact, not valid research. The method and genre of the piece apparently do not align with the journal's focus on research. The editor wonders about my methodology—the piece couldn't possibly be published without Institutional Review Board (IRB) approval. In the assumption I didn't have such approval, whether intentional or not, an act of criminalization takes place. The editor infers I didn't go through the process already—so, without asking, this white woman professor simply presumes I was attempting to skirt the rules. There's no question to answer—they automatically believe I did not seek or possess approval for my use of "data." It did not matter that I already had such permissions. While the rhetoric of this demeaning letter suggests a white fragility about turning down the essay, this editor also prompts me—in possible revision—to pick a side: the essay struggles between wanting to be creative or analytical. A choice must be made here, suggesting a misunderstanding of the very move autoethnography attempts to make to blur the lines between binary perceptions of how knowledge making happens.

What follows adds insult to insult or maybe injury to injury. What seems like the editor's standard form letter outlines "how to write a research essay," following the traditional seven-step model I'm sure we're all familiar with. It explains the model as formulaic but worthwhile. I'm thrown completely by the response. Not only does the push to a systematic model of writing indicate that at the upper tiers of disciplinary knowledge making we still yield to a five-paragraph-essay-like mindset, it also intimates that grown academics submitting to the journal might not be familiar with such models. To judge an apple by an orange's standards reflects a disconnect between where the fields of rhetoric and writing studies have traditionally been and where they might go. As Carmen Kynard (2015) shows, though, our publication apparatuses affirm the racists roots on which our fields stands (3). From the editor's assumption about the ethics of my data collection, to their proposed alternative between creative nonfiction and analytical research essay in revision, to the insinuation that a Black im/migrant remains unaware of the precut formulas for research writing that still form the basis of dominant pedagogies, we can see the distinct hegemonic circumstances autoethnography—and particularly Black and Black feminist autoethnography—faces in finding validation in our fields.

In this chapter, I use this backdrop as the basis for digging into an intellectual history of these marginalizing moves when it comes to autoethnographic texts by Black knowledge makers. I approach the temporal question of the past's relevance to the current reception of Black feminist autoethnography through what Christina Sharpe (2016) calls "the wake"—an understanding of Blackness in a past that is a now in the afterlives of slavery. To do so, I travel backward to call contemporary attention to nineteenth-century US Black women writers and orators whose personal texts about their positionality's intersections with culture laid the groundwork for a Black and Black feminist tradition of autoethnography in the fields of rhetoric, writing, and literacy studies. These texts and the Black women who produced them were, and still are, dismissed through intellectual exclusion—like this white woman editor's dismissal of my tracing of Black/feminist autoethnography in those fields—as unworthy of scholarly attention. However, they have much to teach us about the Black feminist roots, aesthetics, and rhetorics of autoethnography. In highlighting these roots and their communicative technologies, I show the distinct social justice-oriented potentials of autoethnography as a mode for writing studies.

BLACKNESS, REASON, SUBJECTIVITY

Blackness in the Western world arose through the trans-Atlantic slave trade as a concept for justifying the dominating violence of colonialism and capitalism. As postcolonial theorist Achille Mbembe (2017) highlights, white colonialists' goals to conceptualize Black bodies and the difference their Blackness represented as less-than-human objects were formulated with an understanding of these bodies as bereft of "reason." Mbembe explains that when "confronted with the question of Black and Africa, reason found itself ruined and emptied, turning constantly in on itself, shipwrecked in a seemingly inaccessible place where language was destroyed and words themselves no longer had memory" (13). Charting a history for Black autoethnography as I had attempted to do with my study in the previous anecdote, then, was to defy this logic—asking, How can a tradition of Black creative intellectualism exist when Black words and stories conjure no memory? Even today, when these subjects (Blackness and Africa) arise, "words do not necessarily represent things; the true and the false become inextricable; the signification of the sign is not always adequate to what is being signified" (13). Given these histories of Blackness's marginalization and their contemporary manifestations, we might begin to grasp why the white woman editor above questions the truth and ethics of my stories as the basis for autoethnographic thought. To give importance to self-reflective stories about Blackness—to Black testimony—in their white journal would mean a clear demarcation of what might be considered "true" of lived Black experience (and the systemic racism that comes with it). The move to question the ethics of data collection, then, spotlights for this editor the "questionable" methodology of my Black autoethnography while providing grounds for dismissing my testimonial as unverifiable. When I ask a senior white male faculty member in my graduate program if journals regularly assume studies do not have required permission in considering them for publication, he explains he has never been asked for such proof. To legitimize my lived experience of Blackness and Black immigrant-ness, then, I must show my papers. The burden of proving legality, of proving humanity, becomes the work of the Black body, as it has been historically.

This reliance on legal approval for my project (and the assumption that I did not have it) summons ideas about the fraught relationships between US legal systems and Blackness and the philosophical offspring of such relationships. Here is where we should pay close mind to how white law historically treated (and treats) Black women's bodies and the physical and cultural products produced by such bodies. In English colonies, the legal doctrine of *partus sequitur ventrem* dictated that a child born to a woman in slavery would inherit the position of slave from their mother, in contrast to Anglo-European ideologies in which legal status of a child followed the father. This doctrine meant that Black women, literally through their wombs, produced Blackness and the subjugated social position of slavehood. As race and gender as markers of difference evolved through cultural constructions tied to notions of the physical body, so did social conceptions of Black women's position in society. Black women historically carried/on the mark of slave through their physical and cultural products, always raced and gendered as oppressed. As Sharpe (2016) spotlights, living in the wake of slavery means "that inheritance of a non/status is everywhere apparent now in the ongoing criminalization of Black women and children" (15) Kimberlé Crenshaw's (1991) conceptualization of intersectionality derives particularly from the ways the law operates to subjugate Black women because of their complex social positions in relation to identity and personhood. Black women's cultural products, then, under the gaze of white institutions, always already occupy a space outside the boundaries of personhood—devalued, nonhuman, and illegitimate. Their attempts at articulating subjective experience through autoethnographic texts suffer the same fate.

Writing as a technology in the Western world emerged as a marker of reason in opposition to those technologies of "primitive societies . . . governed by . . . 'savage mentality'" (Mbembe 2017, 42). The articulation of subjectivity through writing provided a civilizing force for European potentates to shape "individuals" out of these primitive mindsets after the abolition of slavery. Education provided a basis for this assimilation. The educated former slave, like the colonized African, "could receive and enjoy rights, not by virtue of belonging to a particular group, but because of their status as autonomous subjects capable of thinking for themselves and exercising that particular human faculty that is reason" (87). The aim of such education was to erase difference through a universalization of humanity via subjectivity—I think therefore I am, as the white fathers proclaim. But, in formulating a self through reflective writing, Black women, in historically/culturally existing outside the category of human, as producers of difference itself, find themselves still outside this genre of Western Man. In the afterlives of slavery, their autoethnographic writing necessarily squares the personal with the political. Black feminist thought, which materialized to describe these politics through the Combahee River Collective (2017) and other activist groups and scholars, demonstrates this idea, as it promotes the notion that when Black women get free, all oppressed identities will simultaneously get free. Since autoethnography works at the junctures of the personal and the political, of self and culture, of creative and analytic, we can see how Black feminist autoethnography becomes vital to how it "strives for social justice" (Adams, Jones, and Ellis 2015, 2). Black feminist autoethnography shows "people in the process of figuring out what to do, how to live and the meaning of their struggles" (Bochner and Ellis 2006, 111).

Mary Louise Pratt's (1991) definition of autoethnography as writing that incorporates one's native language along with the "idioms of the metropolis or the conqueror" (35)—while aimed at both one's home community and that conqueror's—pinpoints this intersection between the personal and the political. In using the language of the oppressor in order to be legitimized as a knowledge maker, autoethnography's resistant qualities lie in the ways one disruptively challenges dominant discourse to imagine one's subject position in relation to that dominance (via language, institutions, or identity). Tony E. Adams, Stacy Holman Jones, and Carolyn Ellis (2015) argue that "autoethnographic stories—are stories of/about the self told through the lens of culture" (1). According to these scholars, however, these stories differ from memoirs, personal diaries and journals (online and offline), and even autobiographies in that they overtly "seek to contribute to a scholarly conversation" (Adams, Jones, and Ellis 2015, 36–37). In acknowledging how the academy and what is determined to be scholarly might be raced, classed, and gendered in order to keep out Black women and other marginalized identities by presuming them incompetent, (Gutiérrez y Muhs et al. 2012), it might be useful here to open up this definition further. We might usefully understand how early autoethnographies—particularly early US Black feminist autoethnographic texts—might be not just scholarly conversations but directed at wider society's hegemonic denial of humanity to those outside its normative bounds. Widening Adams, Jones, and Ellis's (2015) definition via Pratt (1991) in this way offers ways to read the rhetorics and aesthetics of Black women's personal writing and how that writing goes about envisioning more just worlds. In the following section, I re/visit Black women's writing from the nineteenth century, specifically early US Black women's writing, to work through these communicative technologies.[2]

That venture emphasizes social justice possibilities for autoethnographic writing based in Black feminist traditions.

BLACK FEMINIST AUTOETHNOGRAPHIC RHETORICS AND AESTHETICS

As Alicia Griffin (2012) contends, spotlighting Black feminist autoethnography "renders Black women more visible in the realm of autoethnography, which in the academy is more often associated with and published by White women" (143.) In a footnote, Griffin points us to an unrecognized tradition of Black feminist autoethnography, explaining that

> Black female activists and scholars such as Sojourner Truth, Harriet Jacobs, Maria Stewart, Anna Julia Cooper, Ida B. Wells-Barnett, Zora Neale Hurston, Fannie Lou Hamer, Ella Baker, Maya Angelou, Alice Walker, Toni Morrison, bell hooks, June Jordan, Angela Davis, Michelle Wallace, Audre Lorde, Barbara Smith, Barbara Ransby, Beverly Guy-Sheftall, Patricia Hill Collins, and innumerable others have been engaged in the art of rhetoric, narrative, and autoethnographic writing for years without the use of formal academic labels. (152)

Indeed, a lineage of Black and Black feminist autoethnographic texts dates back to well before its validation by the academy. And while I have worked to situate this tradition in rhetoric, writing, and literacy studies elsewhere (particularly in relation to Black feminists of the 1970s–90s like hooks, Jordan, and Lorde), going deeper into the past might help us to even further situate that tradition within a longer US Black and Black feminist autoethnographic lineage.

Through the essays of Maria W. Stewart ([1831] 1987), Jacqueline Jones Royster (2000) points out how Black US women, even in 1831, understood both the powerful possibilities for language and learning and the violence of life in the United States (108). On the connections among subject position, humanity, and the institution of trans-Atlantic slavery, Stewart cries out in her essay "Religion and the Pure Principles of Morality," "O you daughters of Africa, awake! awake! arise! no longer sleep nor slumber, but distinguish yourselves. Show forth to the world that ye are endowed with noble and exalted faculties" (28). In this apostrophic address to fellow Black women, Stewart calls on them to recognize their intellect, underscoring the abolitionist idea that humanity proven through the ability to reason could convince white institutions of humanity's universality. The self-advocating exhortation to "awake!" and "arise!" embodies the African indigenous rhetoric of *nommo*, "the intense African belief in the potency of the word" (Gilyard and Banks 2018, 50). Geneva Smitherman explains (1977) that "no medicine, potion, or magic of any sort is considered effective without accompanying words" (78). In speaking life into "you daughters of Africa" through *nommo*, Stewart ([1831] 1987) acknowledges, "I speak as a dying mortal, to dying mortals" (28), perhaps conjuring her eventual material death along with the social death (Patterson 1982) associated with the conditions of the enslaved, this context acutely surrounding the essay. In Stewart's recognition of her subject position relative to such deaths and the potential for intellect to act as a means toward resistance, she demonstrates autoethnography's prioritization of lived experience as a technology of meaning making, a Black feminist epistemological tenet (Collins 2000, 257–60).

Sojourner Truth's famous "Ain't I a Woman?" speech delivered in May 1851 in Akron, Ohio, deploys similar direct address, especially in the version published in 1863 ([1863] 1889). In the titular phrase, Truth rhetorically asks her audience to rethink who gets to fit into the category of woman, declaring no one helps her into carriages, while pointing out she also bears the brunt of harsh manual labor and physical violence, as men do. Truth creates a dialogue through these questions, answering them herself, and even (reportedly) solicits a response from her audience when posing, "Den dey talks 'bout dis ting in de head; what dis dey call it?" (1889, 116). That "intellect" would be the interjecting response to this question sheds light on Truth's "use of dialogue in assessing knowledge claims" (Collins 2000, 260–62) that mobilizes the Black rhetoric of call and response (Gilyard and Banks 2018, 47–50). Truth asks the audience to name the concept that might be used as the basis for reasoning Black folk are human before immediately dismissing it as irrelevant to her articulation of humanity, effectively illustrating how the back and forth of these conversational devices furthers her claims. One such claim, in the 1851 version of the speech, declares "I am a woman's rights," a statement that distinctly folds together the personal and the political. By intersecting her African American Vernacular English with the political discourse of her day, Truth reveals how Black feminist autoethnographic texts can critique dominant notions of humanity and dominant language systems that oppress Black women.

Harriet Ann Jacobs's *Incidents in the Life of a Slave Girl*, first published in 1861, and known as autobiography, brings attention to the sexual assault Black women routinely faced in plantation life. But could we productively read Jacob's slave narrative as an autoethnographic text? In sketching the cultures of enslaved Black women, their customs and habits, the narrative does offer ethnographic descriptions of these women's lives while revealing an awareness of the dominance and violence of sociopolitical institutions impacting them. Jacobs exhibits a critical grasp of the politics of the institution of slavery, recalling how her grandmother loaned her mistresses some money and her mistress could easily take advantage of the loan: "The reader probably knows that no promise or writing given to a slave is legally binding; for, according to Southern laws, a slave, being property, can hold no property." This articulated consciousness of her and her grandmother's position in relation to the material impact of slave laws discloses Jacobs's knowledge of how these laws operated within quotidian exchanges to exploit Black women. Continuing to reflect on her childhood, Jacobs asserts, "The slave child had no thought for the morrow; but there came that blight, which too surely waits on every human being born to be a chattel." In considering how her individual situation reflected the overall circumstances of most US Black children around her, the autobiographic text takes an ethnographic leap to posture the author's experience as a matter of cultural custom.

Likewise, Dr. Anna Julia Cooper's 1892 *A Voice from the South: By a Black Woman of the South* digs into contemporaneous dominant ideologies using the frame of the author's personal experience to advocate for Black women's self-determination. Scholars like Margaret Busby (1992, 136) and Vivian May (2012) claim the volume as one of the first examples of Black feminist thought, the latter explaining that it "tackles the racialized, gendered, and classed meanings of personhood and citizenship" (61). In comparing the circumstances of English women and Black women in the US South, Cooper (1892) highlights—through cognizance of her positionality—the unextended allyship necessary for social uplift of Black southern women. The Black feminist pronounces that "English girls are dispirited and crushed by no such all-levelling prejudice as that supercilious caste spirit in America which cynically assumes 'a Negro woman cannot be a lady.' English womanhood is beset by no such snares and traps as betray the colored girl of the South, whose only crime and dire destruction often is her unconscious and marvelous beauty" (32). Through cross-cultural comparison, Cooper emphasizes the issues with the women's-rights movement while situating her own experience as the basis for such exploration. *A Voice* goes on to call for a kind of coalitional politics familiar to Black feminisms of the later twentieth and earlier twenty-first century in efforts toward gender and racial justice. Cooper (1892) contends, "'I am my sister's keeper!' should be the hearty response of every man and woman of every race and this conviction should purify and exalt the narrow, selfish, and petty personal aims of life into a noble and sacred purpose" (32). By calling out these women in particular, Cooper employs the Black feminist epistemological "ethic of personal accountability," through which, as Patricia Hill Collins (2000) suggests, it is "essential for individuals to have definite positions on issues and assume full responsibility for arguing their validity." In Cooper's dismissal of "narrow, selfish, and petty personal aims," she rejects "prevailing beliefs that probing into an individual's personal viewpoint is outside the boundaries of discussion" (Collins 2000, 265). Through Black feminist rhetoric, Cooper's autoethnographic critique sheds light on the dynamics of her lived experiences in relation to the violent hegemonic politics of the US South preceding the turn of the twentieth century.

Stewart, Truth, Jacobs, and Cooper, through their respective writings and orations, all exhibit how Black women can be knowledge agents, a key aspect of Black feminist thought (Collins 2000, 266–69). While the academy proper might not acknowledge these women (or might acknowledge only Cooper as an intellectual of the group) as such, understanding their texts as the beginning of a tradition of US Black feminist autoethnography affirms the quotidian knowledge making that remains the invisible labor of Black women. If autoethnographers truly seek "to consider the accessibility of their texts, asking what value or benefit our work might have for our participants and readers, as well as ourselves" (Adams, Jones, and Ellis 2015, 44), we must also find ways to recuperate spaces for those who came before—ways to challenge boundaries placed on intellectualism and who is capable of knowledge making. If not, we run the risk of reinforcing the binary of academic and nonacademic rhetorics and literacies that forces excluding reactions to autoethnography in the fields of rhetoric and writing studies.

CONCLUSION

In the age of activist scholars, university centers opening doors in historically Black communities, and "alt-ac" career development in doctoral programs, one might question whether there remains a clear line between the academy and its surrounding ecologies. Still, however, white respectability politics and hegemonic ideologies govern who gets to produce intellectual thought and who gets to be seen as deserving of humanity both inside and outside the academy. The #BlackLivesMatter movement's emergence as a counter to such politics provides enough evidence that such exclusionary ideologies, nevertheless, persist. Here, I delve deep into history to consider the writings and orations of nineteenth-century Black women in order to show how intellectual exclusion, born out of the same logics as biological and cultural racism, haunts the reception of Blackness and Black feminist thought.

By highlighting the rhetorics and aesthetics of these early autoethnographic texts, I seek a through line from them to contemporary activisms that draw on similar communication technologies. The social media practices of call-out culture, for example, parallel the autoethnography's "overt critiques of cultural identities, experiences, practices, and cultural systems" while addressing "instances of unfairness and injustice" (Adams, Jones, and Ellis 2015, 89). Social media posts using #MeToo and #BlackLivesMatter—movements started by Black women[3]—in foregrounding the trauma of lived experiences for the purpose of social justice might well be seen as digital offspring of these Black feminist autoethnographic traditions. Like the narratives of their nineteenth-century foremothers, these personal narratives analyze culture through the lens of the self for the hope of more just futures. They also create knowledge that should not be dismissed as lesser than, untrue, or stereotypical based on white heteropatriarchal conceptions of what it means to consciously be.

NOTES

1. I tell autoethnographic stories from memory, using aids like text messages, emails, and digital notes to fill in details. I acknowledge that stories change with each re/telling. The names of individuals have been excluded to protect their identities.
2. This sketch of selected writing from nineteenth-century Black US women by no means attempts to offer a comprehensive representation of all the rhetorics and aesthetics of early Black US women's autoethnography. The sketch means, instead, to offer an entry point in considering these rhetorics and aesthetics to spark further exploration of what constitutes autoethnography and/or Black feminist autoethnography.
3. Tarana Burke and Alicia Garza, Patrisse Cullors, and Opal Tometi, respectively.

REFERENCES

Adams, Tony E., Stacy Holman Jones, and Carolyn Ellis. 2015. *Autoethnography: Understanding Qualitative Research.* New York: Oxford University Press.

Bochner, Arthur P., and Carolyn Ellis. 2006. "Communication as Autoethnography." In *Communication as . . . Perspectives on Theory,* edited by Gregory J. Shepherd, Jeffrey St. John, and Ted Striphas, 110–22. Thousand Oaks, CA: SAGE.

Busby, Margaret. 1992. *Daughters of Africa: An International Anthology of Words and Writings by Women of African Descent from the Ancient Egyptian to the Present.* London: Jonathan Cape.

Collins, Patricia Hill. 2000. *Black Feminist Thought: Knowledge, Consciousness, and the Politics of Empowerment.* 2nd ed. New York: Routledge.

Combahee River Collective. 2017. "The Combahee River Collective Statement." In *How We Get Free: Black Feminism and the Combahee River Collective*, edited by Keeanga-Yamahtta Taylor, 15–28. Chicago, IL: Haymarket Books.

Cooper, Anna Julia. 1892. *A Voice from the South: By a Black Woman from the South*. Xenia, OH: Aldine.

Crenshaw, Kimberlé. 1991. "Mapping the Margins: Intersectionality, Identity Politics, and Violence against Women of Color." *Stanford Law Review* 43 (6): 1241–99.

Gilyard, Keith, and Adam J. Banks. 2018. *On African-American Rhetoric*. New York: Routledge.

Griffin, Alicia Rachel. 2012. "I AM an Angry Black Woman: Black Feminist Autoethnography, Voice, and Resistance." *Women's Studies in Communication* 35 (2): 138–57.

Gutiérrez y Muhs, Gabriella, Yolanda Flores Niemann, Carmen G. González, and Angela P. Harris, eds. 2012. *Presumed Incompetent: The Intersections of Race and Class for Women in Academia*. Logan: Utah State University Press.

Jacobs, Harriet. (1861) 2004. *Incidents in the Life of a Slave Girl by Linda Brent*. Project Guttenberg.

Kynard, Carmen. 2015. "Teaching While Black: Witnessing Disciplinary Whiteness, Racial Violence, and Race-Management." *Literacy in Composition Studies* 3 (1): 1–20.

May, Vivian. 2012. "Intellectual Genealogies, Intersectionality, and Anna Julia Cooper." In *Feminist Solidarity at the Crossroads: Intersectional Studies for Transracial Alliance*, edited by Kim Marie Vaz, and Gary L. Lemons, 155–72. New York: Routledge:

Mbembe, Achille. 2017. *Critique of Black Reason*. Translated by Laurent Dubois. Durham, NC: Duke University Press.

Patterson, Orlando. 1982. *Slavery and Social Death*. Boston: Harvard University Press.

Pratt, Mary Louise. 1991. "Arts of the Contact Zone." *Profession* 33–40.

Royster, Jacqueline Jones. 2000. *Traces of a Stream: Literacy and Social Change among African American Women*. Pittsburgh, PA: University of Pittsburgh Press.

Sharpe, Christina Elizabeth. 2016. *In the Wake: On Blackness and Being*. Durham, NC: Duke University Press.

Smitherman, Geneva. 1977. *Talkin and Testifyin: The Language of Black America*. Detroit, MI: Wayne State University Press.

Stewart, Maria W. (1831) 1987. "Religion and the Pure Principles of Morality: The Sure Foundation on Which We Must Build." In *Maria W. Stewart, America's First Black Woman Political Writer*, edited by Marilyn Richardson, 28–42. Bloomington: Indiana University Press.

Truth, Sojourner. (1863) 1889. "Ain't I a Woman?" In *History of Woman Suffrage*, Vol. 1, edited by Elizabeth Cady Stanton, Susan B. Anthony, and Matilda Joslyn Gage, 116. 2nd. ed. Rochester, NY: Charles Mann.

Truth, Sojourner. 1851. "Ain't I a Woman?" *The Anti-Slavery Bugle*, June 21.

13

WRITING *WITH* NOT *ABOUT*
Constellating Stories in Autoethnography

John T. Gagnon

As I participate in this conversation about autoethnography in writing studies, I acknowledge there is a good chance you are at least somewhat skeptical about what this conversation means for how we do the work we do. Such a position is understandable. For quite some time, in fact, I did not consider my own work to be autoethnographic and did not want it to be so. My rejection was, of course, rooted in my own orientations, highly inculcated and developed by institutional academia, about what research should be and do and look like—that is, what counted and what did not. My early refusal to embrace autoethnography as an identifier of my work was also centered in fear of my own vulnerability—telling stories of my-self in research seemed to make me too visible. But, over time, that all has changed.

To explain, let me tell you a research story.

* * *

In 2015, I started conducting a research project on the storytelling practices of human-trafficking survivors. At the project's nascence, I described it as ethnographic community-engaged research. I wanted to gain a better sense of the trauma associated with human trafficking, how individuals who had survived such experiences constructed and shared stories about their lives, as well as whether those stories aligned with culturally dominant narratives about human trafficking.[1] As I built and fostered relationships with participants, gathered stories through interviews, and attempted to analyze and write about what I believed I had found, I discovered my initial orientation to the project had been flawed. In sharing their stories with me, the project participants were not merely engaged in recounting facts but actively writing and transforming themselves as they interacted with the stories that also lived within me. Across my research, my understanding about the nature of the

DOI: 10.7330/9781646421213.c013

project necessarily evolved to account for the fact that the interactions between my-self and my research participants involved my embodied stories, too. This recognition represented a moment of researcher disorientation that led me to travel down a new orienting line, a line that led me from merely gathering and analyzing stories to more carefully considering how such stories constellated with my enactments of writing and self-transformation. My own story was a complex one, starting a decade prior, and traversed a line that had taken me from a position in federal law enforcement—where I routinely made life-changing decisions about trafficked individuals—to the role of an academic in which I studied storytelling practices around trauma.

* * *

Sara Ahmed (2006) writes that experiences become available to us "because of the lines that we have already taken: our life courses follow a certain sequence which is also a matter of following a direction" (21). Ahmed's words opened up this research story for me. I say opened up because, in understanding and acknowledging the course my life had taken to meet and interact with my research participants, I found the space to reorient research in a different way: an approach that not only honored my participants but that also included my-self. That reorientation meant I shifted to understand my story as an important reality that impacted how my participants and I interacted. And so the research story inevitably changed. The reflexivity of my participants inspired, and required, reflexivity in my approach. The past and present collided, both within myself and in how my story constellated with the stories of my participants in guiding the process of my own reorientation to writing and to story. Not unlike Mark Noe (2016), who "realized that though [he] had started out studying [his] students, [he] ended up studying [him]self" (90), I began to understand that the work I needed to do was not so much ethnography as something more along the lines of autoethnography. That required a turn inward and a willingness to be externally open about it.

While the lines between and utility of autobiography, ethnography, creative nonfiction, autoethnography, and other overlapping qualitative approaches have been debated across the humanities, the questions of how and why to do autoethnography in writing studies, particularly in trauma-related research, remain underdiscussed. When doing my research with participants who had experienced profound trauma, I was left with no clear guide, no set framework. How could I find a way to responsibly and ethically do research around something as sensitive as trauma when I had not experienced that trauma myself, even though I had spent years steeped in such stories? To echo Noe (2016), "Somehow, I had backed into a journey of reflexivity" (90), and I was not entirely sure what that meant or what the implications were. I knew I could not ignore my own story, but I also did not want to privilege it over that of the project participants. What was the balance? I wondered. I did not want my scholarship to be viewed as an "author saturated text" that was "self-indulgent and narcissistic" (Kirsch 1999, 77). At the same time, as a pretenure academic, part of my own tentativeness to embrace autoethnography derived from concerns about how I would be perceived; after all, in some corners of academia, autoethnography is viewed as risky "because the term is largely pejorative" (Hanson 2004, 185) because it is an approach wherein "the researcher-writer, in revealing his subjectivities to an audience, may find that the audience passes judgment not only on his work, but also on his person" (Alsup 2012, 225).

The stories we tell about autoethnography and writing studies are, like any compelling story, a bit messy. I bring my research story into the mix because the work I do in and around trauma highlights the ways an autoethnographic approach lends itself particularly well to conducting this type of necessarily messy research and scholarship. While many writing studies scholars—Benjamin Batzer (2016), Kendall Gerdes (2019), Cathryn Malloy (2016), and Laura Micciche (2001) immediately come to mind—have examined the ways writing, healing, and trauma intersect in the writing classroom, only a handful—Tamika Carey (2016), Trever Hoag (2018), Thomas West (2000)—have addressed methodological approaches to conducting research at that particular intersection. While writing with Maria Novotny about research experiences with trauma populations, I invoked my respective research stories and shared my personal experiences, making visible the complex interweaving of stories between researchers and participants (Novotny and Gagnon 2018). This making visible of self in research and as researcher is a vulnerable and sometimes messy act but an important one that helps us rethink what our work can and ought to do. By acknowledging researcher stories and positionalities through the deployment of autoethnographic approaches in our research, we can draw meaningful lines of connectivity between researchers and participants. Such connectivity is powerful because it necessarily reorients researchers to ethical practices by laying bare positionality in, orientation to, and reasons for conducting research.

THE CASE FOR CONSTELLATIONAL AUTOETHNOGRAPHY

The question immediately arises, If autoethnography is useful for those of us doing trauma-related research—and those of us in writing studies generally—then how do we actually go about doing it? While the question is a good one, I want to first step back and consider the idea that *autoethnography*, as a term, describes a spectrum of approaches. As Rebecca Jackson and Jackie Grutsch McKinney observe in this collection's introduction, there are dozens of approaches to autoethnography. Within this multiply inhabited spectrum, which tells many stories about autoethnography in writing studies, is an approach I like to call *constellational autoethnography*. The concerns I raise in this chapter's introduction begin to be resolved by linking the cultural-rhetorics idea of constellational practice with that of critical autoethnography.[2] First, the area of cultural rhetorics offers up an orientation to writing studies research that centers on story and on relationality. Phil Bratta and Malea Powell (2016) write that cultural rhetorics is a "practice of constellating" that emphasizes "the encounters that people have with one another within and across particular systems" (under "What Is Cultural Rhetorics?"). Second, Susan Hanson (2004) provides the concept of critical autoethnography, which she describes as an approach committed "to studying other people, but as an account of that process, it bridges the chasm between the autobiographical Here and the ethnographic There and lays bare the dynamics of self-other engagement" (185). Taken together, these ideas coalesce to argue for an autoethnographic approach that is, at its core and in its application, focused on presently describing encounters, the dynamics of those encounters, and attending to the other forces at work that manifest in each encounter.

When I refer to constellational autoethnography, I indicate an approach to research that values the identities of the research participants and researcher, makes clear the relationship between the parties involved in research, and leverages an approach that looks to stories from both to inform the research process, findings from the research, and the presentation of those findings. In applying such an approach, constellational autoethnographers acknowledge their own stories and how those stories engage with those of research participants, as well as the other stories, institutions, and power structures they connect with. Such constellations are centered in making an effort to understand the shared reality participants and researchers inhabit by being brought together to create knowledge and make meaning. Such a constellated framework transcends the merely interpersonal yet still privileges it while recognizing the roles and impacts cultural forces have and do play.

The value of such an approach in researching and writing trauma stories cannot be understated, particularly when the researcher is not, directly, a community member through shared experience. By constellating stories and acknowledging the cultural forces at work, the researcher and participants are able to find common ground through which meaning can be made, creating a research approach that embraces a set of values and perspectives, as described by Jacqueline Jones Royster and Gesa Kirsch (2012), "that honors the particular traditions and subjects of study, respects their communities, amplifies their voices, and clarifies their visions . . . for a more dialectical and reciprocal intellectual engagement" (14). Constellational autoethnography, then, pushes against normative Western research paradigms that dishonor cultural traditions, disrespect communities, and silence voices.

Many objections to autoethnography center on its alleged lack of analytic rigor, the idea being that experiential description of research is not actually research because it is intellectually lazy. Even proponents of autoethnography in writing studies often view it as a sort of soft entrance to academic writing rather than an approach to academic writing that can and should stand on its own. The application of constellations to autoethnographic practice is important because it pushes back against both assertions. Malea Powell (2017), in her interview with 4C4Equality: Writing Networks for Social Justice, explains that constellation is a metaphor of practice that "acknowledges that what we're doing is taking a set of things that exist and putting them together to make a story, to make knowledge. You can't pretend it's linear" (para. 6). This reminds us that our practices—whether they relate to research about writing, teaching writing, or writing itself—are always our stories. One could use such an understanding to argue that those levying critiques against autoethnography are themselves intellectually lazy and lacking analytic rigor because they fail to acknowledge their own practices as stories that happen to also be connected to bodies, including their own, and cultural influences. By viewing constellation as a legitimate scholarly practice, then, we erase "the possibility that there is one linear narrative, that there is one logical explanation or a single change of events. Constellating highlights the impermanence, ambiguity, and subjectivity of making that story in that moment" (para. 6). If we embrace that understanding, then, constellational autoethnography is not just a soft entrance to academic writing but a wholly legitimate scholarly endeavor because it actually makes visible the messiness and nonlinearity of academic writing in general and writing our research, specifically. Moreover, it expands the potential for what we can do as scholars. If there is not one linear narrative to explain a particular thing or event, we may find within that thing or event, and in ourselves, entirely new lines of inquiry, as well as a plurality of interpretations and understandings. This is important because how we inquire, interpret, and understand is at the very center of how we can and do imagine and reimagine writing studies in an ever-changing world.

To explain, let me tell you a research story.

* * *

Having continued to expand my research around the traumas associated with human trafficking, I now make it a point to look backward and inward. That reflexivity is a central part of my practice because I learned something important when I started this work. When I initiated my research, I admittedly viewed stories as discursive events that recounted happenings to people and that were recounted about people. As such, I understood self and story as things that could overlap but that were usually distinctly separate. In many ways, I thought such compartmentalization made my work easier: if I could separate the person from the stories, it mattered far less how I evaluated them. Stories became objects that could be accepted or merely discarded. But, as my research matured through encounters and interactions with my participants over time, I realized separating the person from the story was not possible; to discard stories would be to discard the individuals telling them. To discard my story would be to discard my-self. The impulse to separate person from story was neither sufficient nor appropriate because of its colonizing compartmentalization.

I learned that the beauty of constellational autoethnography is that it embraces these stories, all of them, visible and invisible, known and unknown—in all their human messiness—and honors them. The notion of constellational autoethnography evokes Cherokee author Thomas King's (2008) repetition of the statement, "The truth about stories is that that's all we are" (2). The statement's power resides both in its initial saying and in its repeated use—a continual, persistent reminder. King's words notably make visible the stories that constellate in my research. We each—every participant, including my-self—are stories, embodied collections of stories, and in the telling and writing and combining of them, we find our respective identities and make meaning together. In listening to how my participants addressed identity and self-transformation, I began seeing connections to Thomas King, Joy Harjo, Qwo-Li Driskill, and many other theorists operating in a native/Indigenous paradigm, who emphasize the notion that stories are what we are. In the act of telling their stories, my participants were not merely engaged in a recounting but in demonstrating their present, in-that-moment subjectivity. As was I.

* * *

Reflecting on what it means for how I constructed my own views of the self and how I saw stories at work in the world, such ideas were critically important to helping me rethink and reorient my approach. What I learned by applying this understanding of story was that the stories that lived inside me and my participants, whether told or untold, gave form to identity and constantly negotiated our place in the world, as well as our relations with each other. These stories—particularly when put into the world through writing—constellated with other stories "existing inside other bodies, and in other spaces, places, and times" (Smith et al. 2017, 53). The recognition that stories are who we are rather than mere recountings encouraged me to rethink what I heard when I listened to participants in my research.

DOING CONSTELLATIONAL AUTOETHNOGRAPHY: WRITING *WITH* NOT *ABOUT*

A. Suresh Canagarajah (2012) writes that researchers who use autoethnographic approaches "theorize from the ground up, developing the relevant constructs from their observations without imposing etic (outsider) constructs from their field" (114). What I take Canagarajah to mean is that in doing this type of work, the stories shared by both the researcher and participants may be seen—and valued—as data and as findings in and of themselves, a notion shared in the Indigenous precept that story is theory. Consequently, "the researcher/subject roles are fused in autoethnography" (114) wherein each player "creates frameworks in their language and on their terms" (Riley-Mukavetz 2012, 79), thereby creating a constellating story matrix. This embraces the notion that the fusing, or constellation, of researcher-participant roles in autoethnography is based in stories and, as stories are embodied, emphasizes the lived experiences of all involved. Such emphasis helps us see the nonlinear ways stories are not only constructed in writing and in speech but also actively and collaboratively theorize life experiences and cultural situatedness.

But, you may fairly ask, how do we engage in such constellative practice? I propose we start by listening. The only way to constellate stories with any integrity is by emphasizing listening as a research practice. That might strike the reader as odd; after all, doesn't autoethnography imply a turn toward the reflexive? But true reflexivity, I think, is rooted first in listening. It is only in listening to those we are talking to, to those whose stories are joining with our own, that we can begin to explore and understand the meaning and value of what we are writing. I have found that a significant part of constellating research relationships and finding my own voice within the framework of that relationship—particularly revolving around sensitive subject areas—involves close, careful listening. This orientation to constellative practice emerges from Krista Ratcliffe's (2005) definition of rhetorical listening as a code of conduct that relies on listening for pauses, the articulation of concern, and employing listening as an approach to hear how people encounter one another for the purpose of negotiation. So, building from Ratcliffe, I propose that constellative autoethnography is rooted in and centered on listening practices, which require researchers to reorient from merely listening to take and listening to use to a paradigm that focuses on listening to listen.

Let me tell you another research story.

* * *

Once I realized my work was necessarily autoethnographic in nature, I wanted to locate the proper balance of how to express my-self in the work along with the stories of my participants. Constellative practice offered this balance and opened up the space to create an essential platform of shared meaning making. One of my research participants, whom we'll refer to as Deb,[3] was a survivor of human trafficking who had experienced multiple layers of trauma spanning decades. She was initially suspicious about participating in the project because of my law-enforcement background. There was, lingering in the backdrop of our initial interactions, a question about my motivations, about how I would use her story. As I listened to her, I realized that, for her, knowing my story was the lynchpin in making the decision to participate. It was an element of the research interaction I hadn't fully considered and, as she questioned me, I had to explain the decisions I made, share with her my journey from a law-enforcement career to that of researcher and teacher, and open myself up to her critique. In this process, we constellated around the stories we each had lived. I told her of the stories I had extracted in interrogations, an uncomfortable thing for me to verbalize and yet one I knew was essential to garnering her trust: by giving voice to the tensions in my own life, I opened the door for her to give voice to her own.

Important, by sharing my story and life trajectory—including the underlying goals, rationale, and reasons for my research—with my participants, I was able to better conceptualize what I needed to do to protect my participants. This reflected an enactment of my values: in acknowledging the roles of my own positionality and orienting lines, whether perceived or real, I opened myself to critique, laid bare my positionality, and situated myself as a researcher informed by the stories intersecting and constellating with my own. Jacqueline Jones Royster's (1996) scholarship encouraged me to use an approach that understands cross-boundary discourse and research as complex and messy realities that require "individual stories placed one against another against another" (30). In fact, that might be the best definition of what I understand constellational autoethnography to be: it places my individual story into conversation with the individual stories of my participants and places each of those stories, together, into conversation with culturally situated narratives.

Deb's insistence early in the project on learning more about my background was an attempt to redress unbalanced power relations. By listening to and being responsive to that need, my project created plurivocal ways of interpreting and understanding complex lived experiences. Rather than merely interviewing my participants, I sought to constellate my stories with theirs. As a result, the ideas, issues, and questions that eventually became central were developed and set by the participants themselves. Not merely part of the story, they became the storytellers and in that capacity functioned in a way that transcended mere participation: they, too, were researchers and partners. And as this process unfolded, I acknowledged I wasn't there to write *about*; rather, I was there to write *with* the individuals who had agreed to tell their stories to me. Listening, then, informed the writing process, which was a constellative practice in which my participants selected which interview excerpts they wanted to include, thereby fully expressing their own voices, as well as where and how they felt bits and pieces of my own story could be inserted to make transparent my own motivations and tensions. This listening-based writing allowed for a collaborative endeavor that constellated researcher-participant stories and theorized from the ground up rather than my trying to fit participant stories into a predefined framework based solely on my own analysis and ideas.

* * *

In this sense, constellational autoethnography is a listening exercise: to participants, to self, to cultural influences. In listening to others and other perspectives, as well as to our own responses to those perspectives, we open ourselves as researchers to the self-transformation that comes from constellating stories, and in so doing we mutually engage both in an act of resistance and an activity of hope. The concepts of listening and writing *with* are common suggestions for qualitative research. But these work with/as autoethnography to shape it in specific ways. If autoethnography theorizes from the ground up, it cannot be constructed from a predesigned outline or be based in the researcher's anticipated or assumed findings. Using a constellational approach, we can ask and listen for what our participants think their stories are about, what they think ours are about, and negotiate the presentation of such stories together. As we consider making our own voices heard in our research, we then ask our participants what role our voices should play in interacting with and conveying their stories. Constellating stories is hard work, messy work. It is work that doesn't write itself because it is not linear, neat, or tidy. As a practitioner of and advocate for constellating as a practice, I write of both the benefit and the struggles that come with it. This, too, is a value because we often fail to disclose the messes, the failures, and the tolls research takes on not just participants but on ourselves as researchers. Constellational autoethnography opens up the room to explore those spaces as a legitimate realm of scholarly inquiry and storytelling. Situating research in this way allows the privileging of story and storytelling practices across the research terrain to interrogate and resist totalizing and linear narratives.

My research has been a journey of sorts, a travel story across space and time from when I took stories as a federal officer to listening to stories as a researcher. As I have done this work, I have paused to consider what moments along that journey might mean, have written about them, and have grappled with how I might think about them in relation to the experiences my participants were going through by writing out and telling their stories from the other side of the table. I listened closely to their stories, too, rereading their writing and interview transcripts and relistening, again and again, to audio recordings of our interactions to locate moments of importance sometimes represented by a pregnant silence, laughter or crying, a joke or a side-bar about a valued pet. Listening to my own responses to these moments, both embodied and intellectual, allowed me to focus less on the words and more on the underlying human emotions involved, both my own and those of my participants. As a result, there were moments in which I reevaluated certain portions of my work—moments I had initially discounted as valueless but eventually came to recognize as critical and vice versa. More important, I opened myself to the notion of writing together, of putting my voice into conversation with their voices. In so doing, I learned that in many ways, constellational autoethnography is a form of research and storytelling rooted in the exploration of self that undoes alterity, rendering individual voices relevant and palpable, highlighting the creative and healing power of subject formation through stories that come together. In considering the scenes of self-recognition, of transformation, my participants shared, I was reminded of the stories I was shaped by and of the difference those stories sometimes perpetuated and to which I needed to be responsive.

CONCLUSION

As I have traversed the academic landscape, I have become increasingly concerned by what seems to be, as John Chernoff (2003) describes it, "a limited capacity to comprehend the significance of stories" (6) rooted in lived experience. We might identify a core problem of our own discourse as not being reflexive enough. Such discourse operates top down rather than bottom up by placing a framework around research first rather than constructing it from the stories told by those most involved and most impacted and constellating those with our own and those of the institutions we inhabit. An alternate approach—the approach I adopt and try to model—might more closely consider and account for the stories individuals tell about themselves and put those into honest conversation with the stories we put forward about our work.

One of the specific ways boundaries might be remapped, or transformed, in writing studies is in situating what it means to constellate our stories as researchers with those of our research participants, finding ways to write with rather than write about. I think this is particularly important in the context of doing research in and around trauma, but I believe it to be broadly applicable in work being done across the field. I think we are also confronted with the attendant question of what writing with rather than about means for thinking about building connections in and between research communities while thinking about accountability. By refocusing the lens, my work contributes to ongoing conversations about autoethnography in writing studies by practicing a slightly different way of seeing, of researching, and of writing that is both directly connected with and accountable to individuals who have endured exploitation. Such direct conversation—writing with, not about—helps us, as scholars, think about how autoethnography might be recast within the field to more fully acknowledge lived experience in a way that carefully works with those who know what it means to be exploited while working towards accountability to those who remain in situations of exploitation.

Many of the questions I have grappled with as a researcher were driven by the need to explore and examine the dissonance(s) I perceived between culturally situated understandings about trauma and the unheard stories told by those who have lived through such experiences. So, too, my work tells a story about me, as both a professional and a human being who navigated what some would say is a unique journey, from law enforcer to researcher, from someone who unquestioningly propagated narratives from the perspective of the state to someone who began to question how those narratives operationalized once let loose into the world. It would be easy to remove myself from these pages, to write in a neutral voice, to be standoffish and protect myself behind the walls of language. Indeed, this approach would be in many respects my preference and perhaps more adequately fulfill an expectation of my role as a scholar. But as a scholar who situates myself as a cultural rhetorician, I think it is important to share a bit of myself, just as my participants do, not only because it honors my participants—who share their stories with me—but because of the impact Shawn Wilson's (2008) teaching in *Research Is Ceremony* has had on my scholarly path; he teaches me to impart myself in the telling.

NOTES

1. The project was rooted in longstanding interest stemming from my previous work, both in the field and at the operational level, as a federal officer and program manager for the Department of Homeland Security.
2. This is but one potential approach on the spectrum of doing autoethnography in the field generally. From my perspective, it is especially generative for conducting ethical trauma-related research.
3. Deb is a pseudonym used to protect the research participant's identity.

REFERENCES

Ahmed, Sara. 2006. *Queer Phenomenology: Orientations, Objects, Others*. Durham, NC: Duke University Press.

Alsup, Janet. 2012. "Protean Subjectivities." In *Ethnography Unbound*, edited by Stephen Brown and Sid Dobrin, 219–37. Albany: SUNY Press.

Batzer, Benjamin. 2016. "Healing Classrooms: Therapeutic Possibilities in Academic Writing." *Composition Forum* 34 (Summer). https://compositionforum.com/issue/34/healing-classrooms.php.

Bratta, Phil, and Malea Powell. 2016. "Introduction to the Special Issue: Entering the Cultural Rhetorics Conversation." *Enculturation* 21. http://enculturation.net/entering-the-cultural-rhetorics-conversations.

Canagarajah, A. S. 2012. "Autoethnography in the Study of Multilingual Writers." In *Writing Studies Research in Practice: Methods and Methodologies*, edited by Lee Nickoson and Mary P. Sheridan, 113–24. Carbondale: Southern Illinois University Press.

Carey, Tamika. 2016. *Rhetorical Healing: The Reeducation of Contemporary Black Womanhood.* Albany: SUNY Press.

Chernoff, John. 2003. *Hustling Is Not Stealing: Stories of an African Bar Girl.* Chicago: University of Chicago Press.

Gerdes, Kendall. 2019. "Trauma, Trigger Warnings, and the Rhetoric of Sensitivity." *Rhetoric Society Quarterly* 39 (1): 3–24.

Hanson, Susan. 2004. "Critical Auto/Ethnography." In *Ethnography Unbound*, edited by Stephen Brown and Sid Dobrin, 183–200. Albany: SUNY Press.

Hoag, Trevor. 2018. *Occupying Memory: Rhetoric, Trauma, Mourning.* Lanham, MD: Lexington Books.

King, Thomas. 2008. *The Truth about Stories: A Native Narrative.* Minneapolis: University of Minnesota Press.

Kirsch, Gesa. 1999. *Ethical Dilemmas in Feminist Research: The Politics of Location, Interpretation, and Publication.* Albany: SUNY Press.

Noe, Mark. 2016. "Autoethnography and Assimilation: Composing Border Stories." *JAEPL: Journal for the Assembly of Expanded Perspectives on Learning* 21 (Winter): 86–99.

Novotny, Maria, and John T. Gagnon. 2018. "Research as Care: A Shared Ownership Approach to Rhetorical Research in Trauma Communities." *Reflections* 18 (1): 71–101.

Micciche, Laura. 2001. "Writing Through Trauma: The Emotional Dimensions of Teaching Writing." *Composition Studies* 29 (1): 131–41.

Molloy, Cathryn. 2016. "Multimodal Composing as Healing: Toward a New Model for Writing as Healing Courses." *Composition Studies* 44 (2): 134.

Powell, Malea. 2017. "Interview—Malea Powell on Story, Survivance, and Constellating as Praxis." 4C4Equality: Writing Networks for Social Justice. http://constell8cr.com/4c4e/interview_malea_powell.

Ratcliffe, Krista. 2005. *Rhetorical Listening: Identification, Gender, Whiteness.* Carbondale: Southern Illinois University Press.

Riley-Mukavetz, Andrea. 2012. *Theory Begins with a Story, Too: Listening to the Lived Experiences of American Indian Women.* PhD diss., Michigan State University.

Royster, Jacqueline Jones. 1996. "When the First Voice You Hear Is Not Your Own." *College Composition and Communication* 47 (1): 29–40.

Royster, Jacqueline Jones, and Gesa E. Kirsch. 2012. *Feminist Rhetorical Practices: New Horizons for Rhetoric, Composition, and Literacy Studies.* Carbondale: Southern Illinois University Press.

Smith, Trixie, Katie Manthey, John Gagnon, Ezekiel Choffel, Wonderful Faison, Scotty Secrist, and Phil Bratta. 2017. "Reflections on/of Embodiment: Bringing Our Whole Selves to Class." *Feminist Teacher.* 45–63. Accessed June 15, 2021. Doi: 10.5406/femteacher.28.1.0045.

West, Thomas. 2000. "The Rhetoric of Therapy and the Politics of Anger: From the Safe House to a Praxis of Shelter." *Rhetoric Review* 19 (1–2): 42–58.

Wilson, Shawn. 2008. *Research Is Ceremony: Indigenous Research Methods.* Halifax: Fernwood.

14
CHAOTIC CONSTRUCTIONS
Disabling the Autoethnography

Autumn Laws

I thought I was being clever when I tried to record my tales from the mental hospitals. My stories were at the mercy of my risperidone-diluted memory. When your lived experiences become episodic, the control you thought you had over them is lost. But this need to construct meaning from trauma opens the door to autoethnography.

As a genre, autoethnography places value on recounting and re-envisioning experiences of the researcher/subject, acknowledging the ways subjectivity and identity inform lives. Autoethnography, as I refer to it here, refers to the ways the blending of theoretical scholarship and personal narrative can bring about new ways of thinking about cultures and those within them. In the case of disability autoethnography, the writer attempts to make sense of life with disabilities, drawing on both lived experiences and academic theory. Autoethnography, however, problematizes this construction because it forces meaning onto the disabled body using methods dictated by nondisabled scholars. Because of the ways these expectations are placed on disabled bodies (and queer bodies, and bodies of color, and poor bodies), the narratives that can arise from disability autoethnographies represent not the lived experiences of disabled scholars but often, rather, the expectations writing studies attaches to disabled bodies.

In this chapter, I discuss disability theory and specifically disability life writing. I am choosing to include disability life writing in a chapter about disability autoethnography because of the ways autoethnography, a genre primarily taken up in academic spaces, is not always accessible to disabled people, as the academy has always been a space that reifies ableism. By broadening my scope, I can then account for other disabled narratives that still have ethnographic value in the ways they challenge dominant assumptions about disability and those who live with it. Disability life writing is typically categorized into one of three narrative types: the quest narrative, the restitution narrative, and the chaos narrative (Frank 1995). One of these methods, the chaos narrative, is often overlooked and underused because of the challenges it poses to readers; however, this method of disability life writing mirrors methods used by queer theorists and, I believe, can actively resist the nondisabled expectations other autoethnographic methods might presume.

In this chapter, I explore Chicana and queer composing practices that could provide models of composing disability autoethnographies that resist traditional writing techniques. Similarly to how disabled writers are often expected to perform within ableist constructs, so too are Black and brown bodies and queer bodies subject to such expectations. They are pushing back against white-supremacist and heteronormative writing constructs, and I argue that disability autoethnography can gain something in learning from and expanding on practices of queer and Chicana writers because of the ways these methods resist the dominant narratives in writing studies and make room for the representation of bodies rarely considered within the field. After examining these writing practices, I then examine how exploring these queer and Chicana practices might further expand the boundaries of disability autoethnography/life writing, providing an opportunity to compose a disabled life that isn't dictated by nondisabled perceptions of disability. Furthermore, I stress the necessity of writing studies to pay closer attention to these forms of disability autoethnography/life writing because of how they can more broadly challenge writing studies' conceptions of composition and the writing process more broadly. I see disability autoethnography, in the forms I take up in this chapter, as challenging a presumption that scholarship and writing processes should produce neat and approachable texts. If autoethnography is intended to produce a text that is in some way congruent to the life of whoever is composing it, presuming that text to be easily digestible and coherent simply reifies ableist conceptions of disability that force disabled bodies to be presentable to a nondisabled audience. In bringing alternative methods to the conversation, I see this new form of autoethnography expanding the ways we understand disability autoethnography and writing studies as a whole. In addition to discussing how disability autoethnography can push the boundaries of writing studies, I include snippets of my own creative writing alongside my academic writing throughout this text. This is intended to model a kind of chaotic narrative I recommend disability autoethnography explore while also referencing where the early threads of this project began.

CRIPPING IT

Disability theory, particularly the social model of disability, is invested in understanding how human impairment is treated in the world and how that treatment affects the lives of disabled people. Socially constructed variations deemed *disabilities* determine which bodies are disabled and how social spaces will be made accessible (or inaccessible) to those bodies. Disability life writing, then, calls on composing practices to illustrate and construct the disabled life through writing. In his book *Recovering Bodies*, G. Thomas Couser (1997) explores the different techniques used in disability life writing to construct a portrait of disability intended for nondisabled audiences. Couser writes that disability life writing "promises to foreground somatic experience in a new way by treating the body's form and function . . . as fundamental constituents of identity" (12). Disability life writing highlights how bodies dictate the trajectory of disabled lives. Couser writes about that, saying, "Illness and disability acknowledge that our bodies are not ultimately in control. At the same time . . . we do have considerable influence over the way our bodies are viewed" (289). This move toward life writing in disability is a practice to gain agency, giving disabled people the opportunity to construct a narrative attached to their bodies and, in turn, their lives. But, one must ask, who is that construction for? Does the disability narrative serve as a tool for the writer to reclaim agency in an able-bodied world? Or does the narrative serve as a way to reify the misconceptions of disability for nondisabled readers?

This question of whom disability life writing is written for is significant because it dictates the ways disability life writing—and life writing writ large—is and can be done. Arthur Frank (1995), in *The Wounded Storyteller*, describes three models of disability life writing. These three models—restitution narrative, quest narrative, and chaos narrative—describe a kind of life writing not concerned with the potential ways narratives can be constructed, per se, but rather with the functions of the narratives themselves. The restitution narrative, as Frank describes it, "reflects a 'natural' desire to get well and stay well" (78). In this iteration of disability life writing, the illness/disability is seen as impermanent and merely an obstacle to overcome. Quest narratives tell the story of illness as "the occasion of a journey that becomes a quest . . . [wherein] something is to be gained through the experience" (115). In this iteration of disability life writing, the illness/disability provides some kind of higher meaning to the individual that can be used for personal development. Both the quest narrative and the restitution narrative feed into the pitying attitudes toward disability, constructing a story for nondisabled readers to feel as though disabled people are either obsessed with cure or have something to gain through illness. This model of life writing perpetuates the narrative that a disabled life can only be worth living if there is some kind of reparation for such a dismal existence. These forms of disability life writing is a means not for the writer to represent some truth about their disability, but rather a way for the nondisabled audience to reinforce their misconceptions of disability.

The third narrative technique, chaos narrative, does not utilize the same kind of disability misconceptions as the first two methods. The chaos narrative is a kind of narrative in which "no one is in control" (Frank 1995, 100). This model offers a representation of disability as an identity that fluctuates. The chaos narrative, according to Frank (1995), "traces the edges of a wound," and the story can only be told around that perimeter (98). In tracing this wound, the teller of the chaos narrative must necessarily be disassociated from their own body, unable to recognize the difference between the illness and the self. In a chaos narrative, not only is the telling of the narrative problematized but so too is the listening. Frank writes, "Hearing is also difficult because the chaos narrative is probably the most embodied form of story" (101). However, Frank claims that the downfall to the chaos narrative is that it lacks purpose. The difference between chaos narratives and quest or restitution narratives, though, is that the chaos narrative does not represent the disabled life as concerned with cure or gain. While Frank claims the chaos narrative lacks purpose, the chaos narrative must be honored because failing to honor it would also fail to honor the storytellers themselves (109). I challenge the notion that because chaos narratives lack these priorities—priorities often placed on disabled bodies by nondisabled bodies—the chaos narrative inherently lacks purpose. Resituating the chaos narrative to prioritize not cure or gain but rather the process of composing the self brings purpose to the chaos narrative. And, as Frank argues, recognizing the value in the act of composing the self through chaos narrative allows readers to then value the very writers themselves.

Similarly Margaret Price (2014), in *Mad at School*, discusses the practice of "creative incoherence" as a counterdiagnostic tool when writing about mental disibilities. "Creative incoherence" serves as a kind of life writing that challenges the notions of writing by challenging the notions of disability. Price refers to this disruption of narrative as stemming from the presentation of a narrator who is "strategically disorganized and incoherent" (111) This presentation is useful because, as Price notes, its incoherence "is turned to strategic advantage rather than accommodated as impairment," thereby forcing readers to be responsible for negotiating the incoherency often accompanied by disability, rather than forcing the disabled author to weave their incoherent experience into the fabric of a coherent narrative (181). Creative incoherence can serve as a starting point when writing disability autoethnography, particularly chaos narratives, because it "can also be used to disrupt [the] conventional dynamics of power" of disability (194). While some scholars consider this mode of writing to be inferior to other models of disability life writing, Price recognizes its power, particularly for writing about mental disabilities. Thus, bodies that cannot be composed through traditional expectations surrounding illness and disability writing can rely on chaos narratives that employ creative incoherence techniques. These chaotic bodies are fluid, and the ways writing studies allows for bodies to be composed does not always make space for the representation of a chaotic self. In other words, accepted types of writing allow for some bodies to be composed, but rarely chaotic bodies. To better understand the ways creative incoherence and chaos stories might be taken up by disabled writers, I'd like to explore some examples of those kinds of disability life writing.

Disability scholars have grappled with the tenuous identity of disability, and this tenuousness is echoed in disability life writing. Susannah Mintz (2007) writes in *Unruly Bodies* that "disability is an inconstant experience, its significance to the story of self requiring multiple retellings, repeated narrative shaping" (4). This emphasis on the tumultuous experience that informs life with disability helps design a perspective of disability less concerned with the disability itself than with a life that seems impossible to reduce to a traditional narrative. Mintz calls attention to the possibility of disability narrative working against traditional writing constructions, declaring that "if there is no single story of the embodied self, or no single way to tell it, then the autobiographical mode loosens and slips into what Smith describes as works that embrace the 'polyphonic possibilities of selfhood'" (37). This kind of polyphonic possibility makes spaces for composing one's own experience. In fact, this struggle between writing and the body is not unknown to queer theorists and oftentimes serves as a defining framework for queer composition.

I still go back trying to piece together all the scribblings like the broken skeleton of a warm-blooded mammal.

QUEERING IT

The act of composing any kind of embodied experience in writing always poses problems because of the ways composition is expected to represent dominant narratives. Using queer theory as a starting point, I now explore how queer writers problematize writing and, in turn, serve as potential models for writing the disabled life. In "Queer: An Impossible Subject for Composition," Jonathan Alexander and Jacqueline Rhodes (2011) claim composing the queer self is in itself counter to what it means to be queer. A process of composing queer bodies must reject normative methods of writing studies to represent queerness. Because of the ways writing studies has existed (and continues to exist) as a white, heteronormative, masculine tool of the highly educated, the composed body is often required to represent itself within that restrictive identity. Alexander and Rhodes are interested in challenging that restriction for the queer body, saying, "Queerness has the potential to stretch our sense of not only what can be composed but how it can be composed" (183). By expanding our definitions of what can be composed by whom, we then alter the notions of composition itself. "Composition . . . depends on balance, on even-handedness, on seeming neutrality" (185). For this reason, writing studies tends to serve the dominant, privileged narrative rather than provide space for other bodies and experiences. This practice of troubling writing studies in the ways Rhodes and Alexander propose, though, seemingly, falls into to Frank's (1995) notion of the "chaos narrative," wherein nothing can be resolved. In the case of Alexander and Rhodes (2011), the resolution is not in finding the ability to compose queerness using the writing studies techniques currently available but instead challenging what methods are available to compose in the first place. If the current and accepted means to compose the self can only ever heteronormatize queer bodies and reinforce misconceptions about disability, can there be a method of composing that accurately represents the queer and/or disabled experience? If we are to assume the ways we compose are supposed to somehow represent the experiences of those who are composing, then how can these bodies be represented?

What, then, should disability life writing—and, more specifically, autoethnography—look like? Is there a way the disabled body can use writing studies to contribute to the field of disability without perpetuating the stereotypes of disability? Can writing studies serve disabled bodies? Disabled writers must challenge the typical narratives of disability that cater to nondisabled readers just as queer writers have troubled the dominant, cisheteronormative narrative. Autoethnography can serve to trouble and extend these narratives. The most common means of composing disability, though, typically utilize either the quest narrative or the restitution narrative—both of which contribute to misconceptions about disability. In failing to challenge notions of disability, disability life writing also fails to challenge our notions of writing studies. Instead, disability autoethnography should use tools that draw on queer theory to challenge notions about writing, Frank's (1995) concept of the "chaos narrative," and Price's (2014) description of "creative incoherence." Autoethnography allows atypical (re)constructions of self, thereby making it possible to subvert nondisabled expectations. Therefore, a disabled autoethnography should resist narratives that rely on diagnosis, cure, or medical treatment but rather make use of composing techniques that fall outside traditional writing studies methods.

Refocusing disability life writing to represent the messiness of disability is a critical and necessary move. The disabled life cannot be subjected to the kinds of nondisabled expectations that only make room for a specific disability story. Just as queer life writing is often subjected to cisheteronormative writing studies practices within the academy, so too is disabled life writing subjected to able-bodied writing expectations. Queer and disabled identities must challenge how lives can be represented through writing. How, then, can autoethnography house this style of life writing and these other kinds of lives?

This process of shaping and reshaping is a metaphor echoed in the writings of women whose bodies become their sites and sources of research.

DIS-/RE-MEMBERING IT

In her essays in *Light in the Dark/Luz en lo Oscuro*, Gloria Anzaldúa (2015) presents a model of writing that challenges what can be valued within writing studies. This alternative method can help to reenvision disability autoethnography and the purpose of writing entirely. Anzaldúa refers to this practice as the *Coyolxauhqui* process, which is an act of "re-visioning and re-membering" (124). *Coyolxauhqu* is the Aztec mythic name of the goddess of the moon who was torn into thousands of pieces and scattered across the sky and the earth by her brother. For Anzaldúa, this imagery represents a method of composing one's own dismembered body as a means of healing and empowerment. She writes, "The Coyolxauhqui imperative is an ongoing process of making and unmaking. There is never any resolution, just the process of healing" (20). This act of healing happens not just in the moments of reassembling the body but also in the moments of "dismemberment," when our very existence is threatened by violence. If the Coyolxauhqui imperative is prioritized, then bodies are in constant negotiation and healing through this writing practice. The chaos of restructuring the self is met only with dismantlement and consequent re-membering. In this method, the purpose of composing the self is not valued through a final product, as a final product is impossible through the *Coyolxauhqui* process. Instead, healing comes in the flux of composing. Anzaldúa writes, "Because your reconstructions are always in progress, the world, society, and culture are always in compositional/decompositional states" (43). Not only does *Coyolxauhqui* serve as a metaphor to recognize the equal value of pain and reconstruction, but *Coyolxauhqui* as a methodology provides a space wherein this pain and reconstruction can actively inform research. The *Coyolxauhqui* process is similar to what Trixie Smith, in chapter 11 of this collection, refers to as "collaging," though the *Coyolxauhqui* method is distinct because of its re-membering being born, first, from trauma. This *Coyolxauhqui* process can serve as a possible method for composing disability autoethnography since it can tap into the chaos and trauma often a part of the disabled life.

As you re-member your story, those stories are fit into your research in ways that would not have been possible without that dis- and re-membering.

In the introduction to Robin Boylorn and Mark Orbe's (2016) *Critical Autoethnography*, autoethnography is presented as a practice that relates the writers' experiences to their readers by forcing the readers to consider their own positions. Boylorn and Orbe write, "Autoethnography is predicated on the ability to invite readers into the lived experience of a presumed 'Other' and to experience it viscerally" (15). Autoethnography poses an ideal opportunity to showcase dis- and re-membering composing techniques because of the chaotic nature of a disabled life. The *Coyolxauhqui* process can serve as an example when composing a disability autoethnography to reimagine how those experiences might be written.

Similar to Frank's (1995) notion of the "chaos narrative," the *Coyolxauhqui* process is a complex practice of writing that takes a dismembered body and attempts to re-member it as a form of healing. The chaos narrative also attempts to compose a complex life of disability by resisting traditional resolutions. Anzaldúa's *Coyolxauhqui* process utilizes a practice similar to the chaos narrative by attempting to piece together fragments of a dismembered narrative, continually reordering it as the self continues to be met with violence. Imbuing the chaos narrative with Anzaldua's *Coyolxauhqui* process gives purpose to this kind of narrative because purpose can then reside in the act of composing. I call on disability theorists to learn from this practice, seeing writing as a means of re-membering the disabled body.

So often, the disabled life is morphed to fit nondisabled notions of disability. Our disabled bodies ought to be considered valuable sites of research that don't just reify the medical community's fascination and fetishization of the disabled body but rather challenge ableist notions of what it means to compose a body. Returning to Mintz's (2007) *Unruly Bodies*, we find, "What one understands of disability, femaleness, and identity is continually being unraveled and rewoven. The reading process mirrors, in this way, that necessarily continual revision of self that chronic illness causes" (44). We ought to see why our writing process should mirror this unraveling and reweaving, too. The disabled body cannot neatly fit into our ableist notions of the composed self, just as the queer body cannot neatly fit into our heteronormative notions of the composed self, just as the brown and Black bodies cannot neatly fit into our white-supremacist notions of the composed self. As selves constantly being retold and re-membered, our writing must also mimic this process of, as Anzaldúa names it, *Coyolxauhqui*.

> *Coyolxauhqui informs the chaos story.*
> *Coyolxauhqui informs creative incoherence.*
> Coyolxauhqui informs disability life writing.

AUTHORING IT

In "Autoethnography: An Overview," Carolyn Ellis, Tony E. Adams, and Arthur P. Bochner (2011) challenge the position of autoethnography as a purely scholarly form of writing, saying autoethnography "accommodates subjectivity, emotionality and the researcher's influence on research rather than hiding from these matters or assuming they don't exist" (274). This blending of the scholarly with the personal should itself be a kind of chaos narrative. It resists the powers that determine what is academic and what is not, with the academic bleeding into the nonacademic. Anzaldúa's reference to *Coyolxauhqui* as a form of constructing the self through disparate pathways, and the healing process of destruction means disability autoethnography can re-member experiences that resist traditional, nondisabled writing studies practices.

The disabled autoethnography that relies on creative incoherence, chaos stories, and the *Coyolxauhqui* process represents notions of disability that can challenge how disability is often perceived by the nondisabled public. Challenging these notions is critical for the disabled community, but in challenging these practices, alternative models of writing are created as resistance, as queer and Chicana theorists have already done in the past. By broadening notions of which bodies can be composed, a space is carved out for bodies that don't fall into the privileged position so often represented. But before this space can be carved out, writing studies' privileging of dominant narratives must first be challenged.

Composing the self is a valuable form of scholarship that allows a means of understanding how subjective experiences affect one's own scholarship. Within writing studies, autoethnography can be a tool used to challenge what methods are valued within the field. By providing a space for nondominant bodies to construct their lives through writing, authors can use autoethnography to see how their lives inform/are informed by their scholarly work. This move for stories from nondominant authors to explore the relationship between lived experience and scholarship opens a gate to further question the methods valued within writing studies. Writing studies' traditional composing can restrict the ways bodies appear in scholarship. Disability life writing, for instance, is often pigeonholed into a perception of disability situated in only diagnosis and cure rather than in the tumultuous experiences the disabled body encounters. Drawing from queer theory that resituates conceptions of writing and the bodies that can be composed, the act of representing the disabled life must too challenge writing studies itself. The techniques of writing the disabled life should resist traditional expectations of disability, instead presenting the experience of disability as fluid and inconstant rather than neat and tidy so as to appeal to a nondisabled audience. The practice of composing the body from a disparate collection of pieces that re-member the body, Anzaldúa's the *Coyolxauhqui* process, places value on the process of writing rather than the final product. In other words, *Coyolxauhqui* shifts its focus to honor a process of composing, thereby making room for chaotic and creatively incoherent narratives that derive their meaning through the composition process. Queer theorists also problematize writing studies practices, questioning whether the field's current methods provide a space wherein the queer body can be composed. Disability life writing ought to more seriously consider these Chicana and queer practices as sites that inform writing studies and disability autoethnography to resist power and resituate the ways bodies can be composed and, subsequently, inform the field. The disabled life should not be represented by the nondisabled perceptions that surround disability and therefore should not be reinforced by those misconceptions that continue to compose disabled bodies and lives through those ableist lenses. The disability chaos story and creative incoherence can offer an alternative method for disability autoethnography within writing studies that resists power by producing texts that do not portray the disabled life primarily for a nondisabled audience, but rather represent the disabled life as much through process as through product. In the same ways queer and Chicana scholars have resisted and continue to resist, disability autoethnography that adopts a chaos-story and creative-incoherence method of writing creates room for new possibilities and iterations of disability life writing.

I can talk all I want about re-storying and re-membering this narrative I carry like a skull in my pocket, but all the theorizing in the world will never stop me from waking up in the middle of the night, anxious from the fever dream of a nurse drawing my blood in a bed that isn't mine.

REFERENCES

Alexander, Jonathan, and Jacqueline Rhodes. 2011. "Queer: An Impossible Subject for Composition." *JAC* 31 (1/2): 177–206.

Anzaldúa, Gloria. 2015. *Light in the Dark/Luz en lo Oscuro: Rewriting Identity, Spirituality, Reality*, edited by AnaLouise Keating. Durham, NC: Duke University Press.

Boylorn, Robin M., and Mark P. Orbe. 2016. *Critical Autoethnography: Intersecting Cultural Identities in Everyday Life*. Walnut Creek, CA: Left Coast.

Couser, G. Thomas. 1997. *Recovering Bodies: Illness, Disability, and Life-Writing*. Madison: University of Wisconsin Press.

Ellis, Carolyn, Tony E. Adams, and Arthur P. Bochner. 2011. "Autoethnography: An Overview." *Historical Social Research / Historische Sozialforschung* 36 (4): 273–90.

Frank, Arthur. 1995. *The Wounded Storyteller: Body, Illness, and Ethics*. Chicago: University of Chicago Press, 1995.

Mintz, Susannah. 2007. *Unruly Bodies: Life Writing by Women with Disabilities*. Chapel Hill: University of North Carolina Press.

Price, Margaret. 2014. *Mad at School: Rhetorics of Mental Disability and Academic Life*. Ann Arbor: University of Michigan Press.

15
THE UNTAPPED POSSIBILITIES OF PARTICIPATORY VIDEO AS AN AUTOETHNOGRAPHIC METHOD TO STUDY LITERACY

Alison Cardinal, Melissa Atienza, and Aliyah Jones

Writing studies has a long tradition of using autoethnographic methods for studying writing and literacy (see Jackson and Grutsch McKinney, this volume). These works have usually involved scholars investigating and analyzing their literacy experiences to draw larger conclusions about the force of discriminatory power structures on literacy, language learning, and writing (Canagarajah 2012b; Guerra 2016; Inayatulla, chapter 2 in this collection; Lu 1987; Rose 1989; Young 2004; Villanueva 1993). The field has historically categorized texts like these as literacy narratives, but they adhere to autoethnographic principles since they perform a self, analyze experience, and use narrative as a form of inquiry (Anderson 2006; Ellis, Adams, and Bochner 2011; Spry 2016). While writing studies scholars have used autoethnographic methods to study their own literacies, this method has been used less to study students' literacies (Canagarajah 2012a). Similarly to the texts listed above, some studies of student writing have drawn on autoethnographic principles without explicitly calling their studies *autoethnographic* by using "literacy narratives" or "autobiographical writing" as a way to understand student writing (Alexander 2015; Eldred and Mortenson 1992; Soliday 1994). While autoethnographic writing has served as a source of data about literacies, other approaches to autoethnographic methodology and methods warrant more thorough theorization and development. This chapter describes a particular type of autoethnographic research method(ology)—participatory video (PV)—Alison used with her first-year writing students in a longitudinal study of college students' literacy practices. In this piece, we (researcher and two participant/collaborators) reflect on our experiences working together in this research project. Through the lenses of our experiences, we analyze the possibilities and constraints of using PV to study literacy.

In her longitudinal study, Alison (the researcher) used PV to investigate how college students' literacies move across contexts and how this movement evolves throughout their college careers (Cardinal 2019). Over the course of four years, twelve of Alison's students created over thirty hours of video footage that described, showed, and reflected on their literacies and the significance of those practices in their daily lives. Students filmed at home, at work, in transit, at school, and in digital spaces, among many others. As part of the study, students met in focus groups to discuss their videos, compare experiences, and brainstorm prompts for the following weeks. This article describes the power of participatory video as an autoethnographic method to cocreate knowledge about language, reading, writing, and communication.

Drawing on this study that investigated student literacies, this chapter explores three theoretical questions about participatory video as an autoethnographic method and methodology: (1) Do autoethnographic participatory video methods allow for more agency and empowerment of participants in research studies than traditional research methods? (2) What are the affordances of video compositions for helping to understand the nature of literacy? (3) How do collaborative autoethnographic methods allow for a type of co-construction of knowledge, and how does that process lead to insights into literacy? Through a braided dialogue with two of the participants in the study (Melissa and Aliyah) and the researcher (Alison), we collectively explore these questions. Looking back on our experiences, the authors explore their assumptions and evolving understanding of PV as an autoethnographic method. We end by suggesting how researchers can localize PV and other visual autoethnographic approaches for their own research projects.

OPPORTUNITIES FOR EMPOWERMENT WITH PARTICIPATORY METHODS
Alison

Methodologically, autoethnography operates under anti-oppressive and feminist principles. Because autoethnography does not see participants' perspectives as a hindrance in research, autoethnography embraces their experiences and backgrounds as an important source of knowledge (Chang 2008) and can be used to disrupt Western, colonial, and patriarchal ways of knowing (Ettorre 2017; Gagnon, chapter 13 in this collection; Houston 2016; Laws, chapter 14 in this collection). Participatory video operates under these same feminist and decolonizing principles (White 2003). As a result, participatory-video research is often described as empowering because it decentralizes the researcher and instead centralizes the perspectives of participants as the source of knowledge (Kindon 2003; Lunch and Lunch 2006; Mitchell and De Lange 2012). In the participatory-video literature, empowerment emerges when participants work towards solving a community-based problem. For instance, in Peter Zoettl's (2013) use of participatory video in Brazil, Indigenous people created films about their lives to challenge how they were visually represented in the media. Zoettl claims this project was empowering because the participants were working towards a shared goal. Shirley White (2003) claims empowerment also emerges because participants maintain a measure of control over the research process. Because participants collect data about themselves rather than having data collected about them, participants have more agency than with traditional empirical methods (Bery 2003).

Having read the participatory-video literature, I began my project with the assumption that participatory video would be an empowering experience for my participants as they autoethnographically studied their own literate lives. Instead of me studying them, they acted as both the collectors and interpreters of their literacies. This was especially important to me as a white, cisgender woman because traditional empirical methods in which I (a white person) collect data about my participants (most of whom are immigrants and people of color) could easily reinforce a white colonial power relationship (Tuhiwai Smith 2013; Young 2008). While the literature strongly suggests PV is inherently empowering, I was unsure how or if it would be empowering in the context of the study. As I watched the videos week by week, I was humbled by the amount of work students put into creating these videos and their willingness to let me into their spaces, their thoughts, their lives. What motivated them to put in the work? Was it empowerment or something else? Below, Aliyah and Melissa each define empowerment in their own ways in the context of the study. Aliyah will describe how she felt empowered, while Melissa, under her definition, did not, especially at the beginning of the study.

Aliyah

Empowerment to me means having the ability to use your voice in any way you want. Being part of a marginalized community, your voice can be restricted by wanting to accommodate to the dominant culture. I have had to accommodate to the dominant culture in educational situations because the standard way I communicate with others in my inner community is not accepted. By providing the freedom to use my actual voice through video without worrying about fitting into the dominant culture, this study allowed me to speak about my culture, and my story opens insights into literacy education. The most empowering thing about the process of making these videos was being able to control what I was presenting. Because I am someone from a marginalized community, this project empowered me to raise my unheard voice and offer a knowledge about literacy the dominant culture does not have. For example, I made a video in which I talked about places I felt discriminated against because of my home literacies and the challenges I face trying to navigate the language landscape shaped by dominant cultures. For instance, I was marked down for using African American English in one of my criminal justice courses, and I made a video in response. Analyzing my experience, I say, "If you sound more proper, you're more likely to get what you want. I have to switch, and I just automatically switch when I'm with certain people. I feel discriminated against, but not in a personal attacking way . . . but it's just how society is." Making the videos was empowering because it provided me an outlet to use my voice to talk back to that situation.

Melissa

Although there were eleven other students participating in this project, I didn't feel a sense of community, which made it difficult for me to feel empowered. For me, being empowered is having a sense of purpose and independence. I interpreted this project in a way that I thought it was for Alison's use only, which caused me to feel as if I needed to please her rather than create content meaningful to me.

Throughout the six-week project, I would wait until the end of the week because I wanted to create content I thought would be worth recording for Alison, which made it difficult. I felt pressured to please her. Because of this, there were multiple times I couldn't think of anything worthwhile for Alison, and I resorted to explaining articles I had to read for homework. As a result, many of the videos I've created weren't inspiring to me and others.

The participatory videos were supposed to be seen as an autoethnographic method, allowing participants to take control of research, giving students the power to have a voice and record anything they wanted based on Alison's topics. This eventually allows the researcher to reorient the perspectives away from her towards students. With that in mind, I misinterpreted the purpose of this project and believed these videos were for her benefit rather than a contribution to share my experiences with my community. I essentially gave up my opportunity of feeling empowered. I believe if I found purpose and a sense of community at the beginning of the project, I would have felt more empowered and in control on what to record from the very beginning.

AFFORDANCES OF VIDEO AUTOETHNOGRAPHY
Alison

Autoethnographic methodology and methods are often more graphocentric, assuming the final product will mostly be written. Heewon Chang (2008), in her description of autoethnography as a method, argues for the use of visuals like photos to elicit memories, prompting participants' reflections as they look back on evidence from their lives (109–10), but Chang sees visuals as supplements rather than central tools in autoethnographic meaning making. By challenging the centrality of writing in the analysis and documentation of experience, participatory video provides a multisensory account of literacy (Pink 2015). In my experience as a researcher, looking at graphocentric texts alone, like student writing and interview transcripts, provides a limited picture of literate activity and experience. Literacy is an entanglement of the material (Haas 1996), the embodied (Arola and Wysocki 2012), and the affective (Richmond 2002), which written accounts of the self in one's cultural context don't fully capture. From my perspective as a researcher, videos create an emergent arrangement of bodies, discourse, and self. The videos show the multifaceted nature of literacy activity through the production of the autoethnographic self (Cardinal 2019). While I found value in the video texts as a researcher, I wondered how participants experienced video as a meaning-making and reflecting tool. Melissa and Aliyah expand on my insights into the affordances of video as both an autoethnographic process and product (Jackson and Grutsch McKinney, this volume). Melissa describes how video, as opposed to writing, was a more authentic expression of herself and argues that video uniquely harnesses the power of emotion to connect to her audience and to create knowledge. Aliyah explains how the process of video making works as tool for inquiry and explains how her insights into her cultural identity deepened over time through autoethnographic exploration.

Melissa

In writing, a student's identity is disrupted because we're taught how to write formally. However, this research project allowed us, the participants, to express ourselves and share our experiences through videos. These video compositions gave us the opportunity to show our audience how unique yet similar we are through our literacy practices, giving us the ability to see how we are part of a larger community. From this, as an autoethnographic text, videos build a connection with our audiences because we are able to express our true emotions and opinions, which we show through our facial expression and tone of voice. By expressing our true raw emotions, these videos become a genuine and authentic way to share our knowledge with others.

I grew up in a US military family, so I had to continuously move every two to three years, leaving the life I had just begun and starting over again in a new place. These participatory videos allowed me to be vulnerable because I was able to speak about my story, my background, rather than typing it on Microsoft. Writing is limited because it restricts the modes a writer can use to persuade. These participatory videos abolished those barriers because it allowed me to speak freely, giving me the ability to feel like myself rather than feeling like my identity was stripped away. For once, I felt like me.

In one of my last videos, I was talking about my dad. I began telling a story about a necklace he gave me. As I was recording, I started tearing up, my voice started to sound brittle, and it took me a lot longer to figure out what to say. I specifically chose to talk about my father and my tangible items for that week's topic because I wanted to share how literacy can be seen as any shape or form. In this video, I said, "I have a few tangible items that I hold deeply to my heart because they represent those that I care about or has some significant meaning to me." Growing up in a military environment, I've collected many items throughout the places I've been to because I never had a sense of permanence. From this, tangible items have become an important aspect in my life because they represent bits and pieces of me. It is typically common in military communities to collect items representative of places we've been or hold on to items we find important. The items we've accumulated overseas and over time bring us together because they express our story that we sometimes cannot express in words. With this, we are able to relate to one another despite being an active duty servicemember or being a military dependent, which enables a sense of community. These videos gave me the opportunity to express where I come from. Not only that, they allowed me to do something writing typically does not, which is being vulnerable.

With participatory videos, people can see a different side of me they cannot see on paper. When I talked about my father, my video conveyed a different form of literacy, which allowed me to express my raw emotions. I was vulnerable, which was clearly noticeable on camera; this is typically not noticeable within writing unless expressed otherwise. Being able to express your story through verbal communication, the vulnerability intensifies because you have to remember—remember how the experience was, remember the feelings you've felt, remember how it influenced you. Allowing yourself to be vulnerable in front of people enables people to relate and connect to you. These genuine moments allow you to speak up and share your knowledge. Telling my story about a necklace my father gave me, I knew that if someone were to watch this video, they would feel empathetic or sympathetic because they recognize that they're not alone and that we've all experienced something similar.

Recording myself in front of the camera versus writing a personal story is completely different; the videos show more than writing. I was able to speak freely and normally rather than formally, but most important, the audience can visualize the emotion present within the context of the video.

Aliyah

With participatory video, I was able to use autoethnographic filmmaking as a tool for inquiry into my culture. The process of creating these autoethnographic videos allowed me to reflect on my identity as an African American woman and helped me see the importance of literacy education in shaping who I am. As an African American woman, when I speak, read, and write with others in my inner community, I primarily use Black Vernacular. However, I do things differently when around dominant groups. In one of my videos, I stated that "being a minority . . . you need to be careful of what you do because not everything is working for you, not everything is doing stuff to represent your people."

Through making the videos, I realized I grew up having to conform my literacies to what is considered standard, especially in my experience with the education system. Composing these videos allowed me to see that over the course of my life, I was conforming to the dominant group in order to "succeed" rather than noticing there is power in not conforming. Initially when I started making the videos, I was doing in-the-moment reflecting on my feelings and point of view. Over time, my insights into my literacies grew. Near the end of the study, I made connections from my past to my future by rewatching the initial videos I made. Through this process, I gained a broader point of view about how the dominant culture shaped my educational experience.

AUTOETHNOGRAPHY AS COLLABORATIVE MEANING MAKING
Alison

Traditional autoethnographic methods focus on analyzing an individual's experience as part of a larger community and society. However, with collective autoethnography, a person researches "the self . . . in the company of others" (Chang, Ngunjiri, and Hernandez 2012, 17). Heewon Chang, Faith Ngunjiri, and Kathy-Ann Hernandez (2012) describe the process using the metaphor of a symphony. A member of the symphony plays a single instrument, but they see that when they come together, each individual contributes to a collective harmony. Collaborative autoethnography is a dialogic process (Gagnon, chapter 13 in this collection) that goes back and forth between an individual's self-study and collaborative knowledge making. This process brings out both the differences and similarities of peoples' experience within a single community, leading to rich insights into the self in relation to one's cultural context (Hernandez, Ngunjiri, and Chang 2015). In the context of the participatory video study, we followed this pattern by individually studying the self using video and then engaging in collective knowledge making in focus groups at intervals during the process of video collection. While the participant-collaborators were from a range of racial, ethnic, linguistic, and class backgrounds, they were all university students, navigating the ins and outs of the institution they all belonged to, which provided a basis of commonality. As a researcher, I was curious how these focus groups would affect students' individual inquiry. Below, Aliyah and Melissa explore this question. In Aliyah's response, she describes how the focus groups brought her in contact with another woman in her African American community, and this dialogue provided the opportunity to affirm those whose lives and histories are often ignored (Thornton and Kohlman 2012). At the same time, this interaction challenged some of the ideas she had about the African American experience. Melissa explores how comparing experiences across racial, ethnic, and linguistic lines can enrich one's own understanding of the self through identification and rhetorical listening (Ratcliffe 2005).

Aliyah

Using this autoethnographic method allowed me to co-construct knowledge because talking with others and listening to others' personal experiences sharpened my own viewpoints and helped me think more critically about literacy. The creation process of this autoethnographic method can help participants interpret information more critically because the creation process allows researchers to learn about people's personal worlds.

I got to improve my research experience by utilizing the focus-group meetings to make connections to my African American community. It helped me see that when you know more personal details about people, it challenges the generalizations that can come from being a part of a subordinate group. Before the research study, I assumed there would be generally more family support for first-generation African American women throughout my community because of the systematic oppression that forces academic achievement gaps on African American women (Nelson 2018). I had to check my assumptions after talking with another research participant, Karen, during the focus groups. She and I are both first-generation Black students that share the same community; however, I discovered how differently we grew up and interact with education. I stated, "No one in my family's doing like what I'm doing. So it's all new . . . they're all doing all this stuff for me to be here." Karen then responded, "That's good you have that support because I have zero . . . when you don't have the family support or the financial support, it's like you are literally on an island by yourself."

Collaborative autoethnography allowed me to realize my African American community faces exclusion in a variety of contexts because they can be blocked from telling their full stories. From connecting with Karen, I can see it seems she was blocked from telling her full story because of her family situation, while in my experience I was blocked from telling my full story because the education system doesn't always have an outlet like this research project where I don't have to accommodate to the dominant culture. Without the focus groups, Karen and I probably wouldn't have talked about our situations, and I wouldn't have checked my assumptions. Overall, literacy helps show how we interact with the world. By using collaborative autoethnography, interacting with others in your own culture helps you expand how you author your own story.

Melissa

By participating in Alison's research project and being a part of the focus groups with people from many different communities, I was able to think more deeply about my literacy practices. Not only that, by talking to my fellow classmates, I was able to refine my lens of the outside world to see how different yet similar we all are.

Alison's focus groups were the most engaging part of this project because students were more critical on their videos once we were all together. We were all trying to see how all of our videos represented a form of literacy, but most important was seeing if our experiences connected in some way. For example, in our last focus group, we talked about miscommunication. I explained one of my videos where my sister and I constantly get into arguments because we always think we're saying two different ideas. But at the end, we realize we're speaking about the same idea, but we're using different words to explain it. From my experience, other students spoke about similar experiences they've encountered. A student spoke about how they know multiple languages, which sometimes interferes when they speak their native language because some words do not translate the same across languages. Then another student spoke about how that experience is similar to technology and human interaction such as texting to one another. As we receive texts, we have to interpret our sender's message by how they are feeling, what the subject of the text is, and how they typed it. Through our discussions, I began to realize how our literacy practices are connected to our daily routines. They are simply unnoticeable because they are a part of us, our culture, and we see them as "normal."

Although most of us come from different communities and cultures, we were able to come together and share our experiences. In these collaborative settings, we were able to connect our experiences to one another. However, there were some moments when each one of us found that some of our experiences we've encountered are normal to us, but they might not be the same to other students because they never experienced them or they experienced something else in their culture. Here, we were all able to refine our lens on how we see different cultures around the world. In these group settings, we were able to learn from one another's experience but in some ways find how uniquely connected we are. Our cultures and upbringings define us as individuals, yet we were able to come together as one because we were able to be aware that some of our practices and values are collectively the same.

POSSIBILITIES AND CONSTRAINTS OF PARTICIPATORY VIDEO

After dialoguing about our experiences with participatory video, we agree this method is worthy of wider adoption in autoethnographic research. As our discussion shows, participatory video helps researchers meet two intertwined imperatives, one ethical and one empirical. While we talked about the ethical commitments of one specific participatory approach, there are many other ways to use participatory methods that have yet to be explored in rhetoric and composition

(Kemmis, McTaggart, and Nixon 2013). Video-based research also offers opportunities for new directions and can help researchers examine the material, embodied, visual, and affective nature of literacy (Cardinal 2019; Gonzales 2018; Shivers-McNair 2017; VanKooten 2019). Taking a participatory approach to video data gives both researcher and participants the opportunity to discover different aspects of literacy that composing a written autoethnographic text alone does not. Melissa and Aliyah agree that participants having the opportunity to creatively express themselves in visual and audio modes gave them opportunities to autoethnographically explore their identities and literacies in a way that felt more authentic than in writing. While we agree that overall the process was empowering, empowerment was not a given (Shaw 2012). Researchers must carefully balance the dynamics of power between participants and researcher, the goals of the researchers and participants, and the purposes and uses of the videos in order to create conditions for empowerment. However, another potential problem is that participants might not be invested in the project because they do not see a purpose for the videos if the researcher is the sole audience. In order to avoid this mentality, participatory-video projects would benefit from being designed to be personally enriching for participants. If there is no shared community-based goal as part of a project, we suggest researchers create opportunities for sharing the videos with others to increase participants' investment in the project. For instance, in our project, we are also cocreating a film, presenting at conferences, and cowriting articles like this one. In our case, the project became more meaningful when participants were given opportunities to share their work with outside audiences.

Researchers should also recognize that participatory video as an autoethnographic method requires a great amount of trust. These types of projects require a sustained and in-depth relationship building before, during, and after the project is completed. With writing, a student's physical identity is disguised. However, with video recording, their physical appearance could be exposed, leaving students vulnerable, which requires more care because anonymity is not guaranteed with visual data. Participants should also be able to self-determine how much they reveal and what they show. Researchers should also take extra care working with these videos, publishing about them, and showing them to ensure the process adheres to anti-oppressive and feminist principles throughout the process. Cocreating projects with participants, as we did with this one, is one way to mitigate this potential pitfall. This article, and the project overall, points to the yet untapped potential in collective autoethnographic methods for providing an expansive and ethical exploration of language and literacy.

REFERENCES

Alexander, Kara Poe. 2015. "From Story to Analysis: Reflection and Uptake in the Literacy Narrative Assignment." *Composition Studies* 43 (2): 43–71.

Anderson, Leon. 2006. "Analytic Autoethnography." *Journal of Contemporary Ethnography* 35 (4): 373–95.

Arola, Kristin L., and Anne Wysocki, eds. 2012. *Composing (Media)=Composing (Embodiment)*. Logan: Utah State University Press.

Bery, Renuka. 2003. "Participatory Video that Empowers." In *Participatory Video: Images that Transform and Empower*, edited by Shirley White, 102–21. Thousand Oaks, CA: SAGE.

Canagarajah, A. Suresh. 2012a. "Autoethnography in the Study of Multilingual Writers." In *Writing Studies Research in Practice: Methods and Methodologies*, edited by Lee Nickoson, Mary P. Sheridan, and Gesa Kirsch, 113–24. Carbondale: Southern Illinois University Press.

Canagarajah, A. Suresh. 2012b. "Teacher Development in a Global Profession: An Autoethnography." *TESOL Quarterly* 46 (2): 258–79.

Cardinal, Alison. (2019). Participatory Video: An Apparatus for Ethically Researching Literacy, Power and Embodiment. *Computers and Composition* 53: 34–46.

Chang, Heewon. 2008. *Autoethnography as Method*. Walnut Creek, CA: Left Coast.

Chang, Heewon, Faith Ngunjiri, and Kathy-Ann Hernandez. 2012. *Collaborative Autoethnography*. New York: Routledge.

Eldred, Janet Carey, and Peter Mortensen. 1992. "Reading Literacy Narratives." *College English* 54 (5): 512–39.

Ellis, Carolyn, Tony E. Adams, and Arthur P. Bochner. 2011. "Autoethnography: An Overview." *Historical Social Research/Historische Sozialforschung* 12 (1): Art. 10.

Ettorre, Elizabeth. 2017. *Autoethnography as Feminist Method: Sensitising the Feminist "I."* New York: Routledge.

Gonzales, Laura. (2018). *Sites of Translation: What Multilinguals Can Teach Us About Digital Writing and Rhetoric*. Ann Arbor: University of Michigan Press.

Guerra, Juan C. 2016. *Language, Culture, Identity and Citizenship in College Classrooms and Communities*. New York: Routledge.

Haas, Christina. 1996. *Writing Technology: Studies on the Materiality of Literacy*. New York: Routledge.

Hernandez, Kathy-Ann, Faith Ngunjiri, and Heewon Chang. 2015. "Exploiting the Margins in Higher Education: A Collaborative Autoethnography of Three Foreign-Born Female Faculty of Color." *International Journal of Qualitative Studies in Education* 28 (5): 533–51.

Houston, Jennifer. 2007. "Indigenous Autoethnography: Formulating Our Knowledge, Our Way." *Australian Journal of Indigenous Education* 36 (1): 45–50. doi:10.1017/S1326011100004695.

Kemmis, Steven, Robin McTaggart, and Rhonda Nixon. (2013). *The Action Research Planner: Doing Critical Participatory Action Research*. Springer Science & Business Media.

Kindon, Sara. 2003. "Participatory Video in Geographic Research: A Feminist Practice of Looking?" *Area* 45 (2): 142–53.

Lu, Min-Zhan. 1987. "From Silence to Words: Writing as Struggle." *College English* 49 (4): 437–48.

Lunch, Nick, and Chris Lunch. 2006. "Insights into Participatory Video: A Handbook for the Field." InsightShare. https://insightshare.org/resources/insights-into-participatory-video-a-handbook-for-the-field/.

Mitchell, Claudia, and Naydene de Lange, eds. 2012. *Handbook of Participatory Video*. Lanham, MD: AltaMira.

Nelson, Raina. 2018. "Still Separate, Still Unequal: The Role of Black Women and Girls in the Legacy of *Brown v. Board of Education*." *AAUW*. May 17. https://ww3.aauw.org/2018/05/17/still-separate-still-unequal/.

Pink, Sarah. 2015. *Doing Sensory Ethnography*. Thousand Oaks, CA: SAGE.

Ratcliffe, Krista. 2005. *Rhetorical Listening: Identification, Gender, Whiteness*. Carbondale: Southern Illinois University Press.

Richmond, Kia Jane. 2002. "Repositioning Emotions in Composition Studies." *Composition Studies* 30 (1): 67–82.

Rose, Mike. 1989. *Lives on the Boundary. The Struggles and Achievements of America's Underprepared*. New York: Macmillan.

Shaw, Jackie. 2012. "Interrogating the Gap between the Ideals and Practice Reality of Participatory Video." In *Handbook of Participatory Video*, edited by Claudia Mitchell and Naydene de Lange, 225–41. Lanham, MD: AltaMira.

Shivers-McNair, Ann. "3D Interviewing with Researcher POV Video: Bodies and Knowledge in the Making." *Kairos: A Journal of Rhetoric, Technology, and Pedagogy* 21 (2). https://praxis.technorhetoric.net/tiki-index.php?page=PraxisWiki%3A_%3A3D+Interviewing.

Tuhiwai Smith, Linda. 2013. *Decolonizing Methodologies: Research and Indigenous Peoples*. New York: Zed Books.

Soliday, Mary. 1994. "Translating Self and Difference through Literacy Narratives." *College English* 56 (5): 511–26.

Spry, Tami. 2016. *Body, Paper, Stage: Writing and Performing Autoethnography*. New York: Routledge.

Thornton, Bonnie, and Marla H. Kohlman. 2012. "Intersectionality: A Transformative Paradigm in Feminist Theory and Social Justice." In *Handbook of Feminist Research: Theory and Praxis*, edited by Sharlene Nagy Hesse-Biber, 154–74. Thousand Oaks, CA: SAGE.

VanKooten, Crystal. 2019. "A Research Methodology of Interdependence through Video as Method." *Computers and Composition* 54 (December): 1–17.

Villanueva, Victor. 1993. *Bootstraps: From an American Academic of Color*. Urbana, IL: NCTE.

White, Shirley A. 2003. "Participatory Video: A Process That Transforms the Self and the Other." In *Participatory Video: Images that Transform and Empower*, edited by Shirley White, 63–101. Thousand Oaks, CA: SAGE.

Young, Alford A. Jr. 2008. "White Ethnographers on the Experiences of African American Men." In *White Logic, White Methods: Racism and Methodology*, edited by Tukufu Zuberi and Eduardo Bonilla-Silva, 179–200. New York: Rowman and Littlefield.

Young, Morris. 2004. *Minor Re/Visions: Asian American Literacy Narratives as a Rhetoric of Citizenship*. Carbondale: Southern Illinois University Press.

Zoettl, Peter Anton. 2014. "Images of Culture: Participatory Video, Identity and Empowerment." *International Journal of Cultural Studies* 16 (2): 209–24.

INDEX

academic storytelling, 14
accelerated learning program (ALP), 115–17
Adams, Tony, 7, 11, 12, 21–22, 179, 183, 184. *See also* "Autoethnography: An Overview"
aesthetics, 22, 152, 176, 179, 180, 184
affective, 20, 117, 120–21, 214, 220
African American Vernacular English (AAVE)/Black Vernacular, 181, 216
agency, 42, 74, 78, 93, 119, 133, 201, 211–12; linguistic agency, 126
agentic discord, 151, 156
Ahmed, Sarah, 187
Anderson, Leon, 118, 136, 153, 157n5
"Arts of the Contact Zone" (Pratt), 14, 123, 126
autobiography, 7, 45, 107, 181, 187. *See also* critical autobiography; institutional autobiography
autoethnographic selves, 16
"Autoethnography: An Overview" (Ellis, Adams, and Bochner, 2011), 6, 29, 43, 97, 207, 210
autoethnography, definitions of, 6, 45, 71, 97, 127, 140, 179, 194
autoethnography, evaluating, 21–22
autoethnography, types of: analytic/interpretive, 8, 9, 16, 136, 153–56, 157n5; betweener, 9; Black feminist, 6, 19, 176, 179–80, 183, 184n2; collaborative, 17, 85–87, 217–18; collective, 217; community, 10; constellational, 19, 189–96; critical, 19, 160–61, 172n1, 206; disability, 19, 199–200, 203, 205–9; duoethnography, 10; evocative/heartful, 8–9, 11–12, 16–17, 29, 43, 57, 116, 136, 157n5, 171, 172n1; exoautoethnography, 10; Indigenous, 10; literacy, 18, 126–34; moderate, 10; multispecies, 10; organizational, 10; performative, 10, 107; postcolonial, 10; rhetorical, 10; vulnerable automythography, 17, 45. *See also* Anderson, Leon
autoethnography, autoethnographic vs., 3–4, 5, 12–13, 15

#BlackLivesMatter, 183–84
Bochner, Arthur, 4, 8–9, 11, 20, 136, 157n5, 171, 179, 207. *See also* "Autoethnography: An Overview"
Brodkey, Linda 3, 11, 15

Canagarajah, A. Suresh, 3, 9, 14, 45, 87–89, 97, 100–101, 104, 126–27, 131, 133, 192, 210
Chang, Heewon, 7, 9–11, 88, 140, 153, 157n5, 211, 214, 217
collage, 18, 159, 171
Combahee River Collective, 179
community college/two-year college, 58, 74, 83n5, 115–17, 119, 121–24
complete member research (CMR), 136, 154
contact zone, 133. *See also* "Arts of the Contact Zone" (Pratt)
Coyolxauhqui, 205–8
creative incoherence, 202–3, 205, 207
credibility, 21
crisis of representation, 4
critical autobiography, 14
critical ethnography, 5
critical race theory, 167–68
cultural rhetorics, 19, 85, 160, 189

decolonizing principles, 6
developmental courses, 115–16, 145
disability, 19, 41, 57, 77, 199–209. *See also* autoethnography, types of
disciplinary lore, 151–53, 155–56, 157n3
discussion forums, 120
dominant culture, 127, 130, 167, 212–13, 216, 218

Ellis, Carolyn, 7, 8, 11, 21–22, 95, 136, 157n5, 171, 172n1, 179, 183–84. *See also* "Autoethnography: An Overview"
embodied personal writing, 152
embodiment, 141
emotional labor, 41, 120
empowerment, 43, 122, 128–29, 205, 211–12, 220
ethics, 4, 10, 21, 86–87, 171, 176–77, 187,

197n2, 219; *See also* Institutional Review Board (IRB)
ethnography, 5–8, 10, 187; feminist ethnography, 5

Facebook, 60, 62
feminist principles, 211, 220
first-generation students, 34, 71, 104, 115; first-generation Black/African American students, 218
first-person scholarship, 11
first-year writing, 17–18, 58, 95, 126–27, 144, 210
Freire, Paulo, 20, 72, 77–78, 83n3, 109n6. *See also Pedagogy of the Oppressed*

gender, 5, 17, 53, 72, 119, 142, 178–79, 182; cisgender, 212
Goodall, Bud, 5
Green River College, 116

Harvard Implicit Bias test, 142
hope, 17, 20, 34, 40, 77–80, 82, 124, 160, 184, 195
human trafficking, 186, 191, 193
Hurston, Zora Neale, 6, 11, 140, 180

Indigenous, 10, 19, 54, n172, 180, 191, 192, 212
institutional autobiography, 152
Institutional Review Board (IRB), 10, 71, 108n3, 134n1, 175
intersectionality, 119, 139, 141, 161, 178

Jacobs, Harriet Ann, 180–83

labor, 17, 20, 57, 61, 75, 90, 92, 108n1, 121, 137–38, 150, 181, 183; adjunct/contingent, 57–58, 73, 75, 81; ethics of, 150; graduate student, 58–59, 69. *See also* emotional labor
liberatory pedagogy, 120
life writing, 19, 116, 199–205, 207–9
linguistic diversity, 117
listening, 155, 191–95, 202; rhetorical listening, 124, 217
literacy narrative, *See* narrative
locally valid assessment, 121

materiality, 119
memoir, 7, 45, 72, 77, 161
mental health, 35, 57, 69
mental illness, 29–32, 41–44; bipolar disorder, 17, 29–33, 38, 40–42; psychiatric disorder, 66; psychological distress, 66
methodology, 8, 9, 12, 14, 86, 88, 90, 97, 159, 160, 175, 206, 210–11, 214

methods, research, 7–9, 11–12, 19–20, 86, 88–89, 96–97, 108n2, 127, 139; teaching, 134
Morrison, Toni, 3
multilingual writers, 3, 14, 97, 107, 126

narrative, 6–7, 15–17, 21, 43–44, 57, 68, 78–80, 89–90, 96–98, 104–6, 117–19, 121–23, 128, 132, 139–41, 150–54, 160, 180–82, 184, 186, 190–91, 195, 197; autobiographical narrative, 14, 127; chaos narrative, 19, 200–202, 204–7; critical personal narrative, 3; cultural, 11, 30, 119, 127, 194; disciplinary narrative, 19; literacy narrative, 12, 45, 127–29; personal narrative, 4, 71, 76, 80, 116, 140, 199; quest narrative, 200–201, 204; restitution, 200–201, 204
National Writing Project (NWP), 159–66, 168, 172n3

participatory video, 19–20, 210–217, 219–220
Pedagogy of the Oppressed, 73, 77, 83n3. *See also* Freire, Paulo
performance of identity, 118–19, 140
podcast, 120, 146
positionality, 137, 139, 141–43, 164, 166, 176, 182, 188, 194
positioning essay, 155–56
Powell, Malea, 15, 189, 190
power, 5, 6, 17, 42, 51, 54–55, 72, 77–83, 85–86, 92–93, 97, 100–101, 116, 123, 126, 142–43, 146, 149, 189, 191, 194, 203, 208–12, 216, 220; healing power, 196; of voices, 120–21, 133, 213–14
Pratt, Mary Louise, 14, 97, 123, 126, 127, 132, 134, 136, 179. *See also* "Arts of the Contact Zone"
Prendergast, Catherine, 30, 103

qualitative research, 3–4, 7, 10–13, 87, 97, 127, 153–54, 195
queer identity/theory, 45, 159–60, 199–200, 203–5, 207–9

race, 15, 72, 142; racism, 54, 166, 177, 184
reflexivity/self-reflexivity, 21, 42, 136–37, 139, 146, 154, 164, 187, 188, 191, 193
reform, 18, 115–16, 122, 124, 163, 164, 166, 172n3
representation, 11, 14, 97, 119, 124, 126–32, 139, 141, 200, 203; self-representation, 42, 99, 107, 120, 126, 136; of trauma, 57. *See also* crisis of representation

rhetoricability, 17
rhetorical listening. *See* listening
Royster, Jacqueline Jones, 152, 180, 190, 194

sexuality, 17, 119, 145; *See also* queer identity/theory
subject positions, 45, 179–81
subjectivity, 21, 95–96, 99, 101, 105–7, 177–78, 192, 199, 207

TED talk, 118
translingual approach/practices, 96, 101, 104–5, 107, 117
transnationalism, 100

trauma, 16, 20, 37, 57, 81, 119, 162, 168, 184, 186–191, 193, 196–99, 206; trauma narrative, 141
Truth, Sojourner, 180–81
Twitter, 60, 62

video compositions, 211, 215
Villanueva, Victor, 14, 210

white fragility, 175
white privilege, 120
working-class identity, 85, 88, 92; working-class students, 71, 74; working-class laborers, 86
Writing Program Administration Listserv (WPA-L), 150–51

ABOUT THE AUTHORS

Leslie Akst is an assistant professor who teaches composition, advanced composition, business writing, journalism, and introductory literature courses at campuses in the New York metro area. In addition to her PhD in English, she has a master's degree from Columbia University's Graduate School of Journalism. Her scholarship focuses on writing praxis and the intersections of institutional power and lived experience.

Melissa Atienza graduated from the University of Washington Tacoma in 2020. She received a dual degree in business management and global studies with a minor in Spanish language and cultures. She has presented her authoethnographic work at regional and national conferences in composition studies.

Ross Atkinson is a PhD student and graduate teaching assistant in the Education, Equity, and Transformation Program in the School of Education at Colorado State University. His research interests include examining veteran reintegration, student-veteran education, and methods of critical empowerment for both youth and veteran populations. Ross also facilitates a writing workshop for local veterans.

Alison Cardinal is assistant professor in writing studies at the University of Washington Tacoma. Her research expertise lies at the intersection of participatory and visual research methods in academic and community settings, community-based literacy studies, and social justice approaches to UX. Her work has appeared or is forthcoming in *Computers and Composition, Composition Forum, Communication Design Quarterly, Technical Communication Quarterly*, and multiple edited collections.

Sue Doe is professor of English, recent director of composition, chair of the Faculty Council, and codirector of the Center for the Study of Academic Labor at Colorado State University. She coedited with Lisa Langstraat the collection *Generation Vet: Student Veterans, Composition, and the Post-9/11 University* (Utah State University Press, 2014). Her work has recently appeared in *Reflections, The WAC Journal,* and *Feminist Formations.*

William Duffy is associate professor of English and director of graduate studies at the University of Memphis. He is the author of *Beyond Conversation: Collaboration and the Production of Writing* (Utah State University Press) and his work has most recently been published in *Present Tense, Literacy in Composition Studies*, and the collection *Explanation Points: Publishing in Rhetoric and Composition.*

John T. Gagnon is assistant professor and former writing center director in the Department of English at the University of Hawaii at Manoa. He is a cultural rhetorician interested in human rights and the rhetorical framing of human-rights issues. He teaches courses in composition studies, rhetorical theory and history, and argumentation.

Elena G. Garcia is associate professor in the Department of Literacies and Composition at Utah Valley University. Her research and work revolve around WAC/WID, writing studies, composition studies, writing center studies, and industrial workplace writing. In all of this, her focus is on supporting writers. Guadalupe Garcia, her research partner and coauthor, is Elena's father.

Guadalupe Garcia is a machine operator at a food process factory, where he has worked for over forty years. In his work he uses writing to support his trainees, and he is invested in finding ways that writing can be used to help his factory run more efficiently. Elena Garcia, his research partner and coauthor, is his daughter.

Caleb González is a PhD student in the rhetoric, composition, and literacy program and an MA student in the philosophy and history of education program at The Ohio State University. His research interests include the study of writing programs at Hispanic-serving institutions, organizational rhetorics of higher education, college and university teaching, creative nonfiction, and writing program administration.

Jackie Grutsch McKinney is a professor of English at Ball State University, where she teaches undergraduate and graduate writing studies courses and directs the Writing Center. She is the author or coauthor of *Strategies for Writing Center Research*, *Peripheral Visions for Writing Centers*, and *The Working Lives of New Writing Center Directors*, all of which have won the IWCA Outstanding Book award.

Lilly Halboth is a secondary language arts instructor with a master of arts in writing, rhetoric, and social change and a master of education and human resource studies in secondary education science. Her research interests include equity in secondary education, critical emotion studies, gender studies, mediatization, and critical pedagogies.

Kirsten Higgins and **Anthony Warnke** teach writing at Green River College in Auburn, Washington. As co-writing program administrators, they helped design an equity-focused Accelerated Learning Program to revamp their department's developmental English sequence. Their scholarship has appeared in or is forthcoming from *The Basic Writing e-Journal*, *Teaching English in the Two-Year College*, as well as edited collections on autoethnography in corequisite courses and emotional labor in writing program administration. Their article "A Critical Time for Reform: Interventions in a Precarious Landscape" was selected for the Parlor Press anthology *Best of the Rhetoric and Composition Journals 2019*.

Shereen Inayatulla (she/her/hers) is associate professor of English at York College, CUNY, and teaches courses in composition, critical literacy studies, and autoethnography. Her work has appeared in publications including the *Journal of Basic Writing*, *Changing English*, and the *Journal of Lesbian Studies*.

Rebecca L. Jackson is professor of English: rhetoric and composition at Texas State University. She is coauthor (with Nicole Caswell and Jackie Grutsch McKinney) of *The Working Lives of New Writing Center Directors* (Utah State University Press, 2016), winner of the 2017 International Writing Centers Association Best Book Award. Her research interests include autoethnography, narrative inquiry, and writing center studies, and her previous work has been published in *Writing Center Journal*, *Praxis*, and numerous edited collections.

Aliyah Jones is a first-generation graduate from University of Washington Tacoma, where she received her BA in criminal justice with a minor in law and policy. Aliyah is on a path to law school and has presented work on criminal justice issues and participatory research methods at regional and national conferences.

Autumn Laws received her master of arts from Michigan State University's Writing, Rhetoric, and American Cultures Program. She currently works in healthcare marketing and research, where she maintains her passions for healthcare equity and creative storytelling.

About the Authors

Soyeon Lee is an instructor of English and composition at Houston Community College. She earned her PhD in rhetoric, composition, and pedagogy in the Department of English at the University of Houston and the Graduate Certificate in Teaching Technical Communication at Texas Tech University. While at the University of Houston, she taught first-year writing courses and corequisite developmental writing courses as a graduate student instructor. She will start working as Assistant professor of rhetoric and composition in the Department of English at the University of Texas at El Paso in fall 2021. Her research interests include transnational literacy studies, community-engaged writing, and environmental communication.

Louis M. Maraj is assistant professor in the School of Journalism, Writing, and Media at the University of British Columbia, Vancouver. He thinks, creates, and converses with theoretical Black studies, rhetoric, digital media, and critical pedagogies to specifically address antiracism, antiBlackness, and expressive form. Maraj's book *Black or Right: Anti/Racist Campus Rhetorics* explores notions of Blackness in historically white educational institutions, while his most recent essays can be found in *Prose Studies* and *Women's Studies in Communication*.

Kira Marshall-McKelvey is a PhD student in communication studies at Colorado State University. She studies YouTube and influencer culture. She got her MA in rhetoric and composition at Colorado State University.

Jennifer Owen is a secondary English language arts educator and instructor of English currently teaching high-risk and detained youth at a juvenile detention center. Her research interests include video game and technology integration, digital media and literacy studies, gender studies, and critical pedagogies.

Tiffany Rainey is a lecturer in the Department of English at Texas State University–San Marcos. Her research interests include narrative/counternarrative, rhetoricability, intercultural competence, language rights, and mad studies—all of which promote diversity and inclusion within and beyond the academy. She is currently exploring first-year-English course design that introduces students to researched writing through critical narrative and autoethnography.

Rebecca Hallman Martini is assistant professor of English and writing center director at the University of Georgia. She specializes in writing center studies, writing across the disciplines, ethnographic research methods, and composition pedagogy. Her book *Disrupting the Center: A Partnership Approach to Writing Across the University* is forthcoming from Utah State University Press. Her work has been published or is forthcoming in *Praxis, Computers and Composition, Across the Disciplines,* and *WPA*. She is also the founding editor of the International Writing Center Association's newest journal, *The Peer Review: A Journal for Writing Center Practitioners*.

Marcie Sims is a tenured professor at Green River College in Auburn, Washington. She teaches composition, literature, and film and gender studies. She writes composition textbooks for Pearson (*The Write Stuff: Thinking Through Essays*). Other publications include *Capitol Hill Pages: Young Witnesses to 200 Years of History* (McFarland) and various stories and poems.

Amanda Sladek is assistant professor of English and composition coordinator at the University of Nebraska–Kearney. She teaches basic writing, as well as undergraduate and graduate courses on composition and language. In addition to classroom applications of narrative and autoethnography, her research focuses on literacy studies, language diversity, and first-year-writing/basic-writing pedagogy.

Trixie G. Smith is associate professor in the Writing, Rhetoric, and American Cultures Department at Michigan State University. She directs The Writing Center and the Red Cedar Writing Project. She is a cultural rhetorician whose research is centered in the idea that we're just humans learning with/from other humans with bodies, feelings, lives in and outside the academy.

www.ingramcontent.com/pod-product-compliance
Lightning Source LLC
Chambersburg PA
CBHW031105080526
44587CB00011B/837